Impossible
Dreams

Impossible Dreams

Rationality, Integrity, and Moral Imagination

Susan E. Babbitt

WestviewPress

A Division of HarperCollinsPublishers

ℐ

Chapter 1 is a revised version of "Knowledge and Identity in Toni Morrison's *Beloved*," *Hypatia* 9, no. 3 (summer 1994): 1–18. Chapter 2 is a revised version of "Feminism and Objective Interests: The Role of Transformation Experiences in Rational Deliberation" in Linda Alcoff and Elizabeth Potter, eds., *Feminist Epistemologies* (New York, Routledge, 1993), pp. 245–264. Chapter 7 is a revised version of "Political Philosophy and the Challenge of the Personal: From Narcissism to Radical Critique," *Philosophical Studies* 77, nos. 2–3 (March 1995): 293–318, reprinted by permission of Kluwer Academic Publishers.

"When my faith was hanging" is reprinted from Forugh Farrokhzad, "Windows," in Michael C. Hillmann, *Forugh Farrokhzad and Her Poetry: A Lonely Woman* (Washington, D.C.: Mage Publishers and Three Continents Press, 1987), p. 123, by permission of the publisher.

Published in 1996 in the United States of America by Westview Press, Inc., 5500 Central Avenue, Boulder, Colorado 80301-2877, and in the United Kingdom by Westview Press, 12 Hid's Copse Road, Cumnor Hill, Oxford OX2 9JJ

Library of Congress Cataloging-in-Publication Data
Babbitt, Susan E.
    Impossible dreams : rationality, integrity, and moral imagination / Susan E. Babbitt.
        p. cm.
    Includes bibliographical references and index.
    ISBN 0-8133-2639-7 (cloth)—ISBN 0-8133-2640-0 (pbk.)
    1. Integrity. 2. Reason. 3. Imagination. 4. Feminist theory.
I. Title.
BJ1533. I58B32 1996
170—dc20
                                                                        95-45757
                                                                            CIP

The paper used in this publication meets the requirements of the American National Standard for Permanence of Paper for Printed Library Materials Z39.48-1984.

10   9   8   7   6   5   4   3   2   1

for J.R.B.
1951–1980

And, as we were now almost at the gate of his house, a man of less outstanding eminence, in heart and brain, might simply have said "good-bye" to me, a trifle dryly, and taken care to avoid seeing me again. This however was not Elstir's way with me. . . . He chose therefore, rather than say anything that might have avenged the injury to his pride, to say what he thought would prove instructive to me. "There is no man," he began, "however wise, who has not at some period in his youth said things, or lived in a way the consciousness of which is so unpleasant to him in later life that he would gladly, if he could, expunge it from his memory. And yet he ought not entirely to regret it, because he cannot be certain that he has indeed become a wise man— so far as it is possible for any of us to be wise—unless he has passed through all the fatuous or unwholesome incarnations by which that ultimate stage must be preceded. I know that there are young fellows, the sons and grandsons of famous men, whose masters have instilled into them nobility of mind and moral refinement in their schooldays. They have, perhaps, when they look back upon their past lives, nothing to retract; they can, if they choose, publish a signed account of everything they have ever said or done; but they are poor creatures, feeble descendants of doctrinaires, and their wisdom is negative and sterile. We are not provided with wisdom, we must discover it for ourselves, after a journey through the wilderness which no one can take for us, an effort which no one can spare us, for our wisdom is the point of view from which we come at last to regard the world. . . ." Meanwhile we had reached his door.

—Marcel Proust, *Within a Budding Grove*

When my faith was hanging
  by the weak thread of justice
and in the whole city
the hearts of my lamps were
  being torn to pieces,
when the childlike eyes of my love
were being blindfolded by law's black kerchief,
and fountains of blood were gushing forth
from the distressed temples of my desire,
when my life was no longer anything,
nothing but the tick tock of a wall clock,
I discovered that I must,
  that I absolutely had to
love madly.

—Forugh Farrokhzad, "Windows"

Contents

8 Philosophy and Literature: Recalling the Archangel

Acknowledgments

ALTHOUGH THIS BOOK began as a doctoral dissertation, only Chapters 2 and 3 were, in some form, part of the thesis I defended at Cornell University in July 1991. Nonetheless, the central ideas of the book are those of the dissertation, and I am deeply indebted to Richard Boyd for helping me to complete that work. During the last eight months I spent at Cornell, I was finally able—almost entirely because of Dick Boyd's generous, weekly offering of intense, fruitful discussion and copious written comments—to organize and express more philosophically ideas I had been thinking about almost forever. Dick Boyd reminded me of what education can be and of that most exciting of experiences: the growth of understanding through the sharing of ideas.

I have benefited from comments and suggestions on different parts of this work over the years: I am grateful to the other members of my dissertation committee—Anthony Appiah, Richard Miller, and Nicholas Sturgeon—for their help at that time. I would like to thank Steve Andrews, Richmond Campbell, Jackie Davies, Carlos Prado, Phyllis Rooney, Stephen Sullivan, and Rob Wilson for helpful comments on particular sections. I am especially grateful to Sue Campbell for reading long sections in the final days when her own workload was demanding.

My family has a role in this work that they may not realize. During the nine years before I started studying philosophy, the time during which I learned the most about rationality, they had good reasons for thinking I had none of it. If they were not the people they are, I would not have reentered Canada or the university, and whatever they think of the current work, they'll find it more coherent than arguments I tried to make to them before. My mother has been a particularly important ally and support at all stages of this book. And I especially acknowledge my father and my brother, Bobby, memories of whom make the reasonableness of impossible dreams ever more believable.

Certain important friends have, by their examples, discussion, and encouragement, been crucial to the completion of this work: Mario and Edelgard Dussault, friends from way back, help me to remember that I haven't always been, and should not only be, an academic; Haideh Moghissi and Saeed Rahnema gave me the best examples, when I started teaching and ever since, of what academics and intellectuals can be; Nkiru

Nzegwu has been a continuous source of lively ideas and fresh interpretations; Bill Bousada played pool with me; Ruth Macleod helped me to keep playing music, without which I couldn't do philosophy; Zora Vlajic has given me her poetry, in writing and in action, with her very special vision. I also want to thank my Cuban colleagues—Amelia Suárez, Inés Rodriguez, and Sonia Enjamio—whose friendship and courageous examples help me keep my priorities straight, if I ever manage to.

I am grateful to the Social Sciences and Humanities Council of Canada for four years of doctoral dissertation funding and to the Advisory Research Council at Queen's University for three research grants for work in Cuba. As well, I thank the Philosophy Department at Queen's for arranging my teaching load in the first years so that I had time to get this work started.

Susan E. Babbitt

Introduction

IN 1960, disengaged, apolitical Beat poet LeRoi Jones arrived in Cuba "determined not to be 'taken'."[1] When he returned to the United States, he was thoroughly politicized, strongly denouncing U.S. society—Beat and otherwise—and going on to become an activist on the black and Marxist lefts. For Jones it was involvement with thousands of Cubans in a celebration at the birthplace of the Cuban revolution that transformed him and made him acutely aware of the "thin crust of lie we cannot even detect in our own thinking."[2] In the angry conclusion to his famous "Cuba Libre," Jones suggests that without struggle for genuinely alternative values, practices, and ways of thinking, without a willingness to challenge fundamental social assumptions, "even the vitality of our art is like bright flowers growing up through a rotting carcass."[3]

Why should Jones's experience in Cuba provide grounds for criticizing fundamental beliefs about and assumptions of his entire society? Jones describes his voyage into the Sierra Maestra as a series of epiphanies, without which he may not have been able even to identify that "thin crust of lie." Would Jones have had such an experience as a result of just any involvement with a large group of people celebrating a revolutionary idea? Was he right in allowing such an experience to influence him so drastically, or should he, perhaps, have tried harder to maintain his initial skepticism about the situation?

One of the central focuses of this book is on the role in rational deliberation of the kinds of personal transformations LeRoi Jones refers to, experiences that easily strike some as bizarre and even wrong but that occasionally appear to explain the acquiring of important insight and capacities. Jones's experience was not just an experience of personal change. It was not just the *adding on* of a new perspective and new experiences to those acquired by him thus far. Instead, Jones's was an experience that provided reasons for thinking that what he had previously thought about the world was *wrong*, profoundly wrong. He did not just experience the celebrating Cuban revolutionaries as interesting and happy people; he took his experience of the Cuban people as interesting and happy to provide reasons for questioning the *appropriateness* of standards by which, previously, he had assessed his life—standards according to which these people should be discounted as crazy, suspicious, perhaps even evil.

In what follows I look at the extent to which conditions for knowledge are sometimes constituted by personal relations—including personal states—by who a person is as an individual, and indeed, even by imagination of what a person could be. I suggest that one way to understand Jones's radical change of position is that his personal experiences in Cuba—his relationships to people and the emotions and feelings such relationships induced in him—constituted the bringing about of the possibility for alternative epistemic standards: Jones was transformed to the extent that his understanding of himself was no longer consistent with that which had previously explained his personal choices and actions, and his transformed self constituted conditions for knowledge not available to him previously. In one way, then, I am exploring an aspect of what some philosophers have said about the need for a broader notion of epistemic standards and virtues, the need to consider the epistemic role of community and personal relations.[4] I suggest, though, that such broadening of epistemic notions depends heavily on discussion of certain metaphysical and moral questions, at least if the story to be told about the nature of knowledge is to make sense of some important examples of self- and social knowledge.

There is a long tradition of acknowledging and examining the implications of the thoroughgoing dependence of all intellectual activity on background beliefs and values. How we understand our lives, how we understand ourselves, is dependent upon the traditions of which we are a part. We know things, when we do, because we are rooted in certain practical and conceptual traditions and because we possess specific values and interests. Thomas Kuhn pointed out, for instance, that it is difficult for people to identify a playing card exhibiting a red spade even when they are looking directly at it. If people do not possess a concept of red spades, if they do not *expect* there to be such a thing, they can look at the card without in fact seeing it at all.[5]

One consequence of philosophical insights into the profound context dependence and theory dependence of observation and knowledge claims is that the basic structure of a society—including the nature of its institutions, its norms, values, and accepted ways of thinking—makes some important features of a society, and indeed some of its members, invisible. Certainly, there are many examples of the ways in which language, customs, and attitudes can perpetuate the continued subordination, the treatment as subhuman, of certain groups within a society. When a concept such as "the people" is rooted in traditions of racism and sexism, entire groups of human beings are typically unable to be understood, or even identified, as people at all. Thus, the anthropologist Lévi-Strauss can write, "The entire village left

... leaving us *alone with the women and children* in the *abandoned* homes."[6]

In cases in which social structures and practices make certain possibilities unimaginable, in which standards of reasonableness preclude the understandability, even the identification, of relevant options, acquiring adequate social understanding requires transformation. The social world—including interpersonal relations—often needs to be changed to be understood. In Jones's case, the transformation to himself explains the acquiring of a radical political perspective. Jones acquires values, commitments, and beliefs that make possible an alternative interpretation of his society than that which he had accepted previously. But I eventually argue that the point about knowledge is entirely general, not just applicable to radical criticism: To the extent that knowledge claims are radically contingent upon social, historical, and personal conditions—that is, to the extent that knowledge and our understanding of it are thoroughly dependent upon the development of certain theoretical and practical conditions—there are some things that cannot be understood, or perhaps even questioned, until existing conditions, including personal states, are disrupted and transformed.

●

Perhaps one of the enduring contributions of feminist scholarship to epistemology and ethics in general is the centrality given to questions about personal development. Philosophers, it seems, have always taken for granted that individuals, as knowers and moral agents, possess a sense of individuality, of agency, and that normative notions such as autonomy and integrity can be defined in such terms. There is an assumption, for instance, that when "autonomy" is defined, say, in terms of a capacity to act on principles that are one's own because one has made them so, nothing further needs to be said about the notion of "one's own." But as Claudia Card points out in introducing a collection of essays in feminist ethics, notions of individuality and agency cannot be taken for granted if we acknowledge the consequences of systemic injustice on individuals' capacities for deliberation and choice—indeed, on capacities to be a *self* at all: "If oppressive institutions stifle and stunt the moral development of the oppressed, how is it possible, what does it *mean*, for the oppressed to be liberated? What is *there* to liberate? What does it mean to resist, to make morally responsible choices, to become moral agents, to develop character?"[7] In "The Fact of Blackness" Frantz Fanon describes how his illusions about self-determination crumbled as he began to appreciate the significance of being black, the fact that "not only must the black man be black; he must be black in relation to the white man."[8] Fanon satisfies himself that he has achieved an intellectual understanding of the "black problem." But then, he writes, "The occasion arose when I had to meet the white man's eyes. . . . The real world challenged my claims. . . . It did not impose itself on me; it is, rather, a definitive structuring of the self and of the world."[9]

In Chapter 1, I try to identify some of the philosophical questions raised by the existence of systemic discrimination, especially the relationship between questions about individual rationality and questions about who a person is or can be within a society of a certain moral nature. I propose that individual rationality be understood not, for instance, as the capacity to choose among possible actions on the basis of one's conception of the good but rather in terms of what is required to bring about conditions, in some cases conditions in which one can *possess* a good—at least of one's own—in the first place. In Chapter 1, I discuss Toni Morrison's novel *Beloved*,[10] in which Sethe, the protagonist, has escaped from slavery with three children and joins her mother-in-law and her youngest daughter. During the twenty-eight days she spends in freedom, she learns something about what it means to control her life; in particular, she learns what it means to make her own decisions, to be "selfish" and do things for herself, to commit herself to her children. When she sees her ex-slave master coming down the road to take her and her children back to Sweet Home, where she had been a slave, Sethe takes a handsaw to her youngest daughter's throat and kills her.

•

Of course, one way to explain Sethe's choice to kill her children, just as we might explain Jones's transformation, is that she is simply crazy. Indeed, it would be more comforting, conceptually and perhaps emotionally, if we could dismiss Sethe's act as immoral and crazy. If Sethe's choice is deviant, there need be no questions raised about what she is deviant from. There exists no threat to our understanding of morality or reasonableness; there are only questions about *how* she departed from the norms and why she departed in this particular way.

But if Sethe is not deviant—if Sethe is an autonomous, caring, responsible adult—the question is not why she acts immorally but why, as a *morally responsible adult,* she acts as she does. If Sethe's choice is that of a rational human being who loves her children, the questions that need to be raised are questions not about her but rather about the *conditions* under which it does in fact become reasonable for her to do as she does. And indeed, it is precisely because slavery disallows Sethe's moral action, for it disallows Sethe's moral status, that Sethe decides to kill her children. She decides to kill her children not to go against morality but to claim its possibility. She claims *human* life for her children—life *involving* moral responsibility—and because slavery takes this away, she refuses in the only way available to her to give her children back to it.

If we see Sethe's choice as immoral, perhaps as well intended but misguided, we can save our stabilizing social stock of meanings and values, that which provides the basis not just for social meaning but for what people take themselves to be, our identities. We can maintain, for instance, assumptions about parents and children, in particular about what it means for a parent to take responsibility for her children. And importantly, we can remain secure in our ability to distinguish wrong from right generally, crazy from sane. But if we understand Sethe's choice as that of a loving, morally responsible adult, we have to recognize the profound inhumanity of slavery and of racism generally. In particular, we have to recognize what it means for a system of thoroughgoing subordination and degradation to deny human status to some people and what kind of resistance can be justified by an understanding of such degradation. If Sethe decides to kill her children because she loves them, if it can be reasonable for Sethe to kill her children because she loves them, then there are social systems, of which slavery is one, in which children—very small children—are better off dead, systems in which even a bit of life is worse than death.

I will suggest that we do see Sethe's choice as reasonable and that we must see it as reasonable if we are to acknowledge, as we sometimes do seem to be able to do, the deep-rootedness of racism generally. Thus, we need to look for an understanding of reasonableness that can accommodate her choice. Indeed, the question of whether Sethe does the right thing is not as interesting as the difficulty of raising the question itself. Elsewhere, in a discussion of American literature, Morrison argues that autonomy, authority, and freedom—essential concepts of the "American Dream"—are defined in the American literary tradition in terms of the unfreedom, primitiveness, indeed the invisibility of African Americans.[11] If we ask whether Sethe did the right thing, we have to ask what this can mean in a system in which to her such a concept does not even apply. For the question even to make sense, we have to be able to imagine a description of her situation in which her claims to human status, to self-respect and dignity—indeed, her fundamental moral responsibility to herself and her children—are not themselves taken to be morally questionable.

As I hope will become clear, I take the question of individual rationality to be a question about what constitutes good reasons for an individual's choices and actions, a question that is distinct from questions about moral reasonableness but that involves a moral component. I do not take the question of Sethe's individual rationality, for example, to be a question merely about the *understandability* of her choice. For I might easily come to understand her choice—as resulting from psychological states, certain beliefs, and so on—without thinking it reasonable. Rather, the question of reasonableness is a normative question about whether she possesses good reasons where what constitutes good reasons is determined not just relative to individual aims and interests but also to moral considerations. Individual rationality has often been understood by philosophers not just as the capacity to reason well instrumentally, to find the best means to immediate ends, but as the capacity to deliberate and act according to a conception of one's best interests—one that depends on moral considerations as well as on important idiosyncratic aims and commitments. What I propose as a complication to this picture is that the kinds of moral considerations required for the articulation and defense of *some* people's interests need to be discovered, often through claims—in theory and action—to real personal human worth. I argue that if the notion of individual rationality is to accommodate the pursuit of dignity and self-respect for people whose claims to such goods are denied by the structure of the society as a whole, it must also be a question about personal integrity, about the significance of certain choices in bringing the conditions for such integrity about, sometimes regardless of whether such choices advance interests and aims the individual actually identifies at the time.

In Sethe's case, questions about reasonableness cannot be separated from questions about whether Sethe can *be* as a person at all, about what she must *become* to possess interests and desires that would reflect her real interests in human flourishing. Individual rationality *is* a question, ultimately, about whether a person's choices and actions constitute the best means to her most important ends. But for some people, the very possibility of the right sorts of ends—practically and theoretically—needs to be brought about, sometimes through individuals' claims to value, sometimes through social change. Thus, I argue that individual rationality ought not to be thought of as being defined in terms of ends. In particular, the possibility of ends such as self-respect and dignity, indeed, of human flourishing generally, often needs to be brought about. I argue that in unjust societies, people often have to have the courage to make certain moral claims and must believe them strongly enough to act on them, sometimes at great cost to themselves, before they can discover the general moral conceptions that could justify such claims. Thus, in some cases, individuals have to act and choose *first* before the ends in terms of which the reasonableness of their actions and choices, as *individual* actions and choices, becomes imaginable.

I use terms such as "real interests" and "genuine autonomy" to distinguish between what might appear to be in someone's interests or to constitute autonomous action, given current social conditions, and what is in fact in her interests or what *would* constitute autonomous action if conditions were such that it were possible for her to deliberate as a full human being. In discussing the relationship between rationality and integrity, I intend to try to give substance to notions of real interests and objective ends. I examine these ideas from various directions in the first four chapters, particularly Chapters 2 and 3. One might think, for instance, that my objective interests, as opposed to my perceived interests, are those ends or plans I would have if I were able to consider my important desires and interests in light of complete information and an ability to reason well instrumentally. I argue that such a conception of objective interests, in its various developments, has the result, in important cases, that a genuine sense of dignity and self-respect is not in an individual's real interests. Instead, I argue that objective interests are more appropriately defined in terms of interests and desires an individual *would* have in more just and humane social circumstances, where what constitutes more just and humane social circumstances is a matter for sociological, moral, and political theory and empirical investigation. I argue in Chapter 4 that such a conception of real interests does not justify arbitrary state coercion, as some will fear. In fact, the popular liberal view of real interests, a view employed not only by liberals, is more likely to justify arbitrary state coercion than the view I am proposing. For I argue that the liberal view leaves unacknowledged and hence uncriticizable the imposition by the state and society generally of values and norms for human behavior and expectations that preclude even the conceivability for some people of the pursuit of human flourishing.

Even if we do not think Sethe is right in choosing to act as she does, we cannot come to know her and her deliberations without at least acknowledging that it is difficult to say that she *cannot* be right. For we cannot come to understand her without acknowledging the inadequacy of not implausible standards of (moral and nonmoral) reasonableness and the need to discover alternatives. Another issue of this book, then, is the role of moral imagination—the capacity to envision alternative social arrangements—in defining both individual reasonableness and the objective interests upon which judgments of reasonableness depend. Whereas on one level we might want to classify Sethe's act as immoral, on another level the question of morality just does not apply. It's the wrong question. To the extent that Sethe's choice is understood by readers at all, we recognize that it is hard to know what it would or could mean for her to do what is right—morally or nonmorally—in such circumstances. We understand Sethe's choice, if we do, not because we possess standards of reasonableness (for our standards may not be adequate); rather, we understand it because we know what *love* is. And as a result of Morrison's prose, we see Sethe's choice as a choice of this sort. Sethe's choice, identified as a choice of love and as reasonable for *being* a choice of love, demands moral explanation that may not be readily available, that may need to be discovered.

Thus, I argue that the moral component in questions about individual reasonableness is often a judgment about the moral nature of the society as a whole and hence moral vision of what would constitute a more adequate society. Indeed, questions about the individual whose rationality is at stake sometimes just *are* questions about the moral nature of the society as a whole. Fanon notices that "not only must the black man be black; he must be black in relation to the white man." The problem, he says, is not so much a problem of *imposition* of certain standards, of the existence of oppressive practices and institutions, but that the pervasive influence of such standards results in a "definitive structuring of the self and of *the world*."[12] Whatever Fanon thinks about himself, however he assesses his own worth, he has to do so within a system defined by certain norms of behavior and importance. And he recognizes that it could never be enough to confront racist norms intellectually since it is precisely those norms that defined intellectual validity to begin with. In the end, there will always be the occasion when "I had to meet the white man's eyes,"[13] to defend what had to be defended in terms that disallowed the very premises.

The issue of "blackness," for Fanon, is not an issue of particularity, of *self*, at least not at first glance. Rather, it is a recognition of the social unity that exists, a naming of the standards and values that make it the case that the black man can only "be black in relation to the white man." The "fact of blackness" is an issue because the society is racist, not because of any idiosyncratic commitment on Fanon's part. Fanon's exploration of this fact, a fact about his identity in this particular situation, is not above all a concern for his own identity: On the contrary, it is a concern to understand what kind of society it is that denies to himself and others any possibility for *genuine* individual identity.

The moral component of personal integrity, therefore, also depends on moral imagination, on general beliefs about what *ought* to be possible. By "personal integrity," I understand a normative conception of identity, the *adequacy* of a person's sense of individuality. Identity is a way of understanding oneself, but one's identity is not always adequate for autonomous action: One's self-concept, that which explains the course of one's choices and actions, is not always adequate for effective agency, for choices and actions that constitute the pursuit of one's real interests in human flourishing. I argue that a proper understanding of individual rationality requires an account of the metaphysics of individuality, including an account of the adequacy of individuality. And I propose that personal integrity be defined not primarily in terms of facts about the individual herself but rather in terms of paths of both personal and cognitive development, where the right sorts of paths of development are defined, in part, in terms of facts about the real prospects for human flourishing in a society with a certain structure and history. My criticism of liberalism in Chapters 2 and 4, then, is not that liberalism is too individualistic but rather that liberalism gives the wrong account of individualism, both of what it means for individuals to act in their real interests and of what it means to give primacy to the individual in social and political theory and policy development.

My concern in this book, in particular, is with the rationality, individual and social, of the *impossible dream*. For many people in systemically unjust societies, the pursuit of genuine self-respect, dignity, and autonomy is just that—an impossible dream. To the extent that social structures, ways of thinking and behaving, central values and norms presuppose the subordination of some members of society, human goods like self-respect and dignity are unimaginable for some people. Their pursuit, in practice, is crazy or at least is perceived this way. LeRoi Jones wrote that revolution is for many "one of those inconceivably 'romantic' and/or hopeless ideas that we Norteamericanos had been taught to hold up to the cold light of 'reason.' That reason being whatever repugnant lie our usurious 'ruling class' had paid their journalists to disseminate."[14]

Suppose Jones is right. If "reason," even occasionally, is itself defined by systems of unreason, systems that preclude even the imaginability of genuine alternatives or the plausibility of their pursuit, what is involved in deliberating properly about one's life or about the direction of one's society, particularly in cases in which that society is profoundly, historically unjust? I argue that reasoning well often requires the presupposition—in theory and practice—of an impossible dream. And since I take it for granted that it *is* often reasonable, even advisable, to pursue such dreams, I am attempting to give an account of notions of rationality and integrity that would allow us to see deliberation to that effect, deliberation that could be perceived as crazy, as genuine instances of rationality.

Throughout the book, I appeal to the notion of human flourishing and human truths. To the extent that questions about rationality and integrity must also be questions about what a society and an individual *can* be, judgments about individual rationality are interestingly dependent upon the presupposition of moral truths, upon the possibility of ongoing empirical investigation into possibilities for greater human flourishing. I do not defend a particular conception of human flourishing because I think such a project would be misconceived. Instead, I take the concept "human flourishing" to require empirical investigation, and my aim in discussing the nature of rationality and its relation to questions of integrity is, in part, to contribute to understanding of what such investigation involves. In assuming the existence and discoverability of human truths, I depart from some central tendencies in recent feminist theory. Yet, as I try to argue, the proper expression of some of the most radical insights of feminist theory presupposes just such a notion. I understand the idea of moral truths to express the possibility that some moral beliefs are justifiable in light of other nonmoral beliefs about human beings and societies, as well as by their role in ongoing social, political, and cognitive development—development the successfulness of which, when it is successful, is explained by facts about the (social and physical) world that is the object of investigation. Thus, I do not take an appeal to the notion of human flourishing to require any implausible assumptions about absolute truth or the specification of necessary and sufficient conditions for the defining of such a general term for all situations in all times. Instead, I take such an appeal to depend on the possibility, plausibly assumed in practice, of ongoing discovery of facts about the nature of social structures and their implications for the well-being of specific groups of people at particular times.

In the first chapter, I discuss Drucilla Cornell's remarks about the significance for political understanding of the retelling of social myths and fantasies. In discussing the story of Sethe in Morrison's *Beloved,* I suggest that Cornell's important insights are best expressed in conjunction with a broader epistemological picture addressing the contingency of knowledge claims upon the *bringing about* of more adequate conditions, including conditions having to do with who a person is and can be.

In Chapters 2, 3, and 4, I discuss a popular philosophical view about what it means to be acting in one's best interests, one I take to motivate much everyday thought about interests. I argue that this view, no matter how sophisticated its presentation, cannot accommodate questions about personal and group integrity raised by considerations of the nature and effects of systemic social injustice. People who are familiar with the insights of feminist theory and politics may find these discussions long. However, I do not think these discussions are too long for those who are not familiar with such work. My experience arguing with some (largely) nonfeminist political and ethical philosophers has persuaded me to resist shortening these discussions more than I have. Those who find the points obvious may want to skip these sections or at least the critical parts of these discussions. In Chapters 5 and 6, I begin to address some of the issues of personal integrity and social unity raised by the previous chapters. In these chapters I do not take myself to be presenting a full-fledged account of what personal or social integrity consists in; rather, my aim is to argue that there is nothing implausible or threatening about the idea that integrity can involve the kinds of objective constraints required if the proposal that individual rationality be defined in terms of radical personal and social transformations is not to end up justifying undesirable coercive repression. In Chapter 7, I address directly the epistemological role of personal relations and commitments in radical criticism and attempt to demonstrate the epistemological and metaphysical significance of recent work in this area in some feminist theory. In Chapter 8, I discuss Martha Nussbaum's defense of an Aristotelian account of rationality, one that shares some elements of my own. In pointing out some of the limitations of her account, I try, perhaps unsuccessfully, to draw ideas of earlier chapters together into a more complete picture.

I should mention here that I do not at any point directly address the issue of realism. Often, in presenting some of the arguments of this book and in my fourth-year and graduate course in the philosophy of culture at Queen's, I have received rather strong objections to my commitment to the idea of more adequate concepts (of self, society, morality) and the pursuit of human truths. I do not address realism here because this subject is not within my competence or, currently, my research interests. I do, however, at various points in the discussion rely on the quite extensive literature developing and defending naturalistic, realist conceptions of knowledge, justification, and the individuation of entities. Unless there are some compelling reasons for thinking that this literature fails to, and will not eventually more fully, develop a plausible alternative epistemological view to its foundationalist ancestors, reasons I have not so far discovered, I take worries about my underlying realist commitments to be unfounded.

I

Myths, Fantasies, and Realism:
The Story of Sethe

IN THE OPENING SENTENCES OF *Willful Virgin,* Marilyn Frye writes that the feminist project is impossible and inconceivable within the system of meanings and symbols that defines current societies. In her view, feminism requires "a persistent project of weaving a matrix of meanings, a world of sense, a symbolic order, in which I can place myself and in which I and all women have original (not relational or derivative), positive, liveable meaning."[1] At least arguably, one of the most significant contributions of feminist theory to ethics and political theory in general is this recognition that systems of meaning—the concepts and terms in which information and events are understood, and questions are formulated—preclude the understanding, even the imaginability, of certain important ethical and political possibilities.

But what does it mean for the pursuit of liberatory goals that the systems of meanings and symbols with which we live deny the very meaningfulness and understandability, even the identification, of such goals? What does it mean for the possibility of engaging in good reasoning, for devising and following strategies likely to promote liberatory goals?

Feminist legal theorist Drucilla Cornell is one who explicitly asks the question of what it means to be imposing on the world more adequate unifying concepts, particularly in theorizing oppression.[2] I take Cornell's work on ethics and deconstruction to be epistemologically significant for two reasons in particular: First, she suggests that some questions about essentialism are, in part at least, epistemological questions about how to achieve the right sort of ordered view of the world. They are often questions not so much about what it means to be a sort of person but rather about how best to classify people for the purposes of understanding a situation as a whole. Cornell recognizes what is rarely made explicit in discussions of essentialism, or of what might be called "identity politics"—namely, that understanding the world consists in achieving a unified vision of it and that identity questions are often issues about *how* we impose order on the world. Second, Cornell's treatment of issues of "difference" recognizes, as many such treatments do not, that properly identifying differences presupposes the possibility of properly identifying unities. Cornell's emphasis on myths and storytelling I take to be an important development of the role of the right sorts of unifying concepts for the proper identification of the differences in experiences and interests upon which effective political theory and strategy depend.

In discussing Cornell's remarks about Toni Morrison's *Beloved*,[3] I argue for the following two claims. First, questions about epistemic standards that arise in regard to issues about theorizing oppression cannot be answered without also asking questions about personal and political identities: Defining epistemic goals and standards often involves ethical and political questions about the appropriateness of general beliefs about who and what people are. I argue, for instance, that the significance of Sethe's story as regards understanding slavery presupposes general beliefs about what she *ought* to be able to be and to aspire to.

Second, questions about personal and political identities, about *sorts* of people, are dependent upon consideration of certain epistemic consequences. I suggest that questions about which characteristics and relationships appropriately define a group or an individual depend, in part, on questions about the role of certain kinds of categorization in an ongoing process of understanding and acting effectively in actual social and political circumstances.

I intend the discussion of Sethe to provide a kind of overview for the general argument about the relationship between rationality and integrity that follows. I argue on the one hand that the reasonableness of Sethe's choice to kill her children is explained in terms of the significance of such a choice to her claim to human worth—for herself and her children: Her choice is reasonable in terms of the role of such a choice in a process of acquiring a more adequate sense of self, including certain cognitive capacities, where adequacy is understood in terms of possibilities for acting in her real interests. On the other hand, I suggest that a more adequate sense of self is a result, in part, of actually acting in her interests: What it means for her to possess a more adequate sense of self only becomes evident when Sethe makes certain choices, choices that *constitute* the possibility of her pursuit of self-respect and dignity. Thus, individual rationality is often importantly dependent upon claims to personal worth and value—claims that sometimes constitute the disruption of one's settled sense of self. Moreover, the moral significance of such claims to worth and value is often defined in terms of facts about what does and what does not actually realize the individual's best interests—interests in acquiring a genuine sense of self-respect and dignity.

In discussing the reasonableness of Sethe's choice, I am interested primarily in nonmoral reasonableness, the significance of Sethe's choice relative to her idiosyncratic desires and aims. As I make clearer in Chapter 2, I take the notion of individual rationality to distinguish between cases in which individual agents do and do not act in their best interests, a distinction plausibly employed in everyday talk. In Sethe's case, we might think that she acts not only immorally but also irrationally as an individual. For her choice has a number of undesirable consequences for her, given her personal ends and values. My point in discussing examples such as that of Sethe is that whereas individual rationality depends to some extent on morality, in some cases the moral component is dependent upon the claim to *individual* rationality for certain choices and actions—that is, upon a claim to a conception of the agent and her society according to which her reasons for her choices and actions are indeed *good* reasons for her.

Similarities and Differences

Consider the wonderful image of the opening paragraphs of Elizabeth Spelman's *Inessential Woman* describing the relationship between a certain conception of unities and a desire for intelligibility.[4] In Iris Murdoch's *The Nice and the Good,* Uncle Theo is distressed by the "manyness" of the pebbles on the beach. Spelman writes:

> The beach is a source of acute discomfort to Uncle Theo. While the children's noise and exuberance bother him, what really seems to make him most anxious is the multiplicity of *things*. As if twinness weren't already enough of an ontological disturbance, there are on the beach all those pebbles, each clamoring in its particularity, the totality of them threatening the intelligibility, the tractability, the manageability of the world. Theo is a man who can only negotiate the possibility of plurality if the many can be reduced to a few or, best of all, to one. The horror of the manyness of the pebbles could then be stilled by the awareness that they are all instances of a single thing, pebblehood.[5]

The concern in Spelman's book is not just the fear of manyness; rather, it is the implications of such a fear for the achieving of feminist antiracist goals. For such a fear, Spelman points out, inspires the desire for a certain imposition—the imposition of concepts and standards defined *in advance* of active antiracist, anti-imperialist, antisexist struggle.

Spelman's connection between a problem about essentialism and one about intelligibility is significant. We cannot make sense of our experience or of information without applying unifying general concepts. As emerged from Hume's attempt to give an account of judgments of causality, there is a question about how we judge one experience or entity to be similar to another. Hume suggested that after we have experienced one event being followed by another a number of times, we come to expect the second sort of event whenever we experience the first sort.[6] But he did not provide an account of how we judge those events to be ones of the same sort to begin with. Any two events are similar in *some* respects, but when we make generalizations on the basis of experience of regularities, and when we use such generalizations to find explanations, we make judgments about some respects of similarity and difference being more significant than others. And the problem of essentialism in philosophy, as I discuss in Chapter 6, has been a problem about knowledge, about how or whether we can identify the *real* similarities and differences between the events and the phenomena we are trying to understand.

The problem for political theory is not that there don't exist the kinds of unities Uncle Theo was looking for—unities that can be defined in advance and to which manyness can effectively be reduced. Clearly, there are no such Platonic unities, but this is not the main worry motivating discussions about essentialism. Rather, the problem is, as seems evident in Spelman's discussion, that to the extent that political theorists assume they ought to *look* for things like real essences, they end up defining concepts like "humanity" or "women" incorrectly—in terms, specifically, of the experience and interests of currently dominant social groups. The assumption of real essences seems to be that relevant respects of similarity and difference can be defined a priori, in advance of empirical investigation, and the tendency to define unity a priori precludes proper appreciation of differences that become apparent only as a result of political engagement and struggle.

The worry about essentialism seems to be, in large part, that although there are no essences of the sort Uncle Theo was looking for, we seem not to be able to get along without them or something like them. Indeed, Cornell suggests, importantly, that the problem of defining unities may be the central problem of feminist theory. In her view, "If there is to be feminism at all, we must rely on a feminine 'voice' and a feminine 'reality' that can be identified as such and correlated with the lives of actual women, and yet at the same time all accounts of the feminine seem to reset the trap of rigid gender identities, deny the real differences between women . . . and reflect the history of oppression and discrimination rather than an ideal or an ethical positioning of the Other to which we can aspire."[7] Political theory, especially radical political theory, depends on being able to identify real similarities and differences. More specifically, identifying *real* differences—differences, say, in terms of possibilities for acquiring important human goods—presupposes assumptions about real respects of similarity—similarity, for instance, in terms of human status.

The question of what it means to make claims about real similarities and differences is not the same question as that which preoccupied Uncle Theo.

We need not identify "pebblehood" or "womanness" in some fixed way, in advance of action and engagement, to make nonarbitrary judgments about how pebbles and women are to be classified and related to each other. The issue is one of objective epistemic standards: We want to know whether there are determinate answers to questions about how best to order things and, consequently, of how best to proceed—answers, in particular, that are not simply the result of certain discriminatory traditions. It may be, and I argue in Chapter 6, that the question of determinate epistemic standards is one not about the possibility of defining concepts and standards in advance but rather about the possibility of determining real similarities and differences in the specific context of an ongoing process of development of the right sort, where the "right sort" is defined in terms of the best available general moral and political theories, as well as ongoing empirical investigation. It may be, as Cornell appears to suggest, that the question of objective epistemic standards has to do not with questions about ultimate, fixed unities at all but with the relationship between the raising of certain kinds of questions and the application of certain general categories, and ongoing development of a specific sort in a particular direction.

A Social "Unconscious"

In a recent work, Cornell suggests that because all judgments and perceptions depend on traditions and some traditions are, in large part, racist and sexist, we need to pay attention to the social myths and fantasies that determine certain sorts of interpretations and preclude even the conceivability of others.[8] She calls the underlying myths and fantasies of a society a "social unconscious." Her proposal, roughly, is that we can sometimes derive standards for properly identifying relevant similarities and differences by examining the relationship between the retelling, or reformulating, of social myths and fantasies and political consequences.

Now, what could a "social unconscious" have to do with questions about ethical and political theory development? Cornell identifies as a problem for theories about oppression the tendency to analyze structures and meanings from within the realm of concepts and meanings that are consciously accessible to us—what deconstructionists have called "logocentrism." She suggests that to the extent that feminist theorists take for granted the conceptual machinery that is available and the perceptions and judgments the current conceptual traditions make possible, we cannot expect feminist theory to advance beyond the racism and ethnocentrism that often currently characterize it. Yet it is difficult to see how to effectively criticize such conceptual machinery. Her suggestion is that if we are even to be able to begin to identify the ways in which a society is deeply racist, sexist, and imperialist, we need to examine and retell the myths, or background stories, that explain our seeing and understanding some things and not others.

Consider Cornell's union organizing example.[9] She describes a situation in which the attempt to organize workers in an electronics plant in Silicon Valley, California was complicated by sexual relationships between an African-American man and a white woman who were both members of the organizing committee. After the work of the organizing committee was stopped by the (emotional and physical) tensions that arose around this relationship, it was suggested that the work of the committee could not continue without an explicit discussion of the dynamics of "whiteness" and "blackness" as they had been played out on this particular "theatre of desire."[10] Cornell points out that the decision to engage in examining questions about cultural representations of whiteness and blackness in this struggle was motivated by a realization that available conceptual representations of the conflict were both inadequate and distorting. Traditional conceptions of how to classify public and private spheres fail not only to make sense of the significance of this "private" sexual relationship for the "public" activity of political organization; such a conception of how things divide up also precludes the kind of understanding that is especially significant for this particular project—namely, an understanding of the significance of racist sexual stereotypes for the possibility of building nonracist workers' solidarity.

Cornell's suggestion is not that feminists need to examine the "underlying" myths and fantasies of a society to get it right about political organization. It does not make sense to suggest that theorists should aim to examine underlying myths and fantasies since such myths and fantasies are, after all, underlying. We cannot just go "look and see" what the underlying myths of a society are because we have only those very myths and fantasies upon which to base our observations. Instead, her suggestion is that the *connection* between the retelling of some myths and fantasies and certain political consequences—consequences identified in *action*—provides some basis for judging that some myths and fantasies are better than others and thus for identifying distorting assumptions. For instance, we may find out, when we offer certain alternative stories, that we are able by doing so to draw more appropriate connections, identify more aspects of oppression, act more effectively, and so on.

The idea that acquiring a more adequate understanding requires storytelling is not new; neither is it unique to feminist discussions. Philosopher of science Philip Kitcher argues that successful science provides the right sorts of storytelling resources.[11] Darwin's theory, for instance, provided a family of problem-solving strategies, related by their employment of a particular style of historical narrative.[12] Stories involving descriptions of ancestral populations, modification through subsequent generations, and selection and inheritance of characteristics could be told to answer a host of biological questions. Thus, Kitcher argues that it is a mistake to think of scientific theories as small sets of propositions. What Darwin proposed was a set of storytelling strategies, and his success consisted in the fact that such strategies could be employed again and again to explain complex and diverse phenomena that were in need of explanation.

Abductive inference, after all, is just a kind of storytelling: When Mendel crossed his pea plants and produced certain results, he looked for a story that, if it were true, would be able to explain his results. His story was not arbitrary. He proposed the most plausible story in light of background beliefs—some of which would have been well supported—and observable results. Many have argued that the justification of beliefs is not a matter of the logical relations between propositions but is, instead, a feature of the processes, including psychological processes, by which people arrive at beliefs. And part of such processes is the telling of stories, the invention, in some cases, of alternative ways of unifying the world, of classifying things and experiences as the same or different. Whether such stories are successful depends on whether they correspond to some degree to facts about how the world actually is. If Mendel's stories didn't get at least something right, they would not have been able to produce the kinds of results—in explaining unexpected observations, making connections to other well-supported theories, giving rise to additional questions, and so on—they did produce.[13]

Myths, Fantasies, and Morrison's *Beloved*

In a discussion of *Beloved,* Cornell suggests that Sethe's attempt to kill her children to protect them from slavery problematizes the myth of Medea, an "underlying social fantasy," and that the retelling of this myth makes possible a more adequate understanding of the reality of slavery.[14] The Medea myth (at least on some readings) is a story about a mother killing her children to protect them from the father. The mother kills her children not out of vengeance toward the father but to protect them from the loss of their autonomy. In Morrison's novel, this myth is problematized, according to Cornell, because whereas the mother, Sethe, attempts to kill her children because she loves them, she has been denied a parental relationship to her children by slavery. Indeed, the mother cannot *be* a mother to the children she has borne because they are not hers under slavery. In *Beloved,* according to Cornell, the myth of the "killing mother" is retold, and "the 'meaning,' the deep significance of killing one's children, is problematized, by the slave 'reality' in which the mother is allowed to bear the children but not to 'raise' them."[15] The retelling of the myth as a story in which there is no autonomous life to be denied to the children in the first place, because of slavery, "dramatizes the very difference of the Afro-American mother's situation."[16]

According to Cornell, *Beloved* challenges on a profound level the idealization of mothering as the basis for a unique feminine "reality," an idealization reflected in the Medea myth. As she says, "In the context of slavery, mothering (in the sense of bearing and raising children) tragically takes on its own meaning through the stark denial of maternal control or even of intervention into her children's lives."[17] Now, many will think that in making claims about women's "reality," Cornell is committing herself to the possibility of there being one true story both about what really is in women's interests and about the nature of sexist and racist oppression. Her point about *Beloved*, though, is that we see what is wrong with a basic social myth—a presumption about how women's experience in general is characterized—when we apply it to the experience of an African-American woman and it fails to make sense. But it is not the examination of the myth by itself, or even the claim that this particular myth is the most relevant, that is of fundamental importance here. The significance of the myth is that when we retell it in the right ways, it makes possible the identification of the "very difference of the African-American mother's situation,"[18] where the "difference" is the quite specific ways in which African-American women are oppressed. In other words, the significance of the myth has to do with the consequences of certain kinds of conceptual reordering, whatever the initial motivation may happen to be, for the acquiring of representations more appropriate for proceeding in a certain way.

It is important to notice the significance of the "very difference" here. In Cornell's discussion, the very difference is the *real* difference between white women and African-American women—difference in respect of living conditions and opportunities—within a specific social order. The very difference of the African-American woman's situation is that she is wrongfully and unjustly enslaved. This difference, though, is only a *difference* if African-American women are the *same* as white women in relevant respects—in particular, in respect of being human beings. If we were to think of Sethe in terms of the then dominant conceptual framework, the difference between Sethe and a white woman is that Sethe is *less* than fully human, not that she is unjustly treated *as* human. Difference cannot be defined in terms of injustice if, as in the terms of slavery, Sethe is such that considerations of justice are not applicable. The differences Cornell has in mind here are, presumably, differences between how African-American women and white women are treated within the current social structures—*real* differences. But such differences only become salient when we get it right about the real similarities. And part of what is involved in getting it right about real similarities is effective criticism of the concepts and theories we mistakenly assume in *judging* things and people to be similar or different.

Myth and Realism

There are two questions that need to be raised about Cornell's suggestion about a social unconscious and about the possibility of effectively examining underlying social myths and fantasies. First, in the case of *Beloved*, what explains the application of this particular myth, the myth of Medea, to the story of Sethe? Why try to understand Sethe's story in these terms? And second, why should we think that because the Medea myth fails to make sense of Sethe's experience, it has been shown to be a distortion of reality? Why should we think, that is, that the myth has been problematized by reality rather than, say, by an arbitrarily constructed story? The question to be answered is about how we can properly identify real similarities and differences given that the conceptual and practical traditions upon which we base such judgments are often, among other things, racist. The suggestion is that the relationship between the retelling of certain myths and fantasies and political consequences—the fact that some retelling of stories makes more effective political theory and action possible—provides a basis for such judgments, guiding us to an understanding of women's real interests and the real nature of oppression. But we need to ask how we take some particular relations to have this significance and how, in particular, we take some political consequences to constitute more effective possibilities for theory and action than others.

Cornell suggests that when we try to understand Sethe's story in terms of the Medea myth, we find that the myth fails to make sense of the story. But why would we apply that myth at all, and why should we take its failure to explain to be significant? Why would we draw on *that* particular myth to understand *this* story? We might well not hear the story of Sethe's actions as Cornell does, as challenging the myth of the "killing mother," for we might not interpret the story in ways that would make it relevantly similar to the "killing mother" myth. According to Paul D., after all, Sethe's understanding of how to protect her children—namely, by taking a handsaw to their throats—is unorthodox.[19] In fact, Paul D. thinks Sethe's entire scheme of meanings is unorthodox. Why do we not interpret the story, as Paul D. first does, as a story about a mistake, about an action that failed?

Indeed, according to some not implausible standards, Sethe's attempt does appear to have failed. She goes to prison, Baby Suggs begins to die, she loses her daughter, her two sons leave, and so on. Perhaps a more plausible explanation of Sethe's act than Sethe's own explanation is that Sethe is not a loving mother at all but rather is crazy, unrealistic, and selfish. Yet if the mother is not loving, or if, because she *has* no relation of protection and nurturance, she is not a mother at all, there would be no reason to see her story as relevant to the "killing mother" myth. We might think the killing mother myth does not fit Sethe's story, either because Sethe's story does not involve love or because the story does not involve a mother. And if the myth does not *apply* to the story, the story cannot show it to be problematic.

But, of course, there *is* a connection between the myth and the story. Sethe in fact struggles for autonomy and does to some degree achieve it. At least, she manages to acquire for herself the capacity to deliberate about her situation in a way that better reflects her real interests. If autonomy is, as some have said, that which makes effective agency possible,[20] Sethe acquires autonomy. Indeed, what explains Sethe's attempt to kill her children is, in part, her experience of having decided to leave Sweet Home with her children and having carried it out: "I did it. I got us all out. Without Halle too. Up till then it was the only thing I ever did on my own. Decided. And it came off right, like it was supposed to. . . . I had help, of course, lots of that, but still it was me doing it; me saying, *Go on,* and *Now.* Me having to look out. Me using my own head. But it was more than that. It was a kind of selfishness I never knew nothing about before. It felt good. Good and right."[21] Whereas Paul D. has learned that slaves should love small, should pick "the tiniest stars out of the sky to own,"[22] Sethe chooses to stitch a garment herself from a piece of cloth for her daughter, to commit herself to her child. The connection between the myth and the story is one that exists in terms of Sethe's actions, commitments, and struggle—a connection that cannot be made entirely in terms of available concepts, for Sethe's commitments to love and autonomy do not make sense in terms of a dominant conceptual framework that classifies her as subhuman. But they do indeed make sense in terms of general human needs and expectations—in particular, for dignity and self-respect.

But what makes this story significant in the first place? What makes it relevant to understanding reality? Is it just because Sethe *says* she experiences feeling "good and right" that the story raises questions about what *is* good and right in general? After all, it is not obvious that we should take someone's attempt to kill her children as an indication of how we should understand love and motherhood in general. Sethe's account of her act demands reflection and understanding not just because she tells the story but also because of facts *about* the story, ones she may not herself explicitly acknowledge. Cornell says, for instance, that we cannot understand Sethe's act except in the context of slavery, especially the *tragedy* of slavery.[23] In terms of the conceptual tradition that grounds the practice of slavery, of course, there is no need to try to explain Sethe's act as an act of a mother attempting to protect her children's autonomy. For Sethe is not a mother; indeed, she is not a person. But we do need an explanation of Sethe's act if we understand it in terms of the tragedy of slavery. Understanding the tragedy of slavery requires general beliefs about Sethe as a human being, as a person with certain distinctively human needs and capacities. It is in terms of a story about a human being who loves and is committed to her children, not a story about someone defined in terms of slave conditions, that the act with the handsaw is indeed odd and in need of explanation.

Now, one might think that to say that Sethe's act requires explanation because of what we believe about humanity and injustice begs the question of justification that Cornell, for one, has raised. For the idea of women's "reality" raises questions within feminist theory precisely because we cannot take for granted beliefs we have about such general notions as "humanness." Surely, it would be a mistake to propose that Sethe's act of selfishness be explained in terms of beliefs about humanity and the moral status of slavery if the question to begin with is one about how we can take our beliefs about anything at all to reflect those aspects of reality that are denied by a profoundly sexist, racist conceptual tradition.

The circularity, though, is not necessarily vicious. Cornell's suggestion appears to be that it is the *process* of defining unities and relations in the *context* of an ongoing effort to effectively order the world and act in it politically that provides grounds for making nonarbitrary judgments about real similarities and differences. Such a claim need not involve any assumption of the truth of some particular conception of, say, "humanity," defined in advance of political struggle. Rather, it could be a claim about the role of interaction with the actual physical, social, and political reality in the right sort of modification of general beliefs and concepts. The kind of circularity involved in taking general concepts based on background theory to define the questions a successful explanation of which can be taken to provide, in part, support for those concepts and theories is only a problem if we accept foundationalist epistemological assumptions. If not, such circularity merely expresses the dialectical relationship between theory development and interaction with the causal structures of the world.[24]

The significant feature of beliefs about, for instance, the wrongness of racism is that racism *is* wrong and that, because this is so, naming it as wrong does in fact contribute to the achieving of certain goals. In other words, what distinguishes this belief from some others is facts about what happens to be the case and the relevance of such facts to ongoing developments of a certain sort. The possibility of discriminating between the appropriateness of an explanation in one case and not in the other does not, it appears, require any commitment to the idea that there exists some absolute proof of something like the wrongness of racism. It only requires that there be good reasons for doing so—reasons the adequacy of which is dependent upon the developments and circumstances of a process of a certain sort, namely, one that is, to some relevant extent, characterized by actual engagement with appropriate aspects of the situation. I discuss this feature of knowledge further in Chapter 6.

Problems

The relationship between the right sort of storytelling and the identification of real similarities and differences has some notable consequences—consequences, in particular, for what we take to be of central importance to theorizing racism. First, the very identification of relevant similarities between Sethe's particular experience and others described in a certain way according to general background beliefs itself depends on general background beliefs about human experience. Second, interpreting the consequences of applying the "killing mother" myth to Sethe's story also depends on general beliefs that go beyond what could be gotten from an understanding of Sethe's particular experience alone. Yet if this is so, it is not clear exactly what work is done by something like what Cornell calls a "social unconscious."

We can understand Sethe's story as she understands it, as a story of love, if we interpret her remarks and perceptions in light of our relatedness to and our assumptions about her interest in self-determination. Her deciding to try to kill her children stands out in the novel not as a decision to deprive her children of the minimal conditions for life accorded them under slavery but rather as an attempt to claim for herself something of which, under slavery, she ought not even to have been able to dream. As a "used-to-be-slave" woman it would be reasonable for Sethe to choose, as Paul D. does, to love small, to pick "the tiniest stars out of the sky to own."[25] Yet Sethe chooses to love big, to assume that she can choose to try to "protect" her children. If the reader understands Sethe's act as an act of love rather than as crazy and selfish, she has to be interpreting Sethe's choices in light of assumptions about what Sethe *ought* to be able to dream and aspire to instead of what would be reasonable for her on then current terms.

But on what grounds do we make judgments about what Sethe *ought* to be able to dream? Paul D.'s judgment that slaves ought to pick "the tiniest stars out of the sky to own" is based on a good understanding of the then current situation for African-American people under slavery, as well as on self-respect. His reasons for thinking that used-to-be-slaves should love small is that there is always the risk that what is loved will be taken away, and one has to be able to continue loving.[26] His judgment reflects a desire to fulfill personal ends and interests, as well as an informed awareness of what the likely consequences will be of certain kinds of actions and commitments. Sethe's reasoning about her own situation is not a refutation of Paul D.'s premises; they share similar commitments, and she knows as well as Paul D. does what kinds of possibilities exist for her under slavery. Sethe's reasoning, however, rejects the very formulation of a question of how used-to-be-slaves should love as one in terms of what is most realizable under conditions of slavery. Sethe deliberates about her situation not on the basis of a different perception of the costs and benefits involved in loving her children but rather of a different perception of what the relevant question is. In her view, the issue of how to love is not at all an issue about how best to realize some amount of love and still be able to survive under conditions of slavery; rather, for her, the issue is one about how to *be* such that *real* love is possible at all.

Sethe's deliberation is not easily understood as one of weighing the costs and benefits of acting and choosing as she does. For she cannot know what costs and benefits are relevant to her commitment to the pursuit of human dignity: She cannot know what such a pursuit means. We see from the discussions Sethe has with Paul D. that thinking of herself as a mother is crazy according to terms available under slavery. It is crazy even to *think* of herself as a mother, let alone deliberate as a mother about her options for her children. In making her choice, Sethe claims a possibility for which there is good reason to think she possesses no moral justification, although this does not mean there *is* no such justification. It looks as though she makes a claim that, given the standards of reasonableness available to her under slavery, cannot be rationalized. Epistemically and ethically, then, Sethe's claim is a gamble. She makes a claim on the strength of intuitions that cannot be explicitly justified, probably not even to herself. And it looks as though her making the claim is precisely what is required for the discovery of such justification.

Sethe acts not on any weighing of options but on what she says she knows is "good and right." Now, if the reader thinks Sethe's action makes sense as an act of love and self-determination, she has to be assuming what is impossible under slavery for Sethe even to properly articulate—namely, that Sethe's commitment to real love for her children *is* right and reasonable. In making sense of Sethe's action as an act of love the reader assumes, for one thing, Sethe's full humanity and, for another, the reasonableness of her quest for self-respect and dignity. And such beliefs have no prominent place in the structure of slave society. Understanding Sethe's act as right and reasonable presumes not just different concepts and values but also contradictory ones, ones that provide an alternative interpretive framework from that which makes Paul D.'s judgments readily understandable and Sethe's not.

The significance of the notion of "social unconscious" is that in theorizing about racism and sexism, people have to pay attention to "underlying" social myths and fantasies and how they distort understanding of the ways in which people and phenomena should be classified. But it also seems to be true that we need to be able to offer an appropriate broader theoretical picture—indeed, a moral picture—to be able to identify and make proper sense of underlying myths and fantasies. It is commonly acknowledged that in cases in which an idea contradicts central, well-established beliefs and principles, it will not be understood, or at least believed, without the development of an alternative conceptual picture. For instance, Hilary Putnam points out that Newton's formula $f = mXa$ could never have been overthrown by an isolated experiment: Any experiment that purported to show that such a deep-seated principle was mistaken would be assumed to have somehow gone badly wrong.[27] Only the development of an entire alternative conceptual framework—Einstein's general theory of relativity—could throw such an important belief into doubt. Similarly, the proper identification and interpretation of social assumptions and values often require the development of a radically different social picture—a moral alternative—and such development demands the exercise of moral imagination.

The problem Cornell describes is that we cannot just look and see what underlying myths and fantasies are. She says, for instance, that if we think we can "finally raise the veil and 'see' that women are *fully human*," as Simone de Beauvoir suggests, then what we mean is that we "see" that women can be like men.[28] What we "see" is often influenced by inaccurate distorting assumptions, and we cannot just pick them out because we have only the same tradition of distorted beliefs and concepts on the basis of which to go look for them. Instead, we can come to understand relevant myths and fantasies if we look for the right sorts of alternative explanations and examine the political consequences of their application. The problem raised by Cornell's remarks, though, is that offering appropriate alternative explanations presupposes the possession of alternative values and norms of the right sort—indeed, often an alternative *vision* of what society should be and how it should be divided up, one that permits judgments about how the existing society is *wrong*. And such alternative visions cannot properly be formulated or implicitly presupposed without relying on general beliefs and theories about what such things as humanity, respect, and dignity really are—that is, on the presupposition of the discoverability of moral truths.

The important grain of truth in Cornell's discussion of the relevance of the "unconscious" is that racist, sexist assumptions are *implicit* in fundamental meanings and ways of thinking. Certain concepts, such as that of genuine autonomy for women, are, as Frye suggests, *unimaginable* in current, explicitly available, conceptual terms because the accepted understanding of such terms disallows such possibilities. The problem that arises for Cornell's view is that *how* such fundamental meanings and ways of thinking become challenged and replaced is not explainable in terms of what "underlies" any particular society by itself. For it appears that to explain how it is that we are able to make the connections between false universalizing assumptions and relevant experiences, we often already have to assume some general conception of humanity, dignity, and respect. Moreover, we must be able to appeal to a more appropriate social vision. To the extent that the sexist, racist character of a society itself precludes adequate understanding of certain general concepts, and explicit theoretical and political work needs to be done to acquire such understanding, it is not clear that attention to a "social unconscious" can do the most important work of explaining how people come to understand systemic racism.

Politics of Identity: The Epistemic Status of Identity

The insight represented in Cornell's discussion may not be best expressed as a point about a social "unconscious" but rather as one about the nature of knowledge more generally—in particular, of the role of the bringing about of the right sorts of personal and social conditions in the pursuit of understanding. A couple of points are especially significant about Cornell's suggestion that *Beloved* challenges basic social assumptions about women's reality, making possible a more adequate understanding of the tragedy of slavery. One is that both Sethe's understanding of her own situation and the reader's understanding of Sethe's situation are explained in part in terms of identity—in particular, of possibilities for more genuinely human identities. The other is that the significance of identities in the development of radical political theory and strategies must at least sometimes be understood primarily in terms of broader epistemological questions about objectivity and justification.

As regards the first point: When Paul D. tells her there could be worse things than returning to Sweet Home, Sethe's response is, "It ain't my job to know what's worse. It is my job to know what is and to keep them away from what I know is terrible. I did that."[29] We might wonder, however, how Sethe claims to know "what is" and how she can be so certain about her options. The only reason Sethe gives to explain her actions is that she has experienced what it is like to be free and to act on her own. As she says, "It was more than [me using my own head]. It was a kind of selfishness I never knew nothing about before. It felt good. Good and right."[30] She then describes how she stitched a garment for her daughter and says, "Well, all I'm saying is that's a selfish pleasure I never had before. I couldn't let all that go back to where it was, and I couldn't let her or any of em live under schoolteacher. That was out."[31] Now, this sounds more like a description of her feelings than an account of reasons.

But it might be precisely the absence of an explicit rationalization that accounts for the fact that Sethe does understand and can claim to understand at least to some extent, her situation. For any kind of explicit rationalization on her part would have to depend on a conceptual tradition that disallows Sethe's full existence as a person. What distinguishes Sethe from, say, Paul D. is that Sethe *has* committed herself to loving her children. Moreover, Sethe *claims* this commitment as a part of her identity: She not only makes the commitment, but she also insists on thinking about herself as someone who *ought* to be able to make such a commitment. Paul D. criticizes her for this since in his view a "used-to-be-slave woman" should love "just a little bit" to protect herself.[32] Yet it is because Sethe has made this commitment and acted on it—because she has claimed this commitment as relevant to her individual deliberations—that she can no longer understand herself as she is supposed to understand herself under slavery. And from that perspective, a perspective of knowing what it is like to act for herself, she cannot interpret her options the way she would have previously. She cannot interpret slavery as an option for *her* unless she denies what she is. And when Paul D. hears Sethe speak in this way, he is shaken:

> This here Sethe talked about love just like any other woman; talked about baby clothes like any other woman, but what she meant could cleave the bone. This here Sethe talked about safety with a handsaw. This here new Sethe didn't know where the world stopped and she began. Suddenly he saw what Stamp Paid wanted him to see: more important than what Sethe had done was what she claimed.[33]

What Sethe claims and what is startling, even to Stamp Paid and Paul D., is that she is a full human being. But she is only able to make this claim *because* of what she has done and indeed of what she has become.

Some feminists have understood the emphasis on identity in recent North American feminist theory to be self-centered and conservative.[34] And it is true that in some feminist discussions of difference, theorists have presented the impression that they are concerned about something like a notion of difference per se, with obvious undesirable theoretical and political implications. It is important, though, to consider what some feminists who have emphasized difference and identity have in fact had in mind and how other presentations might more charitably be read. In *Beloved,* Sethe understands things about her life and situation because she has acted in certain ways and made certain commitments. She attempts to protect her children from slavery because, given what she has experienced and the commitments she has made, she cannot conceive of slavery as an option at all for her or her children. The story is about her struggle for identity. Yet the significance of identity in *Beloved* has nothing to do with a notion of identity per se or with affirming particularities. Instead, it has everything to do with bringing about the right sorts of conditions for the understanding of, and action within, a quite specific oppressive context.

What is significant epistemologically about Sethe's struggle is that given that Sethe is part of a social system that thoroughly denies her existence as a full human being, she may not be able to acquire understanding of her self and her situation *as* a full human being *except* by actively pursuing—through personal commitments and alternative storytelling—the realization of certain possibilities: Her understanding of her options as a human being depends in part on her attempting to bring them about. In a situation in which the conceptual background precludes the imaginability of certain possibilities altogether, personal action and commitment, including becoming a certain kind of person, are epistemically significant.

Sethe's understanding depends on her acquiring a certain sort of identity—one appropriate for the pursuit of certain goals within a situation of a specific structure. It turns out that the reader's understanding of Sethe's story is also in some sense dependent on possibilities for bringing about certain sorts of identities or of ways of being. In discussing Buchi Emecheta's fiction, Donna Haraway argues that readers do not bring to a piece of work a set of experiences that "pre-exist as a kind of prior resource."[35] Instead, experience is what becomes articulable through the drawing of "just-barely-possible connections." In Haraway's view, the development of feminist and antiracist discourses requires learning "how to structure affinities instead of identities," by which she means, presumably, that the development of such discourses requires making connections with others' stories and experiences in ways that do not presuppose identities existing in some finished form. But the development of those "affinities"—the ones that make readers' experiences articulable in a way that promotes understanding of racism, for instance—itself presupposes some sense of identity. For to know how things or people are really connected, we need to know what those things or people really *are,* at least approximately. The possibility of discovering the right sorts of affinities presupposes some sense of what the appropriate affinities are affinities *between.*

For instance, if we understand Sethe's story as a story of love, it is because we reject one conceptual framework and relate to the story in terms of alternative concepts and standards. If we understand the options open to Sethe under slavery as various sorts of death, say, we have to be assuming that for Sethe, as for all human beings, living properly involves certain goods, like some amount of control over one's life. But this understanding requires *identifying* with Sethe as a person in terms of a concept of humanness disallowed both by her social framework and, as well, by the current one. Haraway's point is that it would be possible for a reader to overlook the connections that really exist between her own and Sethe's experience if she assumed, say, that her identity in terms of a sexist, racist tradition were adequate and complete. The problem is that to *not* presuppose, in interpretation, such a prior identity, there has to be some reason to think such an identity is *wrong*. And one cannot identify something as wrong unless one possesses some sort of notion of what is right, at least vaguely. This suggests that making the right sorts of connections presupposes at least some *suggestion,* even if not an absolute, complete vision, of what a more adequate alternative identity, and sometimes an alternative community, would be like.

Politics of Identity: Identity Is Epistemically Constrained

This brings us to the other side of the epistemic significance of identity. Sethe knows certain things because of what she becomes. Her process of becoming is epistemically significant to the extent that her being what she is necessarily makes certain options—like genuine autonomy for African-American women—at least thinkable. But this suggests that what makes it the case that one identity, or vision of identity, is better than another is also, in part, epistemically *defined.*

Suppose we think Sethe is right in drawing a connection between her experience of selfishness, the rightness and goodness of it, and her real possibilities for a better life. Suppose we think she is right in thinking that whatever a genuinely human life would be like for her, it depends on preserving for herself, as part of her identity, her experience of loving and being committed to her children. What would account for her being right? Why should we think she is right to take the attitude she does and not accept, as Paul D. does, that she should love "just a little bit?" The answer cannot be that what makes Sethe's actions right is that they lead to the right sorts of consequences, or at least this cannot be the whole answer. For it is hard to see why we should think that the right sorts of consequences have, in fact, followed for Sethe. Some consequences of Sethe's actions are certainly undesirable—her daughter is dead, her mother-in-law gives up and dies, her sons leave.

Perhaps we might think Sethe's actions and attitudes are right because they reflect some kind of essential humanness. We might think, for instance, that Sethe's actions are an expression of an essential human capacity to love one's children and to attempt to protect them. But then, of course, it is not clear why we should see Sethe's actions as actions of this type: If we derive criteria for assessing Sethe's actions from a conception of essential human capacities, it is hard to see why we should take Sethe's killing her children to be an expression of such capacities.

Of course, as readers we do think Sethe is right, at least in some sense, both because of consequences that come about and because she expresses human capacities. But we can only explain why we take some consequences to be more significant than others and why we understand Sethe to be real-izing human capacities if, as Cornell suggests, we understand her actions and perceptions within a particular context—namely, the context in which African-American people rightly and reasonably aspire to resist the specific oppression of slavery. Moreover, to the extent that we think such aspira-tions *are* right and reasonable, we rely on standards and concepts that are not those which characterize present North American societies, at least not as a whole. Thus, if we have intuitions about Sethe's reasonableness, we presuppose the possibility of an alternative moral context or at least an al-ternative understanding of the same context. We exercise moral imagina-tion. It is true that one reason for thinking Sethe is right in her attitude and approach is that she is able to claim what she claims in the face of Paul D.'s and others' doubts. But we need to ask why we think her claiming what she does is significant and right. It has to do, surely, with assumptions, among other things, about the moral nature of the situation—that slavery and racism are indeed wrong—and with assumptions about how such a situa-tion can be appropriately addressed.

Now, some will object to even raising the question of whether Sethe's act was the right one. For such a question might seem, on some understand-ings, to presuppose that there is some one answer to questions about what Sethe should have done in the situation in which she is approached by Schoolteacher. But we need not accept an epistemological view according to which epistemic virtues are defined entirely in terms of the pursuit of ab-solute and complete truth. A more empirically constrained conception of knowledge suggests that questions about truth are not questions about the pursuit of a single, true story about how the world is but are questions in-stead about the pursuit, as far as is possible in actual conditions, of an ap-propriate ordering of the world.[36] What we want to know, and what needs to be answered for the sake of radical politics, is how we make nonarbi-trary judgments about the greater appropriateness of some ways of order-ing and acting in the world over others—in other words, a question about objective, epistemic standards. The (epistemological) point about Sethe's story is that Sethe's acquiring a certain identity—a self-concept—is an ac-quiring of epistemic standards, of a (partial) way of ordering the world. To the extent that knowledge claims are contingent upon circumstances and conditions, Sethe's acquiring of a more adequate sense of self *is* the acquir-ing of more adequate conditions for knowledge. No commitment to the idea that there is some one way in which Sethe ought to have acted is re-quired to hold that it is possible to make a nonarbitrary judgment about the relative rightness of available options, given the circumstances and al-ternatives.

It looks as though to the extent that we think Sethe was not just crazy when she acted as she did, that there were good reasons for her actions, it is because we see her action as a certain sort of becoming within a process of development with a certain direction—namely, the pursuit of self-respect, dignity, and personal integrity. Sethe struggles for an understanding of a situation with certain definite structural features, one of which is its denial of dignity and respect to African-American people. That her struggle and success are epistemically significant has to do, it would appear, with external features of the situation, with the fact, for instance, that what she does and becomes is indeed a defiance of actually existing oppressive structures.

In thinking, if we do, that Sethe did the right thing in some sense, we need not appeal to an implausible notion of eternal, universal principles about what is right, applicable to any person at any time. Rather, principles of reasonableness, like epistemic standards generally, are more appropriately thought of as radically contingent upon particular circumstances and conditions, specifically upon the bringing about of conditions more adequate for Sethe's claim to human worth. In part, Sethe's act is significant because it makes possible her claim to be what she has become—more autonomous and self-respecting. But it also makes possible Paul D.'s capacity to identify possibilities he could not identify previously. (It is Paul D., after all, who tells Sethe at the end of the story that "you your best thing, Sethe. You are."[37])

If it is a consideration of consequences that makes us think Sethe had good reason for acting as she did, it is consequences of a particular sort— having to do with self-respect and dignity—relative to the needs of a particular struggle at a specific time, as well as general beliefs about what that struggle is about. The possibility of judgments about what is *really* in Sethe's interests—as opposed to what would appear to be in her interests given slave conditions—does not presuppose any set of unities of a fixed, eternal sort. This would be the case only, as suggested previously, if one were to take for granted implausible assumptions of foundationalist epistemology.[38] Instead, it presupposes the possibility of acquiring understanding about the nature of oppression in Sethe's society, as well as about what kinds of choices are more or less likely to bring about the sorts of possibilities and conditions required for her greater liberation.

Real Similarities and Differences

So what does this mean for talk about difference and identity—in particular as such discussion arises in the context of concern about radical political theory development? I suggest that one way to understand feminist discussions of difference and identity—discussions generally having to do with personal development—is in terms of a broader picture of the nature of knowledge. To the extent that all knowledge claims are dependent upon practical and conceptual traditions—that we know things when we do *because* of, not in spite of, our rootedness in certain belief and value systems—what people are able to understand also depends on who they are and who they can be. Some critics charge that emphasis on identity issues within feminist, antiracist, and anti-imperialist theory is narcissistic, that it focuses on particular identities and therefore undermines the possibilities for unified liberatory visions (I discuss this in Chapter 7). In fact, however, the "differences" that are in question in such literatures—differences of experiences and interests—are differences that often only become salient to the degree that people are in fact concerned not at all with particularities but with a general liberatory vision.

For instance, gender and race become issues of identity and difference not when people are concerned with themselves *as* women, minorities, or both but, on the contrary, when they are concerned with their possibilities as *human*. A woman is not *different* from men, with respect to being oppressed, unless she can somehow be identified as a person of the same sort—namely, human. But that kind of judgment is only possible in light of at least some kind of more general, unifying vision—one that at least involves some conception of how people *ought* to think of humanity. It is a mistake to think that emphasis on difference and identity in feminist and postcolonialist theory is an emphasis on something like difference or identity per se. For interesting differences—such as gender and race and also age, sexual orientation, physical capacity, and so on—only become significant when a general identity is being *pursued*, namely, a *human* identity. A disabled person who is surrounded by nonablest people may not think of her particular disability as a relevant identifying feature. She may think of her disability as something like eye color: It is a physical feature but not one that figures centrally into her self-concept. But if she enters a discriminatory work environment, she will be forced to consider her disability as an identifying feature. She will *have* to think of herself as disabled to make sense of the discriminatory treatment she receives. A particular difference becomes salient in this case not necessarily because of a concern about difference on the part of the individual but, more plausibly, because of a concern for sameness. The individual does what she does not because she is different but because she is the same in relevant ways—a human being. Some particular differences become salient not primarily because of *the individual* but rather because of *the institution*—more specifically, because of its discriminatory character and commitments.

To suggest that emphases on difference and identity in feminist and postcolonialist theory are narcissistic, as some have claimed, is to misunderstand the difficulties of acquiring adequate understanding of deep-seated institutionalized racism, sexism, imperialism, and so on. The point that has been made persistently and persuasively by feminists such as Cornell is that people cannot take for granted the position—physical, social, psychological, and intellectual—on the basis of which some sorts of phenomena are visible and understandable to them and others are not. The role of social and institutional structures in making some things and people identifiable and understandable and others not suggests that personal and social development and change are often epistemically significant and required. Not only is the view of feminist emphases on identity and difference as narcissistic a *political* mistake; it is also a failure to recognize the kinds of epistemological questions that are raised, and need to be raised, on a nonfoundationalist view of knowledge. Some have recently urged the pursuit of social epistemology and the recognition of the epistemic significance of community.[39] But any recognition of the epistemic significance of community has to lead to the realization that acquiring some kinds of knowledge requires the radical transformation of societies. So, sometimes epistemological questions cannot be settled, or even properly raised, without addressing ethical and political questions *first*. And at least some of these questions will have to do with identities.

In conclusion, at least some part of the acquiring of adequate understanding consists in the development or bringing about of the right sorts of individual or group identities. But part of what is involved in developing the right sorts of identities is consideration of what sorts of capacities and connections—importantly including epistemic ones—become possible as a result. Some would want to say that the appropriate constraints on identity are purely pragmatic—that is, that what determines what an individual or a group should become is just what they need to become to achieve certain liberatory goals. This ignores the fact, though, that people often have to make commitments and take actions *first* before they can begin to identify appropriate liberatory goals. Moreover, making the right sorts of commitments often involves broad theoretical assumptions—a social vision—of at least a tentative sort. Sethe does not do what she does because she has some conception of liberatory goals, and it is hard to say that what she does is *right* entirely on the basis of the goals she achieves. She says she does what she does because she knows what is terrible and what feels "good and right." If we want to say something about what it is that *makes* Sethe's actions the right ones for her in her situation, we have to go beyond the reasons that are explicitly available to her to a broader consideration of her social and historical situation. We have to look at history and at consequences—moreover, at specific aspects of history and certain sorts of consequences. What these are depends importantly, it seems, on general, albeit revisable, conceptions of human worth and dignity.

Cornell's proposal about an unconscious is significant in at least this respect. It seems to be true that some understanding cannot be acquired otherwise than by the bringing about of the right sorts of alternative structures and relations, by challenging in action the concepts and standards in terms of which information is interpreted. According to Sethe, her reasons for acting were that she felt "good and right." But it is possible that the reason she *felt* good and right was that it was *indeed* good and right for her to be able to choose on her own and commit herself to her children. Moreover, it is possible that what made it good and right for her was that it was true that she was oppressed by slavery in specific ways and that her acting and choosing in the way she did really did constitute a defiance. Thus, there are facts about Sethe's situation and prospects, facts about the nature of the social structures and history, that explain in part how she comes to believe what she believes. And it is because Sethe's beliefs are explained, if they are, by facts about the world that they are reliable, or approximately true, and that they can be effectively acted upon. We might understand the idea of an "unconscious," then, as the possibility that people do acquire understanding of their situations as a result of their situatedness *in* those situations, that people in fact acquire and possess more understanding about the reality of their situations than they can actually make explicit. Even though Sethe probably cannot identify and explicate the kind of life that would really be an alternative to slavery, that in which she—an African-American woman—would be able to be genuinely autonomous, she can acquire intuitions and feelings, as a result of her experience, that some sorts of things, in that context, are indeed more "good and right" than others. In the next chapter, I discuss the notion of tacit or nonpropositional knowledge that I take to explain the occasional epistemic reliability of intuitions and feelings.

Perhaps what Cornell ought to have said is not that feminists need to be concerned about a social unconscious, even relationally, but rather that feminists need to be concerned with the *bringing about* of the kinds of relations, circumstances, and states in terms of which what she calls an unconscious and its relevant consequences can effectively be identified. Sethe's story, it appears, is just one example of a struggle for identity that is also a struggle for understanding—understanding that, given the current conceptual framework, could not be acquired any other way than by bringing about certain conditions and ways of being. What this suggests about justification or about good reasons, it seems, is that sometimes the question cannot be answered entirely in strictly epistemological terms; it is at least partly a question about identity and, importantly, about the conditions for pursuing the right kinds of identity. The other side of this, though, is that sometimes questions about identity—especially the adequacy of identity—are not primarily questions about the individuals or groups whose identities are at issue; instead, they are questions about the structure of the institutions or the society, even the global context, in which individuals with interests in real human flourishing have to act and *be* in specific ways to proceed as human beings at all.

2

Transformation Experiences
and Rational Deliberation

I HAVE SUGGESTED THAT THE significance of Sethe's story for understanding slavery and racism requires a role for moral imagination—an appeal to moral vision of how society *ought* to be—that complicates questions about social knowledge and self-knowledge. In this chapter and the two that follow, I discuss at some length a popular philosophical picture of rationality and what examples like that of Sethe imply for notions of self, self-understanding, and social understanding.

I consider in some detail the philosophical development of a notion of individual rationality for the following reasons: First, as Italian Marxist philosopher Antonio Gramsci pointed out, we need to know what a tradition is about before we can move beyond it.[1] The focus of the discussions here is a popular story about what it means to be acting in one's best interests as an individual, a story that is taken for granted in liberal democratic societies in much political theory as well as, often, in everyday deliberations. If, as I suggested in Chapter 1, emphases on identity and personal development in some feminist work are indeed philosophically challenging—perhaps most importantly as regards the nature of knowledge and individuality—it is important to see what the implications of such insights are for traditional stories, such as the one I will discuss. Otherwise, as Gramsci pointed out, the old stories remain in place, unrecognized, surreptitiously undermining the proper articulation of a more appropriate, genuinely alternative worldview.

Second, since my intention in this book is, in part, to explicate the general philosophical significance of some feminist insights, I take it to be crucial to develop such insights into a larger picture—one that makes clear the connection to more traditional epistemological and metaphysical, as well as moral and political, discussions. In insisting on the development of a larger picture, perhaps, I depart from recent trends in some feminist theory and literary criticism against the development of "big pictures" or "master theories." I hope it will become clear, however, that depending on what one thinks about the nature of big pictures or master theories, the pursuit of broader metaphysical and epistemological issues, including inquiry into the nature of rationality, need not involve the legislative and exclusionary tendencies of (positivistic) conceptions of generality based on commitments to a priori justifiability.

Doing the Right Thing: The Standard View

There is a popular view in North American and European philosophical traditions about what it means for an individual to be acting rationally. The standard assumption often is that someone acts or chooses rationally when she weighs her options in light of relevant information and does or chooses that which is most likely to advance more of her aims than other options.[2] This instrumental picture comes in many versions and is developed in different ways in idealizations. Although it is sometimes not explicitly acknowledged, it operates in much discussion about political issues—discussions about how to define people's interests, how to promote and preserve individuals' autonomy, and how to justify radical social criticism.

Consider, for instance, questions about paternalism, about whether to intervene in another person's affairs for that person's own good. If I come across someone about to step onto a bridge I know to be broken, I will intervene and prevent that person from doing as he intended to do. What kind of story would I tell myself to justify such an intervention? Most likely, I would reason that if the person *did* know that the bridge would not hold his weight, he himself would have decided not to step onto it. In other words, I would take my intervention to be justified on the grounds that the person himself would have done as I did if only he had been properly informed.

●

However, most people are reluctant to intervene in another person's affairs, even if they strongly disagree, as long as that person's choices are carefully thought-out and fully informed. In discussions of paternalism and in discussions about justifying wide-scale social policies, it is usually assumed that intervention is justified only to the extent that there is some reason to suppose that the person or people involved are not fully informed or rationally competent and, moreover, that they would have chosen the act in question if only they possessed the right information and were unrestrained and competent.[3]

What is typically assumed in questions about what is best for someone is that it is of fundamental importance what the person's actual desires and interests are. Certainly, no one would say that what is best for someone just *is* what that person actually desires since in many cases people are ignorant, under the wrong kinds of influences, and so on. But we usually think that what is best for someone is *ultimately* defined in terms of the person's actual psychology. Even in sophisticated idealizations of what it means to talk about an individual's good, there is a presumption of a definite starting place, and this starting place is defined primarily in terms of the individual's initial psychology—basic desires, interests, aims, and so on. In the case of entire societies, we might think that what is best is defined in terms of what most members would want if they were supplied with the appropriate resources, including information about inequalities and real prospects for various sorts of reform resolutions, and were in the right position to make use of those resources. Once we have a conception of what is best for an individual or a group, rational action is defined in terms of this conception: An action or a choice is rational if it is the one that is most likely to realize the person's ends or projects when these are suitably specified.

People often employ conceptions of rational deliberation and action in everyday talk. We often distinguish between actions and interests people engage in and possess and actions and interests that are really right for them. We may wonder, for instance, whether the decisions a person makes on the basis of her preferences at a particular time really represent her long-term interests. It may be that the individual's decisions rest on very little information or are the result of dubious influences.

The most interesting and controversial formulations of issues about rational interests arise in relation to cases of false consciousness. In situations involving ideological oppression, an individual may fail to possess preferences and desires that adequately reflect an interest in her own human flourishing. She may have been deprived of information about her personal prospects and, more importantly, denied the possibility to develop the self-assurance and integrity that would allow her to pursue her options if they were made available to her. Sometimes, of course, individuals who are discriminated against in a society are not aware of discrimination, and even when they do become aware, they may not be aware of the full extent to which discriminatory practices affect them. Moreover, the effects of oppression may be such that people are psychologically damaged, possessing interests and desires that reflect their subservient social status. They may fail to recognize that social and institutional structures discriminate against them in deep ways and that, as a result, many of their own perceptions and reactions are not fully representative of their own real needs and aspirations. In such cases we may want to say that an individual possesses an objective interest in goods that go beyond what she would desire for herself even if she were not mistaken about her options or the consequences of pursuing them. We may think, for instance, that individuals have an objective interest in pursuing and acquiring full self-respect and integrity, even in situations in which for some people such goods are both inconceivable and unavailable, given current structures.

Questions about the relation between rational choice and objective interests have been approached in several ways. What might be called the "liberal" approach to the question has been to define rational choice in terms of what someone would choose under various types of idealized cognitive conditions. (I have called this a "liberal" view not just because it is advanced by liberals but because it is characterized primarily by its ultimate preservation of the initial individual's perspective and a certain conception of knowledge. In Chapter 3, I discuss Peter Railton's more Marxist use of the same basic view.) The idea is that an act is rational for a person if it is accessible to that person through a process of rational deliberation where the conditions for rational deliberation are idealized in a suitably specified way. John Rawls argues, for instance, that a person's rational choice is what she would choose if she possessed adequate instrumental reasoning abilities, full and complete information, and the capacity to vividly imagine the consequences of her actions.[4] In his discussion of paternalism Rawls argues that in any judgment about what is good for someone, we had better be able to argue that the individual herself would have so decided if she had been able to choose under the right conditions.[5] Otherwise, it would be possible to rationalize "totalitarian" actions. Rawls's view permits identifying desires and aims as a person's rational desires and aims, even if they are not the person's current desires and aims, but it precludes the justification of actions aimed at making the person into someone she previously wasn't— conversion experiences. As long as a person would so choose if she *were* fully rational and adequately informed, we can say that the choices in question are in her real interests.

The liberal view has the virtue, first, that it apparently preserves the centrality of the individual perspective. It defines rational choice in terms of what the individual herself would choose under idealized conditions so that what might be called a person's objective, rational choice is determined by the person's idiosyncratic initial perspective. Thus, the liberal can say that the idealization defines an *individual's* good as opposed to what is good for all people, or all relevant sorts of people, according to general social or moral theories. Especially in cases in which paternalism is justified on the liberal view by the individual's incompetence or incapacity, the argument is that the individual herself would have so chosen under the right conditions. For instance, we might feel justified in preventing someone from harming himself even though he has reflected carefully on his decision and strongly desires the result. If intervention were justified in such a case, the argument would be that the person would not have reasoned as he did if he had been able to consider his options in the absence of certain psychological constraints or distorting circumstantial pressures. The concern here is that if the individual's goods were not defined in terms of current interests and desires, it could turn out that detrimental processes of brainwashing and other wrongful licensing of intervention could be held to be rational: Such interventions could be said to be in the individual's objective interest.

The second virtue of the liberal account is that it avoids saying that something is in someone's interest if, as a result of just any changes that come about, she ends up desiring it; that is, the liberal view acknowledges the centrality of the individual's perspective but does not claim that just anything a person comes to desire is rational for her. If a person is adequately indoctrinated, subjected to psychological pressure, she will indeed desire the situation that results from the process even if it is, by all plausible accounts, wrong for her. The liberal view suggests that a future desire is rational for a person at a time if it is desirable to her when reflected upon at that time in light of full and complete information and vivid awareness of the consequences of desiring it. That is, it defines a person's good in terms of what the current person, given her basic desires and interests, would choose for her future self if only she could choose under idealized conditions—that is, conditions of full information and capacity to reason well instrumentally. It does not consider relevant to defining someone's good what that individual would choose for herself if she were to become some other person—if, for instance, she were to undergo a conversion experience and come to assess her options in terms of a fundamentally different personal perspective.

Joel Feinberg's discussion of paternalism provides some examples of the levels of criticism accounted for on the view of individual interests I have just described.[6] The idealization intends to make sense of the distinction people often make in practice between more and less desirable forms of paternalistic intervention. Feinberg suggests that the problem of paternalism, for Mill and others, is that the fully voluntary choice or consent of a mature and rational human being is such a precious thing that no one else (especially not the state) has a right to interfere with it purely for the individual's "own good." Some choices, however, are clearly involuntary. Mill's example of the man who is about to step onto a bridge that is known to be unsafe is clearly one of someone making an involuntary choice to land in the river. The choice is involuntary because of ignorance. Other cases are not so clear.

Feinberg considers some typical difficulties.[7] The first situation is one in which an individual requests a prescription for a drug X, insisting that the drug will not cause her any harm. The facts are, however, that the desired drug will cause her serious harm. In this case, of course, the state backs the doctor. Such medical decisions are the territory of medical experts possessing the needed expertise. If someone ingests a drug without being fully informed about its negative effects, she could be said to be acting involuntarily since it is not her desire to be harmed by the drug.

This situation corresponds to the first level of self-criticism rationalized on the liberal idealization. Since it is reasonable to suppose that if she were well enough informed she would not desire what she actually desires, she would be acting irrationally, according to liberal standards, in taking the drug. Although the individual chooses on the basis of her desires, she is not choosing here as she would under ideal conditions of full and complete information.

The second case is one in which the individual knows the consequences of ingesting drug X and wants a prescription for the drug anyway because she wants to harm herself. In this case she is fully apprised of the facts and is suffering no delusions or misconceptions. Feinberg suggests that, nonetheless, the choice is so odd that there exists a reasonable presumption that she has somehow been deprived of her reason. Because we know that the majority of cases in which people harm themselves are not fully voluntary, there is reason to suspect that the individual's choice may be affected by derangement, illness, severe depression, or some other unsettling occurrence. On the liberal idealization, such a person could be said to be acting irrationally because, whatever her other desires and aims, she is less likely to be able to realize them if she gives up her physical capacities: She would be acting against what Rawls calls a "natural good," a good it is in everyone's interest to have because it is instrumentally beneficial.

The third case Feinberg describes is the most difficult for liberal views. Suppose a person knows drug X is likely to cause her harm but desires it anyway because she will get a lot of pleasure from it before it causes her harm. She is willing to take the risk of serious harm to herself to experience the pleasure. In her view, the cost of taking the drug is outweighed by the benefits. Such a choice is not obviously irrational. She may have made a decision on principle that she prefers a short, intensely pleasurable life to a longer period of physical well-being.

In Feinberg's view, this case is troublesome because the person may have a well thought-out conviction toward philosophical hedonism. If her choice is a decision of principle and no third-party interests are involved, it is hard to see on what grounds the state can legislate against her behavior. Of course, if the facts are that the pleasure derived from the drug is mild and of short duration and the resulting death immediate and violently painful, there would be reason to presume nonvoluntariness. But if the basis of her decision is her ranking the value of immediate pleasure higher than the value of long-term physical well-being, it is difficult to criticize her choice and still give primacy to what the person would choose as long as she is relevantly fully informed. For the person is making a reasonable decision based on evidence, given her own values.

According to the criteria set out by the liberal idealization, we can legitimately take a critical position toward a person's individual decisions as long as the conflict between what a person chooses and what would appear to be in her good is a matter of mistaken beliefs or failure to reason well instrumentally. But if the person already possesses correct information and the explanation for her decision is her personal perspective, justified criticism would require saying that there is some position other and better than the individual's from which to assess the full information about the decision and the consequences. The liberal view can make sense of criticizing someone's decision in terms of a more fully informed perspective but not in terms of one that is fundamentally different.

The Problem of Personal Integrity

But there are some important cases in which this conception of what is in someone's real interests gives the wrong result. The central insight of the standard account is that what makes a choice rational for someone is that she herself would choose such an option if she were able to choose under the right conditions: It precludes consideration of what the person would choose if she were psychologically pressured or were to undergo a conversion experience. There are some cases, however, in which the effects of social conditioning on a person are such that if rationality is defined ultimately in terms of a person's current desires and interests, even under conditions of more adequate beliefs, continued subordination and degradation turn out to be in the person's best interests. In cases in which someone is the victim of ideological oppression, the failure to act in what we would think to be her real interests may not be just a matter of her mistaken beliefs and inadequate reasoning capacities; it may also be a matter of her not possessing a sense of her self—or even a self at all—that would support a full sense of flourishing. It is not clear that a person who is degraded and diminished by social conditioning would have reason to choose goods typically thought to represent human flourishing, even if equipped with ideal cognitive capacities and resources.

Consider, for instance, Thomas Hill's example of the Deferential Wife— that is, the wife who is utterly devoted to, and derives happiness from, deferring to her husband.[8] The person in the example does not just subordinate herself to her husband as a means of acquiring happiness; for instance, she does not defer to him in some spheres in return for his deference to her in other spheres. The Deferential Wife defines herself in terms of her subordination. She is proud to subordinate herself to her husband and derives much of her happiness from the fact that she serves him well. As Hill describes the temperament and outlook of the Deferential Wife, aspiring toward being in control of her life would cause her more suffering than would be balanced by the resulting benefits. His proposal is that we can account for our intuitions that she is acting irrationally in subordinating herself by suggesting that she would choose to pursue a sense of self-respect if she were fully informed as to her rights as a moral being and were able to accord the right kind of importance to such rights. Hill uses the example to show that whereas there are some cases in which it is apparently not instrumentally rational for a person to pursue what many would think to be in her best interests, we might still want to say that the person *has* a moral duty to become a fully self-respecting and autonomous human being and that she is therefore falling short of her interests even though she fully desires to be who she is.

Suppose, however, that in fact the Deferential Wife *is* in control of her life and that deferring to her husband *is* the realization of her actual self— not a result of mistaken beliefs about her self. Suppose she controls the life she has, appreciates her rights, and has full respect for what she is; suppose, in other words, that her real problem is that the life she has and the person she really is are diminished and defective because of deep and long-standing forms of social oppression. If this is so, an alternative interpretation of Hill's example is that rather than failing to have the right beliefs about her situation, the Deferential Wife fails to have an appropriate situation—in particular, she fails to possess an adequate self. She fails to possess a sense of herself that, when presupposed in deliberation, would explain genuinely autonomous action. She may not be lacking in imagination or self-concern at all; on the contrary, she may have carved out carefully defined limits as regards deference to her husband and be actively engaged in fulfilling herself in accordance with them. But given her diminished self, what we might consider to be fully self-respecting and autonomous action is not within her imaginative capacity.

Of course, in some formulations of his view Rawls adds the restriction that under idealized conditions the person whose good is in question be concerned about autonomy.[9] He does this to guarantee that it be in everyone's good to become an autonomous, valuing agent. But if autonomy is defined so as to rule out the kind of servility that characterizes the Deferential Wife's relationship to her husband, it may not in fact turn out that, with full and complete information, she would desire autonomy. For given her actual sense of her self, which is the position from which she approaches idealized information on liberal views, she may have no reason to desire *that* kind of autonomy. If her social and historical situation is such that it is part of her identity to be inferior to men—in particular to her husband—deferring to him in all decisions *is* a valuing of her autonomy. She already is autonomous and self-respecting to the extent available to her.

It might be useful at this point to distinguish between autonomy and agency.[10] The Deferential Wife possesses agency. She has the ability to make decisions that affect how things turn out for her and to act on beliefs formed on the basis of evidence. But autonomy is usually thought of as involving more than this. Autonomy is a special kind of agency, the capacity to take control of one's life and to realize one's best interests. The Deferential Wife acts autonomously if her best interests are defined in terms of her actual aims and desires but not if they are defined in terms of moral considerations of human flourishing. Yet if best interests are defined, in part, morally, and the Deferential Wife is indeed diminished, she might not *see* such a concept of best interests as applying to her, even though it does.

Thus one might think Rawls's view can account for people in situations like that of the Deferential Wife by simply building into the model the notion that under idealized cognitive conditions people would desire the right kind of autonomy. But to the extent that some people are in fact deprived of dignity and self-respect in their actual lives, desiring the kind of self-determination we might think characteristic of a good life would depend on their undergoing a change to their actual selves—a change to their sense of themselves as well as a change to the actual interests and commitments they possess. Otherwise, there is no reason to think they should care about such autonomy. If this is so, then, to accommodate the situations of people who are actually degraded, the model would risk giving up the very feature that is supposed to make it a model that preserves individuals' autonomy—the denial of the definitional significance of conversion experiences.

Conversion Experiences

In situations in which a person's self is degraded, the result of the person's choosing under Rawls-type idealized conditions may be a sense of autonomy that is somewhat thin. It is central to the liberal definition of interests that the self which chooses under idealized conditions be untransformed; that is, it is important that the individual's choices be defined in terms of her own perspective. However, in the case of the Deferential Wife, if she is to choose what is best for *her*—even if she has access to full and complete information about what would be good for her under different conditions—she has no reason to choose the kind of autonomy generally associated with fully self-respecting agents. For she is not the sort of agent who can make such autonomous choice an expression of *her* interests. That is, she does not possess the kind of self to which such autonomy could be applied. And if Rawls were to stipulate that under idealized conditions the Deferential Wife desires the thick sort of autonomy, he would have to include in his idealization transformations to her self. For in order for it to be rational for her to desire autonomy in the sense that rules out her habitual servility, her actual sense of self would have to be transformed so that habitual servility is not what defines it. But defining a person's objective interest in terms of a perspective the person might have but in fact does not is just what the liberal view rules out.[11]

The reasons for denying a role for conversion experiences in defining someone's rational interests are clear: For one thing, it would appear to be hard, otherwise, to see how what is at issue is the *individual's* good and not what is supposed to be good for her given some independently defined (moral or nonmoral) ideal. If, under idealized conditions, a person chooses from among her various options from a perspective that is not that of her self at the time but is instead that of what she might be if conditions were different, it is hard to see how such a choice should carry any weight for the actual person whose choices are at issue. Second, if potential psychological transformations are relevant to defining rational choice, it may become possible to rationalize dubious life choices. Not all transformation experiences are beneficial for individuals, and some are quite detrimental. For instance, it might turn out to be possible to say that something is in someone's good because if she were to spend weeks being indoctrinated by a religious or other cult she would then desire the thing in question. A third consideration is the rationalization of undesirable forms of paternalism. Given that after people have been coerced into certain choices they may, in fact, come to desire them, we may be able to say that such coercive interventions are for their own good.

But in some cases, like that of the Deferential Wife or of Sethe before her escape from slavery, a person's coming to possess interests in human flourishing may depend precisely on the kinds of personal and political transformation experiences liberal accounts want to rule out. In fact, it sometimes looks as though the disruption of a person's secure sense of self is just what is required to make a full state of flourishing possible and rational from the individual's perspective. Consider the member of a marginalized group who has the talent to be a medical researcher but who aspires toward a job in the local pharmacy. The liberal view would attempt to account for our intuitions that the person's aspirations are irrational by suggesting that if the person had access to full and complete information, he would know that his low expectations for himself are socially induced and would desire more for himself than a career in the local drug store. But if the person has access to full and complete information, he will find out not only that his aspirations are a result of adverse social conditioning; he will also find out that if he pursues a career as a medical researcher he will suffer harassment, job discrimination, alienation, and so on. Moreover, he will find out that although he has the ability to do such a job well, that fact is irrelevant. For he will not be taken seriously in his work and will spend more of his time fighting civil rights cases than doing what he desired. At least at the drug store he has the possibility of doing reasonably satisfying work and gaining a steady income. If he inserts himself into the medical establishment, he may achieve other goals and acquire other goods, but he may not be acting rationally given his *current* desires and interests.

Now, of course, it may *not* be in his rational interests to pursue a career in medical research. It is certainly sometimes true of individuals that they could not cope with the consequences of pursuing what we would intuitively think to be in their long-term interests as human beings. But there are cases in which a person actually acquires greater self-respect, strength, and a quite different sense of priorities as a result of the effects on her of undertaking just such an apparently irrational pursuit, of going against the grain despite the personal consequences. Sethe's claim to humanity would appear to be of this sort. Certainly, on one level—on a narrow conception of instrumental rationality—Sethe's choice is irrational: Given slave conditions, it is better to love small. But in terms of personal and cognitive developmental processes, where what constitutes development is constrained by facts about human possibilities within her specific society, Sethe's choice is rational. In light of Sethe's real interests in human flourishing, her going against the grain could be considered rational in the more objective sense I have been proposing.

Moreover, it often appears that as a result of the changes to a person's interests and commitments resulting from certain choices, the *failure* to realize initial aims and preferences is of no consequence or even that such failure *contributes* to developmental possibilities of a different sort. For instance, the kind of alienation from community that Sethe experiences sometimes explains important cognitive possibilities. Dorothy Allison quotes Bertha Harris as saying about writing that "the ecumenical, appeasing, side-stepping middle class mind never ever produces a great work of art, nor a great work of politics."[12] It may well turn out that for some cases, such as cases in which people are really not capable of going against the grain, the instrumental model of rationality gives the right answer: It does express what it means for people to act in their best interests when people are really incapable of going against the grain. But it is inadequate as a guiding theory if it precludes the individual rationality of radically going against the grain in general. For it is often just these sorts of choices that some people need to make to identify the possibility of and to pursue real dignity and self-respect.

One might think Rawls could include transformation experiences in his picture by including them under the effects of vivid imagining; he might say that people should be able to imagine the insights acquired as a result of having their condition and situation transformed in specific ways. The basic principle of Rawls's formulation is that a rational person adopts that plan which maximizes the expected net balance of satisfaction.[13] The process of deliberative rationality is one according to which a person surveys her interests and desires in light of information about how she acquired them and what the results would be of acting on them. As he says, "Awareness of the genesis of our wants can often make it perfectly clear to us that we really do desire some things more than others. As some aims seem less important in the face of critical scrutiny, or even lose their appeal entirely, others may assume an assured prominence that provides sufficient grounds for choice."[14]

Rawls is relying here on the work of Richard Brandt.[15] Brandt makes use of a good deal of contemporary psychology that shows that people come to desire and to be averse to things largely as a result of conditioning.[16] In his view, a desire or an aversion is rational if and only if it is what it would have been had the person undergone "cognitive psychotherapy," by which he means a desire or an aversion is rational if it fails to be extinguished by a process of repeated exposure, "in an ideally vivid way, and at an appropriate time, [to] the available information that is relevant in the sense that it would make a difference to desires and aversions if [the person] thought of it."[17] In explaining his concept of cognitive psychotherapy, Brandt draws on information about processes by which desires and aversions are instituted in people. For example, a treatment for alcoholism consists in having a person take a sip of a martini and then either receive, or vividly imagine receiving, an electric shock. Or the person can be made to feel, or to vividly imagine feeling, nauseous as a result of drinking too much alcohol. The idea is that the thought of a martini gets associated with an aversive state, and the person loses his desire. Brandt's claim is that the desire for alcohol can be called "irrational" in virtue of its *not* surviving a process in which the person confronts desires with relevant information.[18]

It is important to note that in both Rawls's and Brandt's discussions, the changes that come about to a person's desires and interests are ones the person herself could choose from her initial perspective. Particularly in Brandt's arguments but also in Rawls's, it is clear that *which* of a person's desires and interests are held up for criticism depends on the individual's own (in some sense) basic view of herself and her situation. Brandt states explicitly that the process of reflection must be one in which the person is not influenced by external factors, such as other people's values, rewards, induced physical states, or whatever.[19] On the contrary, the real test of whether a desire or an interest is rational for a person, according to Brandt, is whether the person would have such desires or interests if she experienced such events in her "native" state—that is, as she is independent of experiencing the effects of social influences (whatever this means).[20]

Moreover, it is important to Brandt's definition of a person's good that the information that is confronted by the person be *relevant* and experienced at an *appropriate* time, and both relevance and appropriateness are defined in terms of the person's own view of herself. For instance, he states that the conditions of relevance for information on his view are that the information be about the "expectable effects of the thing, or about the kind of thing it is, or about how well one would like it if it happened, and so on."[21] As in the case of the alcoholic who submits her desire for alcohol to cognitive psychotherapy, it is as a result of the person's own desire to get rid of a particular desire that therapy is undergone. Moreover, insofar as what counts as *relevant* information is defined in terms of the "expectable effects" of the desire or aversion, it would appear that the process is defined specifically in relation to the person's own experiences with a desire or an aversion.

So whatever criticism is carried out by someone under idealized conditions, it is still true that the person's perspective itself cannot be undermined by that criticism, for it is the person herself in some ultimately untransformed state who defines the conditions under which self-criticism is carried out. It would not appear to be part of Brandt's procedure, for instance, that as part of the process of cognitive psychotherapy a person might be repeatedly exposed to information that would cause her to give up the desires for herself upon which her desire to get rid of her desire for alcohol is based. In other words, she does not, under idealized conditions, undertake to change her ultimate self-image. Neither does she, presumably, vividly imagine herself in situations in which she would acquire new desires and interests—ones that, in her current situation, she does not contemplate. She is not, for instance, repeatedly exposed to information about what her desires would be like if she were part of a different community, culture, economic background, or whatever.

Whereas Rawls does not make this point explicit in his account of deliberative rationality, it would certainly seem unlikely that he would have more extensive personal changes in mind than those implied by Brandt's examples. For if he were to include personally transforming, or conversion, experiences under the effects of a fully vivid imagination, his view of individual rational deliberation would raise a number of questions that he does not address. In particular, he would have to address the seemingly intractable question of why we should think a person should be someone other than she is—that is, of how it is possible to discriminate, on other than strictly moral grounds, between more or less adequate personalities or self-images for some particular person.

Nonpropositional or Implicit Understanding

The second distinctive feature about the liberal view is that the full and complete information assumed in the idealizations is mostly propositional; that is, the kind of information in light of which an individual considers her choices is of the type that could be expressed in words and concepts. The individual reflects on her options in light of a full and complete body of truths that could be put into the form of sentences. The idealizations do not include complete access to a different kind of knowledge—knowledge people possess in the form of intuitions, attitudes, ways of behaving, orientation, and so on. It is true that for Rawls, a kind of nonpropositional understanding is involved in the idealizations insofar as people are able to vividly imagine being in certain circumstances. But his account does not include the kind of understanding a person acquires when her situation is transformed in certain ways—those that provide a person with the resources to begin to adequately understand ideological oppression. This is because this sort of transformation constitutes a different interpretive position; the vivid imaginings provided in a Rawlsian idealization are dependent precisely upon the person's initial interpretive position.

One may think nonpropositional understanding is not included in liberal idealizations because there is no such thing. Yet it seems clear that people usually know things about their situation that cannot be expressed now. There is always something about an experience of a situation that cannot be expressed, even in principle—such as knowing what it is like to see red or to hear a trumpet. Moreover, in certain cases what a person knows as a result of being in a situation constitutes grounds for acquiring understanding of a larger situation, understanding that could not be acquired any other way. Being in a particular personal state and relationship to society sometimes constitutes a kind of understanding of that society that could not be acquired through an examination of the expressible truths about that society. Literary critic Barbara Christian describes something like this knowledge in her discussion of Alice Walker's *The Color Purple*.[22] She cites a passage in which Mister taunts Celie: "Look at you. You black, you pore, you ugly, you a woman. Goddam. . . . You nothing at all." Celie retorts: "I'm pore, I'm black, I may be ugly and can't cook. . . . But I'm here." Celie is nothing according to the categories Mister possesses for interpreting the world. Her existence as a person is an anomaly in his terms because according to the conceptual framework he applies, the concept "people" does not include black women. Christian writes that "Celie's affirmation of her existence does not deny [Mister's] categories of powerlessness; rather she insists that nonetheless she exists, that she knows something as a result of being at that intersection of categories that attempt to camouflage her existence."[23]

But we might think that Celie does indeed challenge Mister's categories, and it is in fact *because* she challenges his categories that she knows something that could not otherwise be known. Celie's experience of existing as a person puts her outside of the categories in terms of which Mister and most of the rest of society make sense of their experience. Not only is there something about Celie's experience that cannot be expressed—that is, something that it is like to be in her situation—but there is also something about her experience that if it could be expressed would contradict presuppositions of the dominant conceptual framework. Celie's assertion of her existence challenges Mister's unifying classificatory system, but it is because her knowledge is, in fact, a way of existing and acting that her assertion constitutes a threat. Her being who she is and her claim to the significance of who she is constitute an interpretive position. If Celie's challenge to Mister's categories were merely verbal or intellectual, it could be answered within the terms of the framework Mister employs, just as anomalies can usually be explained away in terms of a dominant conceptual framework. However, to the extent that Celie's understanding of what it is like to be in her situation consists in her *acting* against the grain of that conceptual framework, her nonpropositional understanding of her position constitutes a critical interpretive position or at least the beginnings of one. As Christian writes, "That contrariness [between prevailing traditional and alternative modes of representing reality] is a measure of health, of the insistence that counter to the societal perception of black women as being 'nothing at all,' their existence is knowledge that relates to us all."[24]

Celie's existing in a certain relation to society constitutes a kind of understanding of that society that cannot be expressed entirely in propositions. For her position constitutes epistemic standards, grounds on the basis of which to unify and interpret propositional information. In one sense the inexpressibility of Celie's experience is explained simply by the difficulty of expressing any experience of what it is like to be somewhere or in some state. But there is more to be said about inexpressibility in this particular case. In Celie's situation, the inexpressibility of her experience is not just another dimension of her expressible experience. What she understands but does not completely express provides, or potentially provides, the interpretive standards that could make an *alternative* expressible version of her experience possible. The conceptual framework available to Celie to deliberate about her situation and actions is inadequate because, for one thing, it cannot accommodate her existence as a full human being. But because Celie knows that she, as an African-American woman, *does* exist as a person, she is not only in a position to identify this inadequacy; if she proceeds, in acting and interpreting her life, *assuming* this knowledge of her existence, she will be able to identify even more inadequacies in the dominant conceptual framework—ones that could not be identified, *usually because they do not have to be identified to proceed,* by someone in a position of relative power. Thus, Celie's being who she is is epistemically significant for one thing because her *proceeding* as she is, her acting and deliberating as a full person, both presupposes and requires the development of explanatory resources that constitute or can constitute a more appropriate evaluative (theoretical) perspective.

Celie's coming to be able to think properly about her life, at least to be able to think about her life as a full human being, depends in part on personal developments, on the bringing about—through commitments and personal relations—of a critical perspective that at least acknowledges her existence. To the extent that Celie's *personal* struggle *explains* her coming to know certain things and that struggle itself is explained by feelings and intuitions she acquires as a result of her situation, Celie's feelings and intuitions are epistemically significant. Indeed, in this kind of case, namely, one in which her intuitions provide perhaps the only possible access to knowledge, Celie's intuitions would appear to *constitute* understanding—a reliable guide to more accurate beliefs and a basis for deliberation and action. As with the example of Sethe, Celie's understanding is contingent upon the bringing about of certain conditions, including a certain personal condition. Sethe knew what she did about her options and her situation because she had experienced the freedom to make her own decisions, to commit herself to her child. Her *feeling* of goodness and rightness was not something she was able to express. But that feeling constituted grounds for revising her previous beliefs about the world, for her rejection, for instance, of Paul D.'s view that "used-to-be-slaves" should love small. Because of what she has become as a result of her experiences—in particular, because of the expectations for her life she has thereby acquired—Sethe can know that slavery is *worse* than death. She knows this in light of an epistemic process constituted in part by her becoming who she is.

One might think nonpropositional understanding is just what Gilbert Ryle had in mind when he distinguished between knowing that and knowing how.[25] It looks as though knowing how is nonpropositional since it does not consist in possessing knowledge of truths about the activity in question: Knowing how requires behavioral competence—being able to react in the right way when confronted with certain events. But the kind of understanding people acquire through some sorts of personal development is not simply the acquiring of know-how; it is the acquiring of know-how of a particular sort—namely, that which constitutes a *position* on the basis of which to apply alternative interpretive standards. There is a difference between, for instance, acquiring a skill because such a skill is necessary for the carrying out of one's basic aims and desires and acquiring particular know-how because it is necessary for *survival,* necessary to proceed as a person at all, to even be able to identify and care about one's idiosyncratic personal aims and goals. In the latter case, someone learns to behave in certain ways not because such behavior fulfills certain aims and desires she now identifies as important but because the situation is such that a certain orientation or set of behaviors is required to be able to continue acting effectively at all. In such cases, to the extent that the acquiring of know-how constitutes the bringing about of an interpretive position, of epistemic standards, it is also the *bringing about* of new sorts of interests and commitments, not simply an instrument toward the realization of ones already identified.

Something like this seems to happen to people who begin to appreciate and adapt to the customs of another culture. They don't see things the way they used to. They come to measure and assess things differently. For instance, many people living abroad for some amount of time sometimes come to realize experientially what they may or may not have known intellectually—namely, that there are other important values, customs, and ways of behaving than those that are typical of their original society.

Of course, one can also avoid acquiring this insight. It is easy for people to travel around and live in different places, hearing other people's views, appreciating their cultures, and so on, while continuing to interpret and assess all of them on the basis of an initial conception of what kinds of things are valuable, what the important questions are, and so on. It was just this sort of thing that seemed to be occurring when a prominent U.S. political philosopher presented a paper in Cuba entitled "Can the Cuban Revolution Survive Without Democracy?"[26] By this he intended, of course, to discuss whether the Cuban revolution could survive without multiparty political systems and a U.S.-style press. Cuban philosophers legitimately responded that however one understands the term "democracy," and there is some question about this concept, one cannot just take it for granted, *without argument*, that it means what it is assumed to mean in existing liberal democratic traditions. Their point was that whatever the more adequate understanding turns out to be, to fail to even recognize—let alone properly address—plausible, competing understandings is a kind of conceptual imperialism, in some ways just as damaging as the militaristic kind.

Third World women at conferences with North American and European feminists have made similar complaints—namely, that women from developed countries tend to take it for granted that what is meant by "democracy," "equality," and so on is just what these concepts mean in the more dominant societies.[27] This is not to say that there are not some culturally defined concepts that are *better* than others but that whether they are better cannot always be established from within one culture alone. It may turn out that it is *only* through engaging personally with, and acquiring ways of behaving and values of, societies with which one hopes to communicate—a process that takes considerable amounts of time—that deep-rooted and sometimes distorting biases of one's own culture can become, to a greater extent at least, both identifiable and understandable. This sort of personal transformation often *is* the acquiring of nonpropositional understanding, the bringing about of practices and conditions that constitute an interpretive position and hence epistemic standards.

The significance of travel for the acquiring of insight should not be overstated. What is important is not travel but transformation—indeed, relevant sorts of transformation. Neither travel nor transformation is necessarily epistemically interesting. Whether these are epistemically interesting depends on their role in a process—both political and theoretical—of ongoing empirical investigation *and* cognitive development. In an influential paper, María Lugones urges white/Anglo women toward a kind of world traveling, where "world" is understood as an experience of a certain kind of identity.[28] In Lugones's view, "Travelling to someone's 'world' is a way of identifying with them . . . because by travelling to their 'world' we can understand *what it is to be them and what it is to be ourselves in their eyes.*"[29] But the metaphor of traveling may be a bit misleading since it is possible to travel and engage in all sorts of ways—even lovingly, as Lugones urges—without acquiring critical understanding. There would appear to be additional questions both about how white people should approach different "worlds" and about how those worlds should understand themselves within a global situation defined in terms of a theoretically distorting capitalist economic order. Nkiru Nzegwu argues that cross-cultural understanding involves an important theoretical dimension in which appropriate understanding of oneself, by those in both more *and* less dominant positions, needs to be arrived at not only through personal engagement but also through argument and theoretical development.[30]

In another Walker story, an African-American woman's understanding of her personal situation again depends importantly on the coming about of commitments and relations that provide an interpretive context. In *Meridian,* the protagonist comes to understand her political goals primarily as a result of her experiencing what it is like to be part of the "togetherness, communal spirit [and] righteous convergence" of the black political movement.[31] Perhaps in part because of her youth, Meridian is unable at first to define her own political commitment. When asked whether she would kill for the revolution, she is unable to make a judgment, lacking a clear understanding of what such a commitment would entail. At the point in the story when Meridian *does* decide that she can kill for the revolution, the difference is not that she has acquired more theoretical understanding; she had quite a bit of that at the point where she was confused. Instead, what is different is *her* situation, particularly her emotional situation. Sitting in the church, feeling the political impetus of the music and the tradition, she recognizes that "the years in America had created them One Life."[32] Certainly, this latter is propositional understanding, but the understanding of this proposition depends heavily on Meridian's changed personal state. The intellectual element of her experience in the church is made possible, it seems, by her emotionally experiencing what it is like to be part of a developing set of social and political interrelations. Her actual situatedness within a network of political and emotional relationships itself provides her with epistemic standards, making interpretations possible that were not so previously. What Meridian acquires during her experience in the church is not knowledge of when and where she would or could kill for the revolution; rather, what appears to be the case is that she has acquired relations, attitudes, and ways of behaving that constitute a more adequate interpretive framework, one she could rely on if she *had* to make the decision of whether to kill for the revolution.

There is an important scientific source for this notion of nonpropositional knowledge. In Kuhn's discussion of scientific paradigms, he treats the acquiring of scientific skills as an acquiring of knowledge.[33] He insists that scientific practices and procedures amount to more than the explicit theories they depend on and inform and that precisely for this reason part of the training of professional scientists must be experimental. Regardless of whether they accept Kuhn's constructivist conclusions about the status of scientific knowledge, philosophers of science are generally agreed that good scientific practice depends on the acquiring of experimental know-how, including good scientific "hunches" and intuitions. Moreover, one explanation for this is that the practices and procedures of science often constitute a kind of nonpropositional, or tacit, knowledge.[34] Now, one reason the role of nonpropositional understanding of this type would be important in explaining scientific progress is that what needs to be explained in regard to the possibility of objective scientific knowledge is how it is that scientists acquire rational standards that guide them to knowledge of a theory-independent world.[35] To the extent that it is uncontroversial that all aspects of scientific practice are deeply theory dependent, the possibility that scientists develop practices and skills as a result of interaction with the physical world would help to explain how it is that scientific standards are appropriate for the investigation of a theory-independent world and are not simply the consequence of the development of a particular tradition. The role of nonpropositional knowledge in explaining reliable scientific practice is thus not *just* the acquisition of skills necessary for carrying out previously defined projects. Rather, it appears importantly to involve the development of standards for defining and evaluating new directions in theory development.

Knowledge people acquire of oppression appears to be of just this sort. If it is true, as it seems to be, that all thinking is dependent upon a person's social and historical situation, there is a question about how people can ever know that their current situation is, in fact, wrong for them. To the extent that people interpret their lives in terms of a conceptual background that represents the status quo, how do they come to learn that that background is, in important ways, mistaken? We might think people know certain social practices are wrong just by appealing to general moral theories. For instance, we might think we can know that racism is wrong by appealing to general principles about the equality of human beings. The problem, though, of course, is that we sometimes lack the appropriate starting point; we sometimes lack the sort of theoretical perspective that would even permit racism, at least some important manifestations of it, to be identified. Virginia Woolf, for example, points out that the question of women's liberation is not primarily a question about whether women can join the procession of educated men, as if the process itself can be taken for granted; rather, it is a question about *the terms on which* women should join the procession of educated men or, in other words, of the *kind* of process that should be joined.[36] The acquiring of more adequate standards for defining what it is that marginalized groups might be able to be part *of* is explained by the role in knowledge of the development of practices, intuitions, and attitudes as a result of engagement, as a result of the regulation of epistemic standards not just by other beliefs but by the world.[37]

Consider again the standard picture of what it means for an individual to be deliberating rationally. It is hard to see how the liberal view could accommodate the understanding someone acquires as a result of *becoming* a different sort of person or an occupant of a different set of relations. It is possible to picture someone having access to all kinds of propositional truths since propositions can be set apart from the deliberator. But it is hard to picture an idealization involving the deliberator having access to the cognitive results of actually deliberating from a number of different positions. The kind of understanding the Deferential Wife would acquire if she were in fact to be in a position of greater self-respect and dignity is not an understanding she would have by surveying this possibility from her current perspective of being a Deferential Wife. For what she would understand by actually being transformed is not what it would be like for the Deferential Wife to be in a different position but rather what it would be like for her not to be the Deferential Wife. It is difficult to imagine what an idealization would be like in which a person had access to the experience of interpreting her life from the position of being a different person. For in order for her to have access to that information, she would have to *not* be the person desiring access. If the idealization were really to include access to the epistemic advantages of transformation experiences, it would have to be an idealization in which many different persons were committed to and defined in terms of quite different situations. To the extent that Brandt and Rawls were to include full access to nonpropositional understanding, their idealizations would begin to become unintelligible.

The problem is that some kinds of nonpropositional understanding, unlike propositional knowledge, just don't add up in the right way. It is not possible for a single person to have a lot of different kinds of it, at least not if the differences are great. A single person can, at least in principle, possess an enormous amount of different kinds of propositional understanding. But a single person cannot possess widely differing nonpropositional understanding and still be one person. Possessing the kind of nonpropositional understanding that constitutes a competing interpretive framework means *being* in a situation—complete with certain values, attitudes, behavioral practices, history, and so on—as well as acting and interpreting events *from* that position.

People learn things about the world that they might not learn otherwise when they are compelled, permitted, or choose to apply to and develop in the world a different set of conceptual resources, practices, orientation, and so on. And often what this amounts to is *personal* change. This kind of understanding is different from the experience of vivid imagination liberals typically include in their idealizations. In the case of someone like the Deferential Wife, it would be the acquiring of new aims and interests altogether that would explain her possession of an individual, rational interest in human flourishing. Vividly imagining oneself in some position does not usually involve transformations. This is why vivid imaginings are often quite different from something like a mind-altering drug experience or a hallucination. When we vividly imagine ourselves in some situation, we are in control of the interpretation of that event to an important extent. At the least, the position of interpretation is familiar. In a drug experience or a hallucination, the control is not always there, so a person often experiences herself in a state of emotion, desire, commitment, or relationship she might not have been able to consider choosing. Not only does someone in such a position experience being in that situation, but she will also experience what it is like to be interpreting the world from that position—to be acting, engaging, and deliberating according to what she is in this other situation. The kind of transformation that would make it possible for the Deferential Wife to properly understand her real possibilities as a person would be one that would provide her with a more adequate interpretive position, and such a transformation would most likely have to be one that transformed her*self*. Celie's nonpropositional understanding would be diminished if she were able to occupy Mister's perspective or even if she were less committed to acting out her own perspective. In Chapter 7, I discuss more fully the occasional epistemic significance of personal relations and commitments.

Now, of course, it is not just in the case of oppressed people that transformation experiences are relevant to the acquiring of more adequate understanding of one's life and situation. Indeed, in any case of self- or social knowledge, the proper interpretation of propositional information may require the bringing about of conditions and circumstances, including a particular condition of oneself. Anthony Appiah talks about what he calls "cognitive incapacity," or the inability to understand propositional information that, if it were to be understood, would require that people change their view of themselves.[38] He proposes, for example, that it is hard for some people to understand that those who get into good schools are often just better prepared, not more intelligent. For if such people were to grasp this information, they would have to see themselves differently. Similarly, it is possible to possess large amounts of theoretical information about oppression and fail to understand what it means for one's own life. If this were not so, there would be no Marxist scholars who would fail to understand the claims of feminists and antiracists about the implications of systemic discrimination for interpersonal relations and institutional structures. And there do seem to be some of these. It is not possible for the relatively nonoppressed to acquire adequate understanding of sexism, racism, or imperialism *simply* by reading or listening to what those who are oppressed by these systems have to say. If the appropriateness of the status quo is taken for granted in one's self-concept and general worldview, an appropriateness relative to which claims about the wrongness or even the existence of systemic oppression are nonsensical, it will be hard to grasp the significance of, or even to hear at all, what is being said. To the extent that all understanding depends on background beliefs and conditions, and to the extent that there is good reason to think that particular background beliefs and conditions involve error and profound injustice, it may be that acquiring adequate social and political understanding *always* requires undergoing some kind of transformation experience, specifically of the sort that results in the unsettling of the knower's sense of self and position.

Rationality Again

The two features of the liberal view noted here—the avoidance of conversion experiences and the inclusion of mostly propositional information—are related in a way that helps explain the inadequacy of the standard view. I have suggested that it is a mistake to think that a person acts autonomously when she chooses in light of correct information on the basis of her "settled preferences," her secure sense of self. For it is often a person's *self* that is diminished and deprived by ideological oppression, and the correction of *beliefs* is not an adequate response. Yet there is definitely a strong grain of truth in the intuition, reflected in the liberal view, that it is wrong to interfere in a person's carefully thought-out choices. It is certainly true that we are often rightly reluctant to try to persuade someone we care about that she is living her life wrongly, that she is mistaken in her view of what is good for her. It is also true, however, that in cases in which we might be reluctant to say such a thing to someone, we would take action to change that person's situation. We might supply her with increased economic resources, introduce her to different social relations, and so on.

The grain of truth in intuitions that it is wrong to tell people how to live their lives may not be that people act autonomously when they act on the basis of their own basic preferences and values and that their choices, therefore, ought to be respected; rather, it may be that it is often insensitive and cruel to try to help someone out of a difficult situation by simply giving her more propositional information. Moreover, it is wrongheaded. The notion that we ought not to interfere with someone's choices does not correctly reflect a concern for autonomy if that person is deprived of the *resources* to act autonomously. This, of course, is recognized by liberal theorists. The problem, though, is that, for some important cases, supplying people with the information they need to deliberate rationally is not a matter of providing increased access to propositional truths; instead, it requires bringing about different, more appropriate social and political situations. Thus, the idea that a person acts or chooses in her interests when she proceeds as she would under liberal, idealized conditions is mistaken both epistemologically and metaphysically: It mistakenly excludes the role of important kinds of nonpropositional understanding in rational deliberation, and it ignores the occasional importance to proper individual development of the bringing about of conditions that transform a person's aims and values.

In the chapters that follow, I argue that when we talk about what it means to do the right thing—either individually or socially—we get it wrong when we assume it is a matter primarily of doing what is right given certain overall or long-term ends or projects, however defined. Moreover, we get it wrong not just in detail but in assumptions about what matters to the pursuit of a more humane way of living. Rather, I argue that appropriate ends or projects are often only identifiable or conceivable as a result of the *bringing about* of particular ways of being and that rationality, therefore, is not a question primarily about acting relative to ends, however defined, but about *being* relative to capacities for acting in a specific sociohistorical situation. It is difficult, though, to put this picture forward as an alternative to the popular liberal view described earlier. This is not so much because the idea of rationality as a fundamentally intellectual matter is deeply ingrained in Western thinking (although it has been challenged by philosophers, such as Aristotle, as we will see in Chapter 8) but rather because there is something apparently undesirable about making judgments about what people are (in a nonmoral sense). One reason the standard picture of rationality is so appealing, even to many feminists and Marxists, is that we intuitively think that what is right for a person or a group has to be rooted in facts about what that person or group currently desires and values. And, as already argued, there are good reasons to worry about claims that what a person or group of persons desires and values should not figure centrally into deliberations about their situation.

It is not true, though, that to give centrality to the desires and interests of individuals and groups—as opposed to some independently defined, probably arbitrary ideal—a picture of rationality needs to give primacy to considerations about the psychology of that individual or group. The grain of truth in the standard picture of rationality is that what someone desires and values *is* relevant to judgments about what is good for her. The mistake in the picture is the assumption that *individuality* and *integrity* can be presupposed, that it is a person's psychological state that primarily *defines* her individuality or integrity. What is overlooked is that individuals' initial psychological states are most likely themselves to be a result of an arbitrarily defined (sexist, racist, homophobic, or whatever) social ideal. It is true, for instance, that the Deferential Wife desires her deferential relationship to her husband. And if she possessed all of the relevant information, it is not clear that she would change her mind. But it is possible that the *she* who desires this deferential state is not acting individually—indeed, cannot act individually—but rather is acting according to socially imposed, individuality-denying, gender stereotypes. I discuss this further in Chapter 5.

The reason it makes sense to think that what is right for the Deferential Wife is what *she* herself would choose for herself if only she possessed the right resources is that the issue at hand is one of *individual* rationality; the issue is what is best for *her*, not what is morally best or best according to some independent ideal. What is missing, though, is acknowledgment of the fact that given the deeply sexist nature of the society according to which the Deferential Wife assumes her identity, there is already no possibility on this picture of *individual* rationality; to the extent that the Deferential Wife is oppressed in her society, considering what she herself would choose under suitably specified conditions is already to consider what is best according to some independent (oppressive) ideal. The motivation behind the dominant conception of rationality is a concern for individuality and autonomy. There is good reason to suspect, however, that for some types of people it is not possible to *be* an individual in the first place, let alone to be in control of one's life, without significant change to the larger situation.

3

Objective Interests, Nonpropositional Knowledge, and Conversion Experiences

I HAVE SUGGESTED THAT A popular philosophical picture of what it means to be acting in one's best interests precludes the rationality of the pursuit of human flourishing for some members of society. Moreover, such a view makes rational for an individual the maintenance of a subordinated state. Peter Railton develops a more sophisticated version of the same philosophical story, one that might be taken to address some of the concerns raised in Chapter 2. In particular, Railton sometimes seems to be concerned about the role of nonpropositional understanding in defining objective interests and, as well, about the role of the development of personality, of something like transformation experiences. Railton intends to offer an account of objective interests, of what it means to be acting in one's good, that rationalizes an individual's *radical* criticism of her own desires and interests. And he appears to acknowledge the importance in defining objective interests of the understanding one acquires as a result not of deliberation but of acting in and engaging with the world. Railton's account is interesting for this project for two reasons: First, the fact that Railton relies on the liberal view to express his more Marxist concerns demonstrates the strong appeal of that view. Second, the inadequacy of Railton's account for the concerns he intends to address demonstrates that the view is not just mistaken in detail; it gets the issues backward.

Railton's Objective Ends

In "Moral Realism" and "Facts and Values,"[1] Railton addresses the question of what it means to talk about an individual's objective good, acknowledging that his is a version of the view of individual rationality offered by Rawls, Sidgwick, Brandt, and Hare, among others.[2] He points out that most formulations of the idea of an individual's objective good avoid taking what is best for someone to be defined entirely in terms of whatever interests and desires someone has. After all, people are often ignorant about the consequences of their choices, are under the wrong kinds of influences, and so on.[3] Rather, the model allows that someone may criticize desires he has if they are inconsistent with more powerful or important desires, or he may, upon receipt of full and complete information, desire not to possess some of his actual desires—even some that are fundamental. Railton's intention is to consider the possibility of the rationality of "radical reassessment of desires,"[4] that is, of the rationality of criticizing the desires a person still holds after thoroughly correcting his beliefs for factual error. Thus, he appears to intend for his account to answer a question that is crucial for radical politics: What do we mean when we talk about people's real interests, given that oppressive social structures distort some people's perceptions not only of their interests but also of their fundamental values?

The account starts off looking very much like standard ones. Railton suggests that defining a person's good depends on an idealized perspective on the basis of which the person's range of choices can be surveyed in light of full and complete information and with proper reasoning abilities. In his most straightforward formulations of his view, he suggests that we consider the initial person as he would be if equipped with "complete and vivid information of himself and his environment, and . . . instrumental rationality [that] is in no way defective."[5] We then ask that person—the idealized initial self—"not what *he* currently wants, but what he would want his non-idealized self . . . to want—or, more generally, to seek—were he to find himself in [his] actual condition and circumstances."[6] The desires relevant to determining the objective interest of a particular person at a time, then, are those of the fully informed and rational individual "regarding what he would seek were he to assume the place of his actual, incompletely informed and imperfectly rational self, taking into account the changes that self is capable of, the costs of those changes, and so on."[7]

There are two issues Railton takes to be crucial to the development of an account of an individual's interests. The first is that an individual's objective good has to be something the initial individual, given her idiosyncratic desires and interests, would find compelling.[8] This is because the intention is to provide an account of an *individual*'s good, as opposed to what is best for someone according to some independently defined moral or other ideal. If a theoretical account does not allow for a connection between the person whose choices are at issue and the objective good, then it would look as if coercive interventions into someone's affairs could be justified. The second issue is that the end has to be determinate, at least in theory. Otherwise, it will look as though for an individual at a time, any choice is just as good as any other. Railton takes the question of an individual's good to depend on the possibility of defining a "point beyond the self," a "toehold" beyond a person's actual ends, that could provide criteria for assessing the relative merits of particular choices.[9]

Railton's suggestion is that a person has an "objectified subjective interest" in virtue of facts about her physical and psychological constitution, her history, capacities, and so on.[10] Such an interest is an extrapolation from the initial subject, taking into consideration facts about how such a person would change under specific conditions, what desires she would come to have, and so on. The initial person would feel compelled by the results of the idealization, even though the objectified subjective interest may be quite different from her current interests, because the idealized perspective—although different from herself—is nonetheless a version of herself.

Railton develops his view as follows: We give to the actual individual, A, unlimited cognitive and imaginative powers and full factual and nomological information about his physical and psychological capacities, circumstances, histories, and so on. Included in this information is understanding the person would acquire if he were to undertake one or some of his options. We then ask idealized A what he would want *for* A.[11] For example, Beth, the happy and successful accountant, desires to be a writer.[12] As Railton describes her, Beth suffers no failure to imagine her expectations for the future, and she does not fail to reason well on the basis of the information she has available to her. It may be prudentially rational for Beth to undertake to be a writer, given her current perspective, but as it turns out, Beth does not have the skill or the temperament to be a writer. In Railton's view, the perspective on the basis of which an appropriate judgment can be made about whether Beth should attempt to become a writer would be that of a changed Beth—one who had full factual information plus the advantage of having experienced the results of trying out her various options.

Now, it is not immediately obvious how this example differs from the kinds of cases that could easily be handled on standard idealizations, the ones discussed in Chapter 2. Presumably, if Beth possesses full information and contemplates it vividly, she will know that she lacks the skill and the temperament to be a writer and will decide not to pursue that option. On the standard view, what would make Beth's choice irrational, if it is, is that with the proper cognitive resources Beth would not choose as she does. Presumably, what Railton adds to this view is the notion that the idealized perspective in terms of which Beth's real interests are defined includes changes that would have come about to Beth as a result of having gone through certain experiences. Thus, Railton's critical perspective is defined not only in terms of full and complete information and instrumental reasoning capacities but also in terms of some understanding acquired experientially—of the experiential information the initial individual would gain in the course of acting out the option in question.

Given the similarity of Railton's account to standard accounts of an individual's good, it is important to try to identify why he thinks this model adds anything significant to the standard view and why, in particular, he thinks his view is more radical or at least rationalizes more radical self-criticism. The answer would appear to involve two features of his account. The first has to do with his remarks about the development of self-knowledge. He suggests, for instance, that a person's desires sometimes evolve not as the result of "an ideally rational response to the receipt of ideal information" but rather as the result of "largely unreflective experimentation, accompanied by positive and negative associations and reinforcements."[13] Thus, "an individual whose wants do not reflect his interests or who fails to be instrumentally rational may . . . experience feedback of a kind that promotes learning about his good and developing more rational strategies."[14] Lonnie, for instance, feeling low, desires milk.[15] But Lonnie would in fact be better off, given his physical condition, drinking water. Railton suggests it is Lonnie's acting in a certain way that brings about the result that he eventually desires water instead of milk when he is in a particular state, a desire that turns out to reflect his long-term interest in well-being. The example shows, Railton says, "not only wants being adjusted to interests, but also behavior being adjusted to newly adjusted wants. Without appropriate alteration of behavior to reflect changing wants, the feedback necessary for learning about wants would not occur."[16]

These remarks about self-knowledge are significant. One of the features of the standard picture of a person's good is that the idealization mostly includes knowledge of a propositional sort, as I mentioned previously. Now, it is true that for Rawls and Brandt, there is an important role for vivid imaginings. The understanding a person receives through vividly imagining herself in certain circumstances is sometimes partly nonpropositional; that is, it is knowledge of what it is like to experience something, knowledge that cannot always, even in principle, be expressed in propositions. What is significant, however, about these idealizations is that the vivid imaginings are always interpreted from the person's initial perspective, defined in terms of her own values and norms. Railton's remarks suggest at least the possibility that the acquiring of behavior and attitudes is not something to be assessed *in terms of* the person's initial standards and values but that such acquiring of behavior might provide a *basis* for interpreting experience and information.

Such remarks could accommodate the fact that in situations of oppression, it is the acquiring of more adequate *standards* through personal experience and change that explains a person's being able to properly interpret her experience. For an important part of oppression is the internalization by the oppressed person of standards and values that deny her own humanity. Sethe explains her decision to try to kill her children to protect them from slavery by referring to an experience, an experience of deciding for herself. But we know from the story that Sethe's experience of deciding for herself, given her background as a slave, changed her. It was an experience of being "selfish" that she had never had before, had not even been able to dream before. From the perspective, first, of knowing what it is like to act autonomously and, second, of *claiming that possibility for herself,* Sethe cannot interpret the world as she did previously. She cannot think, as Paul D. does, that she should "pick the tiniest stars in the sky to own" because she cannot—because of what she has become—occupy the perspective Paul D. adopts. To the extent that the concepts and standards Sethe has available to her under slavery deny the possibility of what she has become, her rational deliberation about her life and her choices cannot be entirely intellectual. An important element in her deliberation is the process according to which she in fact becomes a different person.

The second point is related. It is important to the standard view that the perspective in terms of which available choices are defined be the individual's *own* perspective, not, for instance, a perspective someone would have if she were psychologically pressured and converted to some moral or political conviction different from her own.[17] But as we have seen, in some cases a person's being able to properly identify her options depends precisely on her being converted or significantly transformed. Railton, in contrast to the standard view, sometimes appears to be suggesting that *personal* change is relevant to the acquiring of more adequate understanding. For instance, in describing a process in which desires change because of interaction with the world, Railton says that such an occurrence sometimes constitutes "a way of seeing things . . . and . . . a tendency to interpret or explain things in certain ways rather than others."[18] This is why, he says, when a person's beliefs are altered to the extent that his desires change, "the agent's outlook itself shifts, with the result that the landscape he previously perceived changes and his desires, which had felt at home in that terrain, become unsettled."[19]

Problems

But Railton's intentions are not always clear. As he describes his notion of wants/interests mechanisms, the point apparently is that such mechanisms correct desires and interests in unanticipated ways; they correct desires that would not be corrected through attempts to make one's belief and desire system more consistent. Railton's story about Lonnie, however, is not an example that demonstrates possibilities for radical self-criticism. Lonnie's problem is one of false belief: He believes incorrectly that drinking milk will make him feel better. It would appear that the examples Railton should consider here are ones in which the operation of feedback mechanisms is required to explain how a person ends up being able to see something as good for himself that he would not have been able to see as good for himself simply by acquiring more propositional information, more true beliefs—for example, cases in which feedback works on rational *standards*. In other words, if feedback mechanisms are to play a role in rationalizing criticism that would not be rationalized on the liberal view, Railton should consider examples involving choices that would intuitively strike us as rational and that could only be rational with the application of quite different standards.

Resisting ideological oppression would be a good candidate. Someone who has been subject to adverse ideological conditioning is someone for whom the correction of beliefs for factual error provides inadequate resources for choosing and acting in her real interests. The desires and beliefs a person has as a result of ideological conditioning would be of the kind a person would not have reason to criticize just by considering such desires and beliefs in terms of consistency with other preferences and desires. For it is likely that the person's entire psychological system reflects a diminished sense of self. Instead, what would be required for her to get some handle on the ways in which the system as a whole is wrong is a different set of standards—standards, for instance, according to which what is considered acceptable for her is in fact wrong.

Feedback mechanisms, it would appear, ought to be able to explain the acquisition of more appropriate standards. But if Lonnie, for instance, were not deciding whether to drink milk but were instead trying to plan his life from a degraded social position, how would the appropriate determinate perspective be specified? Suppose Lonnie does not possess the relevant sorts of desires and interests to start with. Suppose Lonnie does not *care* about the kinds of goods that would, by some plausible account, constitute the pursuit of human flourishing.

We need to consider in more detail how Railton's idealization might work. Consider again the later Beth (following Railton's terminology, we might call her "Beth+"), who is the objectified version of an early Beth who is trying to decide whether to become a writer or remain an accountant. If Beth+ were the end result of a process in which earlier Beth undergoes the actually transforming experiences of attempting to become a writer, Beth+ will be someone different than would be the case if she were the end result of undergoing the experience of remaining an accountant. Yet there is no reason given for why the experiential insight and character development Beth gains through attempting to become a writer should be preferred as a basis for assessing options to the insight she would have gained through experiencing the other set of events since both options are equally open to her. Perhaps in this case Beth might have acquired the same relevant insights by continuing as an accountant as she would have by attempting to become a writer—namely, insights that would have persuaded her that she is not suited for a life as a writer.

But what if her situation were less straightforward and in fact she is not suited to being either an accountant or a writer? Suppose Beth has some abilities she comes to care about as a result of the psychological pressuring tendencies of the experience of trying to be a writer. Suppose, in other words, that even though Beth is not cut out to be a writer, the experience of trying to become one is just the kind of experience she needs to undergo to acquire the kinds of values that would allow her to live a better life—to take more control of her life, possess more self-respect, and so on. On standard accounts, it would turn out that the options later Beth, so defined, identifies for her earlier self would not be considered rational for earlier Beth to pursue. For earlier Beth, according to the example, would not *care* about such options, and the desirability and usefulness of such choices for earlier Beth would depend on later Beth's *transformed* perspective. The standard view defines an individual's good in terms, ultimately, of what she is now; it precludes considering as relevant to a *definition* of her good what she would want if she were somehow transformed. It is not clear, though, that Railton's view does any better with this kind of case. Since he says nothing about what would make some transformations better than others, it would appear that to the extent that Beth+ were to come to possess the appropriate perspective for deliberation under idealized conditions, her doing so would be a fluke.

The most obvious interpretation of Railton's idealization is that Beth act out the options that are most important to her. If Beth+, as an extrapolation of initial Beth, is to represent a single perspective, the special advantage Railton's view has over the standard one is that the position according to which someone's good is defined includes the experiential advantage gained from living out a particular subset of that person's desires. Moreover, the criteria according to which desires are to be included in the subset would appear to be, first, that the desire be one the person has and, second, that she considers it important.

But this drastically limits the adequacy of Railton's account for cases in which people are members of oppressed groups. It may be the case that Beth acquires appropriate nonpropositional understanding as a result of the experiences she undergoes in attempting to become a writer. But if it turns out that it is wrong, by plausible accounts, for Beth to be a writer but that Beth comes to gain appropriate insight into her interests as a result of her attempt to do so, the only explanation for the rationality of undergoing such experiences in the first place is that Beth happened to have the kind of desire that would have that particular result, even though the object of her desires turns out to be wrong for her.

Suppose the earlier Beth were not an accountant but someone like the Deferential Wife Thomas Hill describes, someone who defines herself in terms of subordination to her husband but who may possess the talent to be an accountant—or a writer. That is, suppose she is someone who is happy and proud to be servile to her husband and, partly for this reason, possesses no interest in developing her talents, whatever they are. Moreover, what if the reason Beth is happy and successful in what she does is that her sense of what happiness and success amount to is deeply skewed by the influences of a misogynist, capitalist society? On standard idealizations, Beth would know that she has certain talents. The problem is that given her current sense of herself, she would have no reason to be motivated by this information. For according to the values and norms in terms of which she possesses her identity, being subordinate to her husband is expected, normal, and adequate. This again is the problem with the standard view. Railton's proposal about the role of feedback mechanisms appears to offer an answer to this. But if a person's good is defined in terms of the information she would gather through the living out of options she currently cares about, it is hard to see how it would accommodate the rationality of the kinds of actions and choices the Deferential Wife would have to take to acquire the right kinds of desires and interests. The problem is that in some cases, people don't possess or even care to possess the relevant sorts of desires.

It also cannot be the case that under idealized conditions Beth acts out several different options to see which has the best results for her sense of self and integrity. If actually living out the options is to involve epistemically relevant transformations, as well as the acquisition of propositional information, it cannot be the case that Beth ideally lives out several options—at least not if the options are different. For it would be hard to see how her good could be defined in terms of her choices as several different persons. Indeed, the idealization begins to become conceptually problematic if Beth+ is to have access to the effects of trying out several quite different options. For Beth would have to survey the results of living out her different options from somewhere. If she surveys them from her initial perspective, she does not gain the epistemic advantage of a more adequate interpretive position. If she surveys them from any one of the transformed perspectives, she takes a chance on picking the right one. And to the extent that she occupies more than one perspective, the view begins to fail to make sense.

A second answer to the question of how the critical perspective is defined is offered in "Facts and Values." Rather than emphasizing the individual's undergoing certain experiences, Railton suggests that the idealization be a theory-assisted extrapolation from facts about the individual. The suggestion is that part of any comprehensive psychological theory will be an account of the factors that influence which desires the person forms and how these desires evolve in response to various sorts of changes, including changes in beliefs.[20] In Railton's view, an idea of an appropriate idealized self could be gotten simply by correcting each erroneous belief and examining how the person's desires and other beliefs would change as a result. He claims that the idealization is even more plausible to the extent that the person's nonbelief properties are kept fixed.[21] He means by this that we start with a fixed set of facts about the individual's psychology, physiology, and circumstances that is the "reduction basis" of his dispositions to desire. We then consider lawlike regularities linking beliefs, desires, and other features of individuals and the relevant "initial conditions." In Railton's view, we hold the reduction basis for a person's idealized hypothetical desires as nearly fixed as possible when asking what someone *like* the given individual would come to desire—or come to want that he pursue were he to assume the place of his original self.[22] If the basis for determining a person's good is a set of underlying facts and not the person's current desires, Railton thinks the only risk of indefiniteness in a model involving conversion experiences would arise from the absence of adequate general principles about the interrelation of desires and beliefs.

This later development of Railton's account of an individual's end is somewhat less interesting with regard to the possibility of justifying radical self-criticism. Whereas in the earlier account there is at least the suggestion that Railton intends to develop the implications of considering the role of nonpropositional knowledge amounting to personal change—the idea developed in Chapter 2—in this account it becomes much less likely that this is his intention. In the idea of a theory-assisted extrapolation, Railton takes as his starting position the facts that account for the initial person's psychology, physiology, and circumstances. He then defines the proper perspective in terms of how the person's desires would change if each of his beliefs were corrected for factual error. Railton says that the determinacy of the view is assured by the fact that the nonbelief properties of the person are kept fixed.[23]

Yet the nonbelief properties are precisely what need to be changed for some people to even begin to imagine their real options. In particular, it is often the case that the entire social structure, including fundamental norms and values, needs to be changed for the right kinds of options to become *available* or sometimes even imaginable. What is striking about Sethe's situation as an individual is that her perception of her options, her understanding of the ways in which slavery denies her possibilities as a human being, depends on changes that have come about to her as a person, changes to who she is—her relations, interests, desires. But it is also striking that Sethe has to struggle to maintain her sense of who she is to be able to continue to understand herself the way she does. Paul D. says, after he has understood what Sethe has done, that "more important than what Sethe had done was what she claimed."[24] For what Sethe claimed—her humanity—was crazy from the point of view of her community. As readers, we understand Sethe's choice because we know something about slavery and because we have the advantage of Toni Morrison's prose. But it is hard for Paul D., who shares Sethe's background and social position, to understand her choice. For Paul D., "what [Sethe] meant could cleave the bone."[25] In the absence of certain kinds of conditions or at least the capacity to exercise radical moral imagination, some possibilities are not thinkable at all; they cannot make sense.

In *Playing in the Dark: Whiteness and the Literary Imagination,* Toni Morrison provides an indication of the extent to which imagination is limited by social conditions.[26] She suggests that if, as readers, we look carefully at the ways in which important U.S. writers have told their stories, have had to tell their stories to be understood, we can see how contemporary imagination is constrained by the existence of certain social practices and traditions. In Hemingway's *To Have and Have Not,* for instance, Harry Morgan, the central figure of the story, is occupied at the time the fishing boat he commands enters more promising fishing waters. The problem for Hemingway, Morrison points out, is "how to acknowledge that first sighting [of flying fish] and continue the muzzling of this 'nigger' who, so far, has not said one word."[27] Rather than have the black man speak, Hemingway writes that Harry "saw [that the black man] had seen" a patch of flying fish. Thus, Morrison points out that Hemingway chooses to saddle himself with a construction that is improbable in syntax, sense, and tense to avoid assigning agency to a black man—to tell a story that could be heard by his readers. Morrison's point is not that Hemingway is racist but rather that writers are constrained by the imaginative capacity of their readers. And when we look at how writers tell their stories, we can learn something about the nature of social and historical traditions and structures that explain such capacities. To the extent that Railton's idealization requires that nonbelief properties be kept fixed, it is hard to see how it can accommodate the rationalization of some of the most important kinds of individual choices, rationalization that often requires the disruption of nonbelief properties and their replacement through the bringing about of a radically different situation.

Of course, Railton does intend his theory-assisted extrapolation to account for the need for social change in order for people both to be able to deliberate more adequately and to be able to act. The application of principles of lawlike regularities to the initial "reduction base" is presumably intended to account for the effects on a person's basic desires and interests of acting and being acted upon in different (even radical) ways. But where do these principles of lawlike regularities come from? In particular, what defines regularities? In Sethe's society it is "regular" for slaves to pick "the tiniest stars out the sky to own." It is "regular" for slaves to love small. To reject this sort of "regularity," at least to reject the idea that such behavior *is* regular, Sethe has to do and to think things that are quite *ir*regular, even drastic, according to the norms. One has to wonder about the effectiveness of applying Railton's laws about regularities to the problem of distinguishing between better and worse paths of development for a particular person if the salient regularities are defined in terms of his reduction base. For if the reduction base describes an unjust society, the regularities involved may be of the wrong sort altogether for defining behavior expressive of someone's genuinely human development. Moreover, if the relevant regularities are not determined by the initial set of facts about the person's state and situation, it is not clear what purpose the reduction base serves in Railton's idealization.

As I mentioned at the beginning of Chapter 1, questions about similarities and differences, about how to appropriately unify events and experiences, have been central to some work in feminist and antiracist theory. Thus, Drucilla Cornell, for instance, stresses that political understanding requires the identification and criticism of relevant "underlying" social myths and fantasies. But whereas I suggested that Cornell is right to stress the importance of retelling some of the unifying stories that constitute the theoretical background of social practices and institutions, identifying *relevant* myths and fantasies presupposes moral vision—judgments about how things *ought* to be and hence of what would constitute a more adequate sort of society. In other words, judgments about *relevant respects* of importance in radical criticism often require the possibility, at least in imagination, of radically alternative social arrangements. In taking the notion of relevant respects of regularity for granted in his idealization, Railton would appear to be begging the question of the kind of moral vision required to properly *identify* such regularities.

If the reduction base is to explain the rationality of the experiences someone undergoes to acquire appropriate insight into her situation—insight that could account for the kind of radical self-criticism someone like Sethe is involved in—it must include facts that go beyond the person's current individual situation. It must include facts about the history of the oppression of certain types of people, as well as facts about the possibilities for a better life that would come about if the society were other than it currently is. Indeed, to the extent that it is an appropriate reduction base for the individual, it would have to be a reduction base for the entire society and its component parts. But if the reduction base is of this sort, it is hard to see how it could define the interests of a particular individual in a determinate way, as Railton intends. That is, it would be hard to see how the reduction base would limit the number of options or sets of options that could be said to be in an individual's best interests.

Suppose Railton were just to stipulate that the appropriate end for a person be defined in terms of the kinds of personal and social transformations that appear to be necessary for the acquiring of critical understanding. And suppose he were to have in mind in proposing a theory-assisted extrapolation that the appropriate perspective, defined in terms of the acquisition of nonpropositional information amounting to transformative personal changes, can be accounted for in terms of general laws. That is, he might have in mind that the theory-assisted extrapolation show how an appropriate perspective for a particular person—defined so as to include insight relevant to possessing an appropriate political perspective—can be derived from facts about that person at some one time. It is true that if what is best for someone is defined in terms of transformation experiences, including social transformations, then an individual's objective interests at a time may not be recognizable by that person as she is at that time. Perhaps the theory-assisted extrapolation may be intended as an argument that through the application of general social and psychological laws, it can be shown that the unpredictable resulting perspective is nonetheless traceable to the person's initial self.

But if this is so, the theory-assisted extrapolation is not a response to the worry about determinacy Railton is addressing. The problem of determinacy Railton describes is that raised by David Velleman—namely, that a particular individual, confronted with a body of full and complete information, can approach it from all kinds of directions.[28] Railton's response is that the question of a particular person's good is not a question about the results of confronting full and complete information; rather, it is a question of defining a personality. This seems right. But if the theory-assisted extrapolation is designed just to show how epistemically defined perspectives are connected to particular individuals through actions and circumstances, there is no resolution to Velleman's problem. For any number of perspectives could be attached to particular individuals by way of external circumstances and conditions. The problem is to show how for any one individual there is a determinate perspective or even a set of perspectives. Again, to the extent that Railton answers the indeterminacy problem, he appears to have eliminated any significant role in the defining of objective interests for acquiring the kind of understanding that would explain the rationality of pursuing human flourishing for some groups of people.

Objective Interests Defined in Terms of Specified Ends

As Railton has set up the issue—indeed, as Rawls, Brandt, and others have also set up the issue—a suitable theoretical specification of *ends* defines the relative merits of particular choices.[29] But to the extent that the nature of an entire social structure can deny the possibility of full personhood to some groups of people, the person whose psychology and circumstances are the basis for *defining* that end is sometimes not the right sort of starting place. Railton is concerned to show that, on his account, a person's objective interest is something she would be motivated by, even if that interest is not, in contrast to Rawls, defined in terms of her current fundamental desires and interests. This is because Railton is concerned to avoid justifying the same sorts of undesirable paternalistic interventions Rawls is concerned to avoid. He does not want it to be a consequence of his view that undesirable paternalistic interventions can be justified on the grounds that the individual involved will come to desire the end in question after she has been suitably coerced. However, when we consider the nature of oppressive societies and the effects of those societies on what people can be as individuals, there is reason to think that insofar as the "end beyond the self" *is* one the initial person would be motivated by, it is not likely to be an end that represents her real interest in pursuing human flourishing. If a person is a member of a deeply discriminatory society and happens to be a member of a group that is discriminated against, the full articulation of her individual interest in human flourishing would not be something that in her current state she would identify with or perhaps even understand. For the values and norms in terms of which such an end would be properly articulated would not be those that define her initial society. What I have tried to suggest in mentioning Toni Morrison's discussion of American literature is that some possibilities are just not imaginable in certain terms and require the bringing about of alternative norms and values, or at least the presupposition of such norms and values in imagination, to even make sense.

In assuming that the issue of an individual's objective good is a question about the specification of an end that is traceable to the motivational system of the initial person, Railton's account precludes the rationality of the pursuit of human flourishing for some members of society, just as Rawls's account does. Railton tries to avoid this problem by introducing a role for something like the nonpropositional understanding people acquire as a result of transformation experiences. But this, of course, raises the difficult question of why some transformation experiences and not others are significant—what Railton considers to be the determinacy problem. I have suggested that to the extent that Railton answers this question, he denies the particular epistemic significance of transformation experiences in the pursuit of human flourishing in important cases.

The picture of rationality assumed in both Rawls's and Railton's accounts is one according to which an individual's rational choices are defined in terms of an idealized end or set of ends: The individual herself would, under the right kind of conditions, choose certain ends, and the ideally chosen ends provide criteria for discriminating between more and less rational choices at a time. For Rawls, the Archimedean point—or the idealized end point—is what the initial person would choose for herself under conditions of full and complete propositional information plus adequate instrumental reasoning abilities. For Railton, the Archimedean point is an idealized perspective defined in terms of full and complete information, including some nonpropositional information. Whereas Railton's view adds the restriction that the person choosing under idealized conditions be choosing *for* her initial self, it is still true that ends chosen by an (extrapolation of the initial) individual provide criteria for defining the individual's rational choices at a time.

It does not matter to the structure of Rawls's idealization that he is mostly speaking of plans rather than ends. Rawls distinguishes his view from "dominant-end" views, according to which some one end—like political power, social acclaim, or the maximization of wealth—takes priority over all other goods. Instead, he suggests that the rational plan for a person includes and orders a plurality of aims. Happiness, for instance, is an end for most people that is included in their choice of plan.[30] The point is that the definition of a rational plan for a person provides criteria for ranking a person's options at a time. Railton, in his definition of a point "somewhere beyond our ends," has in mind the objective defense of a person's choices at a particular time. He says that whereas people make choices on the basis of personal preferences, we often like to think there is more to our choices than the strength of current desires. His answer to the possibility of defending rational criteria is the definition of A+—a version of the person whose desires would be appropriate given corrected beliefs.

But if the acquisition of nonpropositional information is in fact a development of the self, then this picture gets things the wrong way around. In cases in which the acquisition of nonpropositional understanding explains the possibility that it is individually rational for people to pursue their real interests in human flourishing, the objective end for an individual becomes identifiable only *after* the individual makes what turn out to be objectively rational choices, choices that also make it possible for the individual to *care* about her best interests. This does not mean we would have to say of the Deferential Wife that she does not have an interest in human flourishing, as I have argued the liberal views would have to say. Rather, we would say that the Deferential Wife is improperly self-defined, that she is degraded by oppression, and that she possesses an interest in human flourishing in virtue of her possibilities for more *adequate* self-definition—possibilities she might not now be able to envision or even, perhaps, care about. An adequate conception of objective interests needs to include a normative conception of self-definition, and if it does, it will turn out that there can be no determinate answer to the notion of a person's good in advance of personal and political transformations. Railton's concern about indeterminacy is, I propose, misconceived.

The problem with the picture of rationality adopted by Rawls and Railton is not that as the idealized end is defined, the wrong kinds of considerations are employed in determining rational choices. That is, the problem is not primarily that the idealized end is *incorrectly* defined, although it is. The deeper problem with the picture Rawls and Railton assume is not its epistemological difficulties but its metaphysical ones or at least the metaphysical problems that are implied by the epistemological ones. The more serious mistake in the picture of rationality assumed by the idealizations discussed is that the picture gets wrong the metaphysics of individual development and its consequences for the nature of self-knowledge. In defining rational choice in terms of what an individual does with information, the standard picture assumes that in some sense it is unproblematic who the individual is. Yet to the extent that acquiring nonpropositional understanding constitutes the coming about of someone's more adequate self, the question of rational interests is not a question about what an individual does *with* full and complete information; at least, if the issue is about *individual* rationality, the more important question is about what adequate (nonpropositional) information does *to* the individual. To the extent that questions of individual rationality are about what is really best for the individual and not about what is good for her given current (oppressive) conditions, the idealizations of Rawls and Railton are not merely incomplete; they would appear to fail to address the question of individual rationality altogether.

The question of objective ends (or plans) for a person is not a question about the relationship between an individual (with certain desires) and a body of information. At least, it is not primarily so. It is true that there are some cases in which the difference between what a person actually desires at a time and what is in her interests can be explained by considering what she would want if she were better informed. But the cases in which the picture fits are ones in which self-development is not an issue. And this is perhaps why the picture has been so popular among philosophers for so long: Academic philosophers have, until very recently, been almost entirely white and male. And if one is white and male, one doesn't encounter quite the same difficulties related to self-development in a racist, misogynist society as one would if one were not white and male. In Chapter 5, I explore in more depth some questions about individual development raised by the implications of systemic injustice for self-understanding, implications of the fact that, as lesbian activist and writer Dorothy Allison writes, "throughout my life I have felt that I was fighting off some terrible, amorphous confusion about . . . what I have a right to do or want, what was dangerous and what was vital."[31]

The formulation Rawls and Railton have given to the question of objective ends ignores questions about the adequacy of the individual's self and integrity and the strong desire people often have to *discover* a more adequate sense of personal integrity. I have argued that in both cases the idealizations offered do not accommodate cases in which an individual's failure to possess an adequate sense of self and integrity is explained by the existence of a systemically discriminatory social system. I want to emphasize, however, that the point is entirely general. It is often relevant to people's choices, whatever their social situation, what certain options will do to them as persons. For instance, it is common for people to undertake certain choices not primarily because the choices lead somewhere in particular but rather because the conditions that will be brought about by such choices will enhance the person's possibilities for making proper choices in the future. In particular, a person may undertake certain actions to acquire more appropriate conditions for determining what proper decisions amount to in her particular case: She may, for instance, need to gain more confidence, a stronger sense of self-esteem, better judgment, broader or perhaps more focused interests, or whatever. Education, certain kinds of travel and many personal relationships get chosen for what they will contribute to a person's capacity to choose rather than for what they contribute to the achieving of predetermined ends.

Moreover, what it means to be able to choose appropriately is to be in the right sort of state. Education of the right kind makes people into certain kinds of personalities. If an individual goes through the educational system and comes out without a desire to learn or to think critically or without any confidence or ambition, we would think the system had failed no matter how much information the person possesses. Indeed, in some cases, people have to come to acquire a certain sense of self to grasp information. For instance, Arlene Stairs argues that one of the most difficult and urgent questions as regards indigenous education in northern Canada is how to provide students with what she calls a "future picture," a vision of themselves *as* native people, fully participating *as* persons within a society that respects who they are.[32] Stairs points out that there has been a tendency in indigenous education to bring the elders into the schools to teach students about indigenous traditions and values. But such practices have little educational value if the students cannot see that the information being transmitted to them applies to *them*. Unless they can not only see themselves in a certain way but also be brought to *care* about seeing themselves in a certain way, the information provided to them has no useful application. Stairs's point is that providing students with the imaginative capacities to see themselves as a certain kind of person is not just a good thing for educational systems to aim for; at least for some people, and perhaps in general, it is necessary for proper learning to occur at all.

It would appear that in situations of individual deliberation, there is a strong sense in which people want to *become* the right kind of person as a result of choices and not simply to *do* the right thing, however defined. Of course, it need not be the case that people who make choices primarily for reasons of personal development and the acquiring of insight have no ends in mind. But it is often true that people's ends are very vague and, more-

over, that they are *supposed* to be vague. It appears to be more common for
people to want to take certain actions to give more precise content to some
of their vague ends than for people to want to possess a set of very precise
ends so they can be sure to take the right actions. It is at least unusual, but
often rather weird, to encounter someone who regularly makes choices primarily to reach previously specified ends. More important, it might even
seem weird for someone to *desire* an idea of her ideal end or set of ends to
be able to make the right choices. The problem with the standard model of
individual rational choice as applied to ordinary cases of rational deliberation is not that it is implausible for practical reasons—lack of information,
for instance—that an individual be able to define her ends in any precise
way in advance of taking action. There also seems, more importantly, to be
something perverse about the idea of someone desiring an idea of her ideal
end in order that she be able to make the right decisions. We might even
think someone who set about trying to define an ideal end in order to make
the right choices was lacking in cognitive capacities—for instance, in the
imaginative capacities required to make proper use of circumstances.

Objective Interests Defined by Paths of Development

The position I will be defending is one according to which rationality is in
the first instance a property of paths of development, not of particular ends.
And real interests, rather than *defining* rational standards, are defined *by*
the paths of development that are individually rational in the sense described. Some will think, perhaps on the basis of what I said just above,
that I am embracing a kind of existentialism. However, as I hope will become clear, the view I am presenting should be seen against the background
of a broader epistemological and metaphysical project, one involving normative claims about both self-understanding and personal development.
For instance, the personal development in question is defined in terms of
facts about possibilities, including epistemic possibilities, for the bringing
about in particular situations of more adequate conditions for human flourishing. As I discuss in Chapter 4, there will be many who will worry that
the significance of personal transformations in questions about individual
rationality implies that arbitrarily coercive interventions can turn out to be
in someone's individual interest. But, as I will argue, this kind of view assumes that there is no distinction between the types of processes that generate and sustain beliefs, decisions, and actions more conducive to human
well-being and those that do not. I will be arguing that some types of
processes *are* conducive to cognitive and moral progress and that others are
not, that there are indeed facts about this matter.

I should say at this point, perhaps, that the aim here is not to provide a definition of rationality that can sort cases of rationality from those of irrationality for all people at all times. If this is possible, and I don't think it is, it is not clear that it would be interesting or important. What I do think is necessary is an examination of what sorts of concerns figure into individual or social deliberations about rationality, of what such a process ought to involve. My concern is with the sorts of questions that need to be asked in the pursuit of real individual or social interests, with the kind of story that is told and that ought to be told to justify choices and actions taken in the pursuit of such interests.

If, as I will argue, individual rationality is a feature of certain processes of development, importantly including cognitive development, the formulation of the question of individual rationality offered by Rawls and Railton is wrong in general and not just wrong for cases involving oppression. The question of individual rationality is not that of the theoretical end, or plan, for a person that would provide criteria for deciding which choices are more or less rational; rather, the question is that of what kinds of actions and engagement would bring about conditions of greater insight and possibilities for liberation. Often when we talk about "right choices," they are ones that have the consequence of bringing about a more enhanced life situation in ways that might not have been able to be predicted on the basis of the individual's actual desires. In particular, the conception of rational choice that is assumed on Rawls's and Railton's views ignores the value that acquiring new interests and desires has in itself. In Chapters 5 and 7, I look at the significance of desire, including erotic desire, in personal and political understanding. I look at some of the philosophical implications of the fact that, mistakenly in Dorothy Allison's view, "so many people divide the erotic and the everyday into such stubbornly separated categories."[33] To the extent that there is an important issue about acquiring interests and desires that is fundamental to a person's capacity to choose properly, it would appear that rationality is more fundamentally about what a person should *be* rather than of what a person should *do*.

Getting It Backward

The rationale for discussing Railton's modification of the view discussed in Chapter 2 is to suggest that the model itself does not work. There is something wrong with the formulation of the question of objective interests and individual rationality that Rawls, Railton, and others employ. To the extent that for some people, perhaps all people, appropriate options need to be discovered as a result of the *bringing about* of alternative sets of relations and conditions, the formulation of the question of objective interests as one about the specification of an "end beyond the self" seems to get the issues backward. Insofar as a determinate end beyond the self is defined in terms of the salient facts about or the psychology of the initial person or even of the initial society, such an end cannot explain the individual rationality of the kinds of choices people often have to make to pursue human flourishing—choices that disrupt, rather than realize, fundamental desires and interests. Moreover, insofar as particular actions and engagements often *bring about* the conditions for choosing and understanding more adequate sorts of options, it is not an individual's objective interest that explains the rationality of particular choices; rather, it appears to be the individual rationality of particular choices that explains the possibility of an individual's objective interest.

This, of course, raises the question of what the right sorts of actions and engagements are. Moreover, insofar as the kinds of actions and engagements in question are often radically transformative ones, it looks as though there is a risk that we can say nothing much at all about whether some actions are more appropriate than others for a person or a society in particular. I deal with this question in more detail in later chapters. Let me just say here that the central worry provoked by the suggestion that the *adequacy* of a person's sense of integrity and individuality is an issue for individual rationality is that it makes rationality dependent on judgments about what people *are*. And one might think there can be no nonarbitrary grounds, beyond strictly moral considerations, for claiming that what or who someone is is a mistake. It should become clear that this may not be such a serious worry once questions about the nature of individuality, especially the social rootedness of individuality, are addressed more fully. In any case, there is sufficient evidence available to suggest that some ways of being for some kinds of people certainly *are* better than others. The question of appropriateness of an individual's integrity turns out not to be such a difficult question if we consider, first, what such a question involves and, second, how much is known about what kinds of changes the bringing about of which is likely to bring greater liberation to certain kinds of people and thus permit their living and acting as genuine individuals.

What Railton seems to ignore in his metaethical account is that there are questions about what constitutes integrity and individuality that are intimately connected to questions about the rationality of choices and actions. This is so even though he suggests elsewhere that questions about the social nature of the self should be central to some ethical questions.[34] Much recent work in feminist ethics and moral psychology has taken seriously the connection between questions about identity and issues about moral justification—both personal and political. Yet Railton misunderstands such work. In a pompous review of twentieth-century metaethics, Railton (with

Stephen Darwall and Allan Gibbard) takes himself to be answering dominant (feminist) criticisms of moral theory when he points out that

> it would also appear that we owe much of what seems admirable in modern
> societies—movements for political democracy and universal suffrage, for the
> emancipation of slaves and women, for the elimination of racial, ethnic and re-
> ligious discrimination, for universal social provision of basic needs, and for in-
> ternational law and human rights—in significant measure to universalizing
> and generalizing pressures that have precisely gone against the grain of some
> entrenched (and still powerful) particularistic moral conceptions and individ-
> ual and group commitments.[35]

Thus, he understands the criticism of moral theory to be a criticism of universalizing and generalizing pressures that go against the grain of entrenched conceptions.

Instead, such work in feminist ethics and some of the work being done in
moral psychology, as I discuss in Chapter 7, raises precisely the kinds of
questions that need to be raised if it is going to be possible even to *identify*
the "entrenched particularistic moral conceptions" that, as Railton acknowledges, prevent movement toward liberation. What has been recognized in much feminist work in practice and not even acknowledged in
Railton's work in theory is that there are questions about what the relevant
universalizing and generalizing pressures are generalizing *about*. And these
questions often cannot be answered except by paying attention to evidence,
for instance, about people's lives and what is involved, say, in trying to live
one's life as a human being if one happens to be poor, lesbian, disabled,
black, or aged. Railton says that generalizing pressures of ethics have gone
against the grain of entrenched views. Perhaps the reason he has not appreciated the implications of (empirically constrained) work on personal identity for ethics is that he has not acknowledged that it is often necessary to
look at the messy details of particular lives and struggles to know what
those grains are.

4

Leading Life from the Inside:
Individuals, Minority Rights,
and Some Problems
About Indeterminacy

IN CHAPTER 3, I suggested that the difficulty of accommodating concerns about personal development into political philosophy almost certainly has to do with the fact that philosophy has not, until very recently, been done by people for whom there exists any problem about claiming their own humanity. Philosophers such as Railton have had some intellectual interest in the issue, but they have not had to think, in the course of day-to-day life, about the fact that, as Toni Morrison points out, "the timeless and timely narratives upon which expressive language rests, narratives so ingrained and pervasive they seem inextricable from 'reality,' require identification."[1] It is because it has seemed so hard to get philosophers to recognize the interest and seriousness for philosophy of the fact that social visions—the American Dream, for instance—can often *presuppose* the inferiority of some members of a society that I will discuss one more recent work in moral and political philosophy, one involving the notion of individual interests. In this case, the account focuses on social rationality, on the story to be told about the interests of a group, particularly minority groups. It is a work that, although certainly influential, has struck at least some readers as—in some important respects—surprisingly naive about the nature of oppression of some minority groups and the implications of oppression for what people need to do, and to be seen to be doing reasonably, to live well.

In *Liberalism, Community, and Culture,* Will Kymlicka argues that liberal theory possesses the resources to accommodate the significance of cultural community for individuals' identities, development, and choices.[2] He points out that recent attacks on liberal theory have saddled liberalism with highly simplistic and implausible notions of self-hood and suggests that liberal individualism, when properly understood, requires recognizing the group rights of cultural minorities. Kymlicka's view is interesting because he offers a sophisticated conception of liberal individualism. He attempts to demonstrate that a more plausible reading of liberal individualism can be employed to answer some of the worries raised against liberal theory. His view is useful here because he defends a conception of social rationality, of how to define the best interests of a group, relying on a notion of individual interests similar to that discussed in the previous chapters. In what follows I argue that the value of cultural communities for minority groups does indeed pose a problem even for more sophisticated contemporary liberal theory just because the significance of conversion experiences and nonpropositional understanding does, as already argued, pose problems for liberal accounts of individual interests.

More than Rawls, Ronald Dworkin, and others, Kymlicka endorses a role for the state in promoting justice for oppressed groups: He defends the necessity of political action to change the social structures that perpetuate sexist and racist understanding. There are two main threads to the following discussion, each related to points already made and intended to demonstrate further both the popularity and the wrongheadedness of the view of individual interests described in the preceding chapters. The first is a discussion of the view of essential interests Kymlicka takes to be uncontroversial. The second is an examination of some of the implications of such a view for justification of political intervention—in particular, for the idea of state neutrality.

It looks very much as though the strong appeal of the view of interests Kymlicka takes to be uncontroversial is explained by a worry about the indeterminacy that would be implied if individual interests were defined not in terms of individuals' settled desires and preferences but rather, at least occasionally, in terms of desires and preferences individuals *would* have under different social conditions. In discussing this worry, I argue that in insisting on state neutrality, at least in a social system that is already profoundly unjust toward some groups of people, Kymlicka disallows rather than preserves the centrality of individuals in the justification of social policies. I do not argue, as many have about liberal views, that the account is too individualistic but rather that it rests on a mistaken understanding of what it means to give primacy to individuals.

It may be objected that my criticism is misdirected because Kymlicka is not concerned with oppressed groups *within* a culture but rather with equality *between* cultures (e.g., between the English and the French in Canada). If this is true, then I would argue that in fact Kymlicka has the *wrong* concerns if his argument is meant to apply, as he claims it is, to the aboriginal peoples of Canada. If his concern is simply for the rights of equal groups within a culture, then I would argue, following John Danley,[3] that its application is limited and rather uninteresting. I suspect, though, that he intends his argument to apply to *oppressed* minority groups, in which case I would suggest that to the extent that he is not concerned with the issues addressed here, he should be.[4]

Individual Interests

Kymlicka's view of cultures as contexts of choice expresses a conception of essential individual interests that he takes to be uncontroversial. He is probably right that the view is uncontroversial, but he is wrong about the view. Or so I am arguing. He takes essential individual interests to be defined in terms of what is required for an individual to lead her life "from the inside, according to [her] beliefs about value," when current beliefs about value that are mistaken can be revised. In his view, "No life goes better by being led from the outside according to values the person doesn't endorse" (p. 12). Lives only go better when they are being led from the inside, according to the individual's own beliefs about value. So individuals have an essential interest in making choices on the basis of their own strong values and interests—with correct information—not on someone else's. Thus, Kymlicka's defense of cultural membership as a good is careful *not* to risk justifying the overriding of choices an individual would make for herself on the basis of her stable context of choice, with true beliefs.

This notion, of course, has a definite appeal. Certainly, we do usually think individuals are better off if they make their own choices, even if these might not be the best ones according to some preferred standard. The account of essential interests Kymlicka offers is appealing because it expresses the intuition many people have that it is wrong to interfere in other people's choices—that it represents a lack of respect for their autonomy—as long as those choices express basic ends and values. The value of particular cultures in the formulation of social policies, in Kymlicka's view, is determined by the resources individuals need to lead their lives "from the inside"; it is not supposed to be defined in terms of any particular conception of what individuals ought to be.

The problem, though, is that if the value of cultures is defined in terms of the resources people need to lead their lives from the inside, it is in fact already defined in terms of a particular notion of what people ought to be. For people lead their lives from the inside by basing their choices on the identity they have as a result of having been shaped in and by a society defined in terms of some particular norms and values, norms and values one has accepted for oneself on the basis of one's own social situation—the relationships that define it, the ideals it prescribes, and so on. Yet these values and norms are precisely what someone struggles against if she is a member of an oppressed minority in an unfair society and desires a more adequate sense of integrity. They are also struggled against, or ought to be struggled against, if one is a member of a more favorably situated group and wants to engage in more humane and equitable relations.

In Kymlicka's view, it is uncontroversial that "no life goes better by being led from the outside according to values the person doesn't endorse" (p. 12). But why not? Why should the lives of people who have been persuaded that they are inferior not go better if they are guided by ideals that represent their real value as persons? And why should the lives of those who have been persuaded that they are superior not go better if they are guided by ideals that express a more humane social vision? It is not at all obvious that just any individual would—or could—*endorse* values that represent a genuinely more equal society, at least not before certain radical changes were brought about to the social structures and systems of meanings. For to the extent that the current society is defined in terms of racist norms and values, it is not obvious that just any individual could *understand* such values. But it *is* reasonable to think lives would go better if changes were brought about to the social structures that would make genuinely nonracist, nonsexist ideals plausible. Why should it always be the case that lives go better only when they are led from the inside on the basis of beliefs and values people have inherited as a result of their membership in a certain society? Why should it not be the case that some other social arrangement makes meaningful more appropriate sets of options?

Kymlicka's response, it seems, is that if some social arrangement other than the current one would be more likely to provide more meaningful choices, such a possibility should be presented in the free and open cultural marketplace. If a socialist society, for example, would provide a better social arrangement, then it should be able to win out in the cultural marketplace.[5] Kymlicka thinks good ways of life are more likely to establish their greater worth, and individuals are most likely to accept responsibility for their choices, when the state is constrained by justificatory neutrality, when, quoting Rawls, individuals cannot "use the coercive apparatus of the state to win for themselves a greater liberty or larger distributive share on the grounds that their activities are of more intrinsic value."[6]

This response is naive. The coercive apparatus of the state is already at work imposing a view about which activities *and people* are of greater intrinsic value. Kymlicka's glib response to Thomas Nagel and Adina Schwartz that of course socialism would do better in a society that produces more socialists, that "every way of life would do better in a society designed to ensure that no one had conflicting preferences,"[7] is unfair. It misses the point that the "neutral state" in a capitalistic, racist, misogynist society imposes meanings and values on society that make it difficult for people even to understand what, say, a socialist, nonsexist, nonracist system would be like, let alone to prefer it. Again, as I argued in regard to the liberal idealization of objective interests, it cannot be a question of *adding on* some new meanings and values; it cannot just be a question of pluralism: There exists a prior question about the nature of the broader practical and conceptual framework—the standards it provides and the values it presupposes—in terms of which any new information, meanings, and values are to be identified, interpreted, and applied.

Kymlicka thinks the question about state neutrality is a question about whether people are capable of discriminating between good and bad ways of life: If individuals are unable to make these judgments in social life, then state perfectionism might be the appropriate way to enable people to discriminate among different conceptions of the good.[8] It may be, though, that the question is not about whether people can discriminate between good and bad choices; rather, it may be about what kinds of resources people require to have those *good* choices available to them to be deliberated about properly to begin with. Kymlicka's view appears to presuppose that current social structures are adequate, at least as the grounds for proper rational deliberation. He takes for granted their *epistemic* adequacy. And one could think otherwise. The epistemological difficulty, which I discuss further later, is that if social change is constrained by the requirement that it be justified in terms of what individuals can endorse "from the inside" with true beliefs, individuals may never be able to find out just how inadequate their current system is for large numbers of people.

Cultures as Contexts of Choice

The primary worry of both liberals and critics of liberalism regarding the significance of particular cultures is that the protection of cultural communities might conflict with the liberty of individuals: If cultural membership is considered a good, it is possible that the protection of certain *kinds* of cultures might be taken to justify repression of individuals. Kymlicka's response is that protecting particular cultures enhances individual liberties by providing individuals with suitable choices, information, examples, and so on. He argues that since liberals acknowledge self-respect as a primary good, they ought to acknowledge the value of cultural membership. For it is the "cultural community within which individuals form and revise their ends and ambitions" (p. 135).

Kymlicka argues that his defense of cultural membership as a good is not an illiberal notion because it does not legitimize changes to a culture that would threaten the existence of the culture as a (stable) context of choice (p. 167). In his view, changes that do not threaten the existence of a context of choice are ones, such as changes to French Canadian culture in the 1960s, that "occurred *because of* the choices that francophones themselves made from within their (stable) context of choice" (p. 167). Changes that do threaten the existence of a context of choice, on the other hand, are ones like those that brought about the demise of aboriginal culture "*in spite of* the choices of aboriginal people" (p. 167). If cultures are defined in terms of particular practices and values, when changes come about to those practices and values—changes, for instance, in religious and political practices—we would have to say the culture has ceased to exist. On Kymlicka's view of culture as a context of choice, "the cultural community continues to exist even when its members are free to modify the character of the culture, should they find its traditional ways of life no longer worthwhile" (p. 167). Thus, cultural change does not threaten the existence of the culture, and hence does not risk overriding individuals' dependence on such cultures, as long as the right sorts of change are ultimately defined in terms of members' choices.

To make more precise the problem about standards mentioned earlier and its significance for questions about social rationality—about standards for defining the interests of a group—it is important to consider Kymlicka's notion of equality. Following Rawls and Ronald Dworkin, Kymlicka favors a resource-based theory of equality as opposed to the view that rights should be distributed equally. He uses Dworkin's shipwreck example to show why the value of cultural membership cannot be accommodated on a color-blind, liberal, egalitarian distribution of resources and liberties and how he thinks it might nonetheless be accommodated on an accepted liberal view of equality. In Dworkin's example, we are to imagine a vessel shipwrecked on an island with the available resources to be auctioned off to the passengers, presumably all from the same culture. Each passenger starts with the same amount of money, and the final costs of goods reflect the cost to others of the choices individuals make about how to lead their lives. This exemplifies the relationship between responsibility and equality: We are responsible for our ends and hence for adjusting our aims and ambitions in light of the legitimate interests of others; the costs to others of the resources we claim should figure in each person's sense of what is rightly his and in each person's judgments of what life he should lead (pp. 187–188).

What Kymlicka adds to this scheme is the suggestion that we suppose there are two ships at the island, one bigger than the other. After the goods have been fairly auctioned off according to individuals' choices about the good life and the cost of those choices to others, it is discovered that the two ships are of different nationalities. This results in the difficulty that the members of the smaller ship, once they have disembarked from their ship, are deprived of the opportunity to execute their chosen lifestyles in their own cultural context. Kymlicka argues that equality requires that the members of the minority culture be recompensed for costs incurred in securing the existence of their cultural context, a cost that is not incurred by the larger group.

Kymlicka's defense of cultural communities as contexts of choice preserves the liberal commitment to individualism. For such a commitment, contrary to some critics, does not involve any denial of social influences on individuals' ends and commitments (pp. 15–16). He points out that the liberal view does not presume that individuals can *perceive* a self prior to its ends, as Michael Sandel's criticism, for instance, suggests (p. 51). Rather, liberals hold that "we understand ourselves to be prior to our ends, *in the sense that no end or goal is exempt from possible reexamination*" (p. 52).

Now, one might wonder what it means for individuals to understand themselves prior to their ends. The particularly liberal claim about individuals, it appears, has to do with the *significance* given to social influences in individuals' deliberation. Kymlicka responds to Charles Taylor (cited in Kymlicka) that liberalism does not deny that communities are a "given" in individuals' choosing and affirming of projects. The difference between the liberal position and others, in his view, is that liberals do not take this "givenness" to be a reason for mistrusting individuals' judgments about the value of their projects as long as those judgments are relatively unimpeded and undistorted: "The liberal view operates through people's rationality—i.e., it generates confidence in the value of one's projects by removing any impediments or distortions in the reasoning process involved in making judgments of value. The alternative view operates behind the backs of the individuals involved—i.e., it generates confidence via a process which people can't acknowledge as the grounds of their confidence" (p. 62).

The liberal commitment to individualism, then, is a commitment to a view about how individuals' choices and interests are *defined;* they are defined in terms of reasons individuals can or would endorse if they were free from impediments and distortions rather than in terms of a conception of the good promoted "behind the backs of the individuals involved" (p. 62). The state possesses positive duties to provide resources for individuals to choose from rich and meaningful arrays of choices (e.g., p. 79), but "governments should not use the superiority (or inferiority) of anyone's conception of the good as their reason for any state action" (p. 80).

The reason for this restriction is clear. If states were permitted to promote someone's good behind her or his back, an individual's good would be defined in a way that the individual might not be able to endorse on the basis of her settled preferences. And this would make it look as though any kind of totalitarian, repressive government could become justifiable in terms of individuals' best interests. Kymlicka's commitment to liberal neutrality endorses interventionist state action to promote the principles of justice. However, any other kind of intervention should be justifiable in terms of individuals' interests in, first, being able to lead their lives "from the inside" in accordance with their beliefs about what gives value to life and, second, in being free to question those beliefs, "to examine them in the light of whatever information and examples and arguments our culture can provide" (p. 13).

An Epistemological Problem

Let us consider more carefully the notion of context of choice. In Kymlicka's view, the state has an obligation to provide the resources for people to be able to choose from a rich and meaningful array of options.

Consider the situation of the two main characters in the film *Thelma and Louise* (Ridley Scott, U.S.A., 1991). The film tells the story of two women trying to flee the country because one, Louise, has killed the man who tried to rape the other, Thelma. Distrusting the justice system and discovering what it is like to take control of their own lives, Thelma and Louise eventually drive into the Grand Canyon to their deaths rather than give themselves up to the authorities. Given what we know about Thelma and Louise's situation from the movie and on the basis of what is known about sexism generally, it is not obvious that their choice is unreasonable.

Now, we might wonder what it would mean for Thelma and Louise to be able to choose from a rich and meaningful array of options. Some people object to this film because it shows two women reacting to an oppressive situation by adopting the very patterns of behavior that characterize the system that oppresses them—violent ones. Such critics presumably wanted instead to have seen a resistance to such patterns of behavior. They might have wanted to have seen Thelma and Louise refusing to participate in the very norms and values that characterize the system that oppresses them, that makes expectations of justice unreasonable. But what would it have meant for Thelma and Louise to have resisted without using violence? What options *might* there have been for more effective resistance, and what would such resistance amount to? Should Thelma and Louise have been more caring, perhaps, as women are typically supposed to be? Claudia Card, for one, argues that the virtues that have typically characterized women's interactions—caring and nurturance, for instance—are in fact ones that have been used to oppress women.[9] What sort of choices *could* constitute rich and meaningful ones when the very norms and values that *make* choices rich and meaningful—social norms and values—either presume women's inferiority or require their annihilation?

Two issues need to be separated here. One is an issue about the appropriateness of violent behavior. The other is the struggle for autonomy. The appropriateness of violence seems not to be the issue in the film. For the reality is that it is this very appropriateness that defines the society, makes salient certain options, and provides the terms in which those options are interpreted. The tragedy of the movie may be that the social structures and ways of thinking that make questions about the appropriateness of violence meaningless are those that frustrate the real pursuit of autonomy for large groups of people. The affirmation of personal worth and the pursuit of self-respect in this film are indeed admirable. But it is not clear what it would mean for Thelma and Louise to achieve their ends in a society in which the dominant interests and ends preclude even the imaginability of their real success.

Suppose the context of choice that would allow Thelma and Louise to choose freely from among a rich and meaningful array of options is one that fully values what they are or are trying to be—independent women. In the absence of available examples, it is difficult to know what this context of choice would be like. It is difficult to imagine a cultural context in which the options available to women—at least those that can be chosen by women without their being seen to be crazy—would be rich and meaningful expressions of human worth. And suppose it is true, as Nancy Sherman argues, that "human flourishing" is a concept the content of which has to be discovered through anthropological investigation into the needs and circumstances of particular communities.[10] Suppose, in other words, that to find out what it would be like for women to be able to choose meaningfully in deliberating about life plans—to be able to evaluate options in light of concerns like self-realization and the pursuit of human goods—it is necessary to investigate social values, the representation of history, the structure of institutions, and the implications of those institutions for well-being. Luce Irigaray says, "The first question to ask is therefore the following: how can women analyze their own exploitation, their own demands, within an order prescribed by the masculine? *Is a woman's politics possible within that order?* What transformation in the political process itself does it require?"[11] If Irigaray is right, for some people the very idea of rich and meaningful choices will require challenging and reformulating—indeed, re-sisting—some quite basic social concepts and principles.

Kymlicka acknowledges that it is difficult to know what it would mean to have a nonsexist society:

> It's unclear what institutions and practices would constitute the best non-sexist spelling out of the ideals underlying the principle of neutral concern. The assumptions of women's inferiority are deeply embedded in many of society's institutions, from the teaching of sex roles to children to the public devaluation of domestic labor. Removing them will require changes not only in the access women have to social positions, but also in their ability to shape and define those positions. (p. 92)

Yet whereas this is certainly true, the implications of such embeddedness are more interesting than Kymlicka acknowledges. For one thing, it is not clear that liberals can say, as Kymlicka supports Rawls and Dworkin in saying, that sexist and racist contexts of choice are disallowed on the liberal view because they conflict with the principles of justice (e.g., p. 83). For if, as Toni Morrison says, "timeless and timely narratives ... [are] so ingrained and pervasive they seem inextricable from 'reality,'"[12] it is not clear that sexist and racist contexts of choice will always be easily identified. If sexism, say, is embedded in some of the concepts and terms in which information and events are understood, including conceptions of justice, it cannot simply be taken for granted that considerations of justice, in the abstract, will show us how to eliminate it.

Kymlicka is right that removing assumptions of women's inferiority will require more than giving women access to society's institutions; it will also require giving women the ability to shape and define those institutions. In other words, women's liberation is not a question about *including* women as full members of the society as it is now; it is also a question about what that society is supposed to be. But again, this point is more complicated and interesting than Kymlicka acknowledges. He does not discuss what it means in practice for members of oppressed groups to attempt to achieve such shaping and defining. Patricia Williams points out that not only can certain possibilities not be properly understood within a system founded on, say, racist assumptions but also certain kinds of people cannot exist *as people* within such a system:

> My parents were always telling me to look up at the world; to look straight at people, particularly white people; not to let them stare me down; to hold my ground; to insist on the right to my presence no matter what. They told me that in this culture you have to look people in the eye because that's how you tell them you're their equal. . . .
>
> By itself, seeing into me would be to see my substance, my anger, my vulnerability and my raging despair—and that alone is hard enough to show. But to uncover it and have it devalued by ignore-ance, to hold it up bravely in the organ of my eyes and have it greeted by an impassive stare that passes right through all that which is me, an impassive stare that moves on and attaches itself to my left earlobe or to the dust caught in the rusty vertical geysers of my wiry hair or to the breadth of my freckled brown nose—this is deeply humiliating. It rewounds, relives the early childhood anguish of uncensored seeing, the fullness of vision that is the permanent turning-away point for most blacks.
>
> The cold game of equality staring makes me feel like a thin sheet of glass: white people see all the worlds beyond me but not me. They come trotting at me with force and speed; they do not see me. I could force my presence, the real me contained in those eyes, upon them, but I would be smashed in the process. If I deflect, if I move out of the way, they will never know I existed.[13]

How does someone begin to shape and define an institution if the norms and values that deny her very existence are also the norms and values in terms of which shaping and defining have to take place? Kymlicka ignores the interesting question about how the right sorts of shaping and defining are to be determined, discovered, and pursued—in particular, about whether any interesting shaping and defining can take place at all on the basis of certain current "social stock[s] of meanings and beliefs" (p. 81).

Now, it is true that Kymlicka rejects the view of some liberals that agreement is fundamental to defining justice.[14] And his doing so indicates a concern for the injustice involved in the conditions under which such agreement is secured, conditions that might disallow the formulation or at least the expression of important differences. Kymlicka acknowledges that emphasis on agreement ignores the fact that people are differently advantaged in terms of rational competence and that, therefore, some people are better able to articulate their interests than others.[15] Thus, Kymlicka favors an interest-based rather than an agreement-based view of justification. But if Patricia Williams, for example, cannot be seen to *exist* as a human being within a conceptual system, what would it mean for social policies formulated and defended largely *within* that system to be representing her real interests? Can she even be understood to possess essential interests within a system of meanings and values that denies her humanity? Surely, Kymlicka does not have in mind the interests she is supposed to have given current conceptions—interests that reflect deeply rooted assumptions about her inferior social status. The problem as regards social justification in cases of oppression is not just that some people are disadvantaged in terms of rational capacities, as Kymlicka acknowledges; rather, it is that some people cannot figure as rational agents at all.

Ian Hacking argues that prior to the development of certain categories for sorting people and behavior—what he calls "human kinds"—it is not possible to pursue some kinds of understanding. Hacking argues that human kinds, as distinct from natural kinds, can transform the way people see themselves, the way people understand the world, and, as well, their possibilities for acting. The category "sexual harassment" would be a human kind: It sorts behavior in a way that makes it possible for people to understand their lives differently and to act in ways they could not have done previously. Before there was a category "sexual harassment," women were indeed sexually harassed. There was the behavior, and there was the harm. But people could not understand interactions *as* sexually harassing before there was a public conception for categorizing these actions in this way.

Hacking thinks human kinds, unlike natural kinds, involve a certain kind of impossibility. The existence of certain kinds of behavior and people depends on the existence of certain kinds of societies or at least of certain practices within a society. "Sexual harassment" would not make sense as a way of classifying behavior if it were taken for granted that women are *supposed to be* objects for men's sexual aggression. The existence of a specific human kind is contingent upon the existence of circumstances and interests that make that sort a *relevant* human kind. So, for instance, "it was not possible for God to make George Washington a pervert. God could have delayed George Washington's birth by over a century, but would that have been the same man? God could have moved the medical discourse back 100-odd years. But God could not have simply made him a pervert, the way he could have made him freckled or had him captured or hung for treachery."[16]

Now, of course, it is true that George Washington could have done what would later be considered perverted. But Hacking's point is that George Washington could not have *been* a pervert at that time. He could not have been treated as one, understood as one, and have chosen from options that reflected his being one. When Hacking says there wasn't that way of being to be chosen, he means it wouldn't have been possible for George Washington to think of himself as a pervert, at least as we now understand "pervert." Similarly, someone who is degraded and diminished by systemically unjust social practices *can* choose to deliberate about herself and act according to a sense of herself as a full human being. But as Frantz Fanon said after acknowledging his intellectual grasp of the "black problem," the occasion always arose when "I had to meet the white man's eyes"[17]—that is, to make his claims within a situation that denied him agency in the first place. In a society in which there does in fact exist discrimination, even the most self-assertive person, if she is a member of a group that is discriminated against, must think of herself as discriminated against, at least occasionally. For she will have to do this if she is to properly explain to herself the kinds of reactions she receives and to deliberate sensibly about her options. If she *denies* to herself the existence of systemic discrimination, she will get at least some causal relations wrong. She may, for instance, attribute blame to herself for certain kinds of treatment when the proper target would have been institutional or social structures. As I discuss in Chapters 7 and 8, people do sometimes choose what is not there to be chosen, contrary to Hacking, but this is not possible without significant personal and political change or at least the claim to its possibility in both belief and action.

Of course, Kymlicka is committed to transformative politics as regards questions of justice. But he seems to think that social transformations, except transformations required by the principles of justice, should be ones people should be free to accept or reject on the basis of their stable context of choice. It is not clear, though, that people should be free to accept or reject changes to ways of thinking and behaving upon which the freedom, even the claim to humanity, for less dominant members of society depends. The response to this cannot be that people are not free to reject *this* sort of change because sexism and racism are incompatible with the principles of justice. For there wouldn't be this sort of change even to be considered as just or unjust *before* political action brings about changes to the stable con-

text of meanings and values: If sexist assumptions are embedded in the social context of meanings and values, they are not understood as sexist assumptions; rather, they are norms. This is part of what systemic discrimination means—namely, that everyday linguistic and social practices can
presume the nonexistence as persons of some sorts of people. For instance,
at the beginning of this book, I quoted Lévi-Strauss's report (cited in
Michard-Marchal) that "the entire village left . . . leaving us *alone with the
women and children* in the *abandoned* homes."[18] Discrimination that is
built into social norms and values requires work to be identified. Appeals to
principles of justice, however defined, are not going to be enough if such
discrimination is not identified as *in*justice to begin with. Changes to social
structures may be required before the sexism that has always been there
comes to be understood and treated as sexism.

For instance, it would seem reasonable to think that part of what would
constitute a meaningful context of choice for black women in this (North
American) society would be the availability of positive images of their history, bodies, sexuality, beauty, and so on. And yet, as Julie Dash, director of
the film *Daughters of the Dust* (Julie Dash, U.S.A., 1991), points out, there
have been no such images in North American film and television.[19] Surely,
an important part of the explanation for this has to do with the fact that
the larger society is constituted mostly of whites. And if we are to take seriously Toni Morrison's essay on American literature, the self-definitions and
values of whites depend heavily on the invisibility of the work and writings,
indeed the bodies, of blacks.[20] It would appear that Julie Dash's film and
other such works are part of an effort precisely to disrupt the stability of
the dominant context of choice so that members of the larger society can
begin to see different sorts of things as meaningful. It is hard to see the
sense in which freedom to accept or reject these changes to norms and values should be an issue here. For the aim is precisely to redefine meanings
and values so that *rejecting* certain changes is in fact *not* a meaningful option.

If by "rich and meaningful" is meant choices that reflect opportunities to
pursue human flourishing, such a context of choice is not always one that
can simply be added on to the currently available options. On the contrary,
the meaningfulness of some sorts of options for some people requires that
other sorts of options for other people in fact *not* be options. Indeed, the
changes that need to be brought about to make certain options meaningful
at all are often ones that are intended precisely to *undermine* the meaningfulness of other options altogether. If the work of people like Julie Dash still
leaves people free to reasonably accept or reject proposed changes to the
social context of meanings and values, such work would appear to be un-
finished.

Perhaps Kymlicka would think that the success of feminists, blacks, gays,
and others in bringing about certain changes to social values provides evi-

dence for his claim that the cultural marketplace, rather than the state, provides the most effective means of combating oppression. If so, this would reflect a disappointingly limited view of what liberation requires. Many people think it is not possible for the oppressed groups of North American cultures to achieve liberation under the current social system. Black lesbian feminist activist Barbara Smith points out that anyone who thinks about it can see that it is

> simply not possible for any oppressed people, including lesbians and gay men, to achieve freedom under this system. Police dogs, cattle prods, fire hoses, poverty, urban insurrections, the Vietnam War, the assassinations, Kent State, unchecked violence against women, the self-immolation of the closet and the emotional and often physical violence experienced by those of us who dared leave it made the contradiction crystal clear. Nobody sane would want any part of the established order. It was the system—white supremacist, misogynistic, capitalist and homophobic—that had made our lives so hard to begin with.[21]

Suppose this is true. And suppose some other social arrangement—one defined in terms of different norms and values—would provide more adequate resources for people to identify and deliberate about choices. Suppose also, as seems plausible, that the very imaginability of such an arrangement requires conceptual resources not provided by the current conceptual background. The point is that given that conditions favorable to such norms and values often need to be *brought about,* it is not clear that within Kymlicka's cultural marketplace, constrained as it is by the stability of the social stock of meanings and beliefs (except in cases in which social members choose to change their context themselves), we would ever be able to discover this.

The liberal commitment to providing the resources for free choosing and revising of projects, if such resources are to allow for the pursuit of human flourishing, should require in some cases a commitment to bringing about the social changes that would make *relevant* the classifications necessary for pursuing adequate understanding of injustice. Now, Kymlicka says the liberal position is distinguished by its commitment to rationality, to confidence in individuals' judgments about the value of their projects, as long as those judgments are relatively unimpeded and undistorted (p. 62). Yet surely people's deliberations will be impeded if they have the wrong sorts of categories. Now, perhaps liberals would say that the liberal commitment to provide resources for autonomous choice includes a commitment to ongoing efforts to provide social members with the right sorts of categories. But in at least some cases, the bringing about of the right sorts of categories is not consistent with a commitment to preserve the stable context of choice in terms of which other social members acquire their identity and find their choices meaningful. It would look as though either unimpeded and undistorted deliberation will be deliberation in terms of the current social stock of meanings and beliefs that, at least in an unjust society, would disallow the imaginability of an important range of choices and hence preclude autonomous choice for some people. Or the liberal commitment to rationality should also be, at the same time, a commitment to the appropriate sorts of transformative politics—some of which, in a society in which people's actions and identities *presuppose* racist and sexist norms and values, would surely have to occur "behind the backs" of the individuals involved.

The epistemic significance of social structures and fundamental social meanings and values provides one reason for thinking Kymlicka's use of Dworkin's shipwreck example to illustrate the problem of equality for minority groups is misleading. The example is interesting because it is one in which the people of the smaller culture formulate their choices and choose their life plans in the culture as it develops independently of the larger culture. To the extent that their choices and life plans will be made meaningful by different sorts of meanings and values, it looks as though the arrival of the two ships at the same island should provoke a question not about equal distribution of resources and liberties, as Kymlicka suggests, but about the terms according to which resources and liberties are defined in the first place—about the perspective, in other words, in terms of which the *relevant* respects of equality are defined.

Suppose the members of the group on the smaller ship had formulated their life projects in a nonracist, nonmisogynist, noncapitalist social system. Would the members of the group on the larger ship even be able to understand them? Suppose, for instance, that the smaller ship contains a community in which homosexual relationships are the norm or at least a culture in which heterosexual relations are not taken to be the only natural way of interrelating. Suppose that for such people, the necessary resources for the realization of life plans include liberty to maintain and develop a culture in which gays and lesbians are recognized and treated as full human beings, are represented in the symbols of the society, are respected for what they are, and so on. In Kymlicka's example, the members of the smaller group choose their ends before becoming involved in a society dominated by the larger group. If the larger culture is anything like our current homophobic one, it would probably be difficult for members of the larger group to see the resources required for the realization of the choices of members of the smaller group as resources at all.

By "rich and meaningful choices," one could have in mind the choices that are made meaningful by a society that presumes the inferiority of the group in question. But if "rich and meaningful" means those choices that adequately reflect people's real interests, the question about how resources are to be distributed must be preceded in cases of oppression by questions

about what the nature of the society is within which those resources are resources to begin with. If current capitalist systems do not permit human
flourishing for all members of society, as appears to be true, then it is possible that the meaningfulness of the choices of the members of the smaller
group—if they were members of a group relevantly different from the
larger group and the larger group was something like our current social system—might well depend on the existence of social, political, and economic
structures of a radically different sort than those presupposed by the aims
and interests of the members of the larger group. Are the members of the
larger society to be asked or required to accept changes to their cultural
context that would make them, in effect, members of another society? Or
must the members of the smaller group reformulate their interests and aims
so their real interests in human flourishing become inexpressible and, eventually, unimaginable?

Cultural Politics

At least arguably, the significance of recent work in cultural politics lies in
the insistence that individuals' interests cannot properly be defined in terms
of the identities people inherit as members of an oppressive society:
Questions about how a cultural group defines itself and how it is represented are issues in important part about how to define the real interests of
people who are members of that group. Anthony Appiah, for instance,
raises the question of what constitutes the unity of Africans struggling
against racist discrimination. He points out that attempts to define African
unity in terms of "common heritage" end up presupposing the viability of
race as an identifying feature, an assumption that concedes the validity of
racist assumptions of European literature and history.[22] "Race" as a unifying feature reinforces the notion of "race" as a feature that distinguishes
some human beings from others, an assumption antiracists have an interest
in opposing. Yet one would not want to deny that there is something that it
means to be oppressed as an African, something that is different, say, from
what it means to be oppressed as a disabled person. One would not want to
deny that there are some real similarities among Africans, some basis for
the identification of shared interest. As I argue in Chapter 6, an assumption
of some sort of real unity is taken for granted in political discussions, even
by those who explicitly argue against such an assumption—in particular,
those who worry about essentialism. This invites philosophical questions
about what such unity consists in, questions Kymlicka's account sometimes
seems to beg.[23]

   Kymlicka is certainly not wrong in claiming that cultural membership *is*
important in providing a context of choice for individuals' deliberations,

but it seems clear that some cultures and some particular representations—in political theory and historical accounts—of such cultures are much more significant in this respect than others. And unless something is said about why some kinds of cultural contexts are to be preferred as contexts of choice for some people and not others, even when people choose such contexts, there is the risk that the justification of social change in terms of individuals' interests, as Kymlicka defines individuals' interests, justifies continued oppression rather than genuinely autonomous choice.

Part of Kymlicka's problem is the difficulty of defining cultures. He acknowledges that questions about how to define culture are complex.[24] Kymlicka defines "culture" as "the existence of a viable community of individuals with a shared heritage (language, history, etc.)" (p. 168). Yet as already mentioned, there are questions, or there ought to be questions, about how commonalities are defined. As in his discussion of equality, Kymlicka does not take seriously enough questions about how standards are defined: He does not take seriously enough the fact that relevant respects of commonality, like relevant respects of equality, are defined in terms of a notion of what the society is. And if a society is unjust, there are reasons to resist taking its standards for granted.

The relevant question about minority cultures here may not be that of how to characterize the cultural communities that are there. At least as regards questions about social justice and individual interests, there seems to be a more interesting question about what sorts of communities *ought* to be there. Rosemary Brown writes that she became brown when she came to Canada, not when she was growing up in Jamaica.[25] Her identification with blacks in Canada is not explained primarily by facts about her individual interests; rather, it is explained by the racist character of the Canadian society in which she is to *pursue* her interests. Should that cultural attachment be the one that should be protected for her to choose freely? We might think instead that she would be choosing freely, in an appropriate context of choice, if she did not have to pursue such an identification—if, in other words, the larger society, the nature of which explains her identification with such a group, were other than it is. Thus, there is also often a normative question about identity—directly relevant to questions about group interests—that Kymlicka does not begin to address.

Justification and Problems About Indeterminacy

What explains the significance of the requirement in liberal theories that justification of social policies be constrained by what people can endorse "from the inside," with true beliefs? Even though Kymlicka acknowledges the role of the state in addressing cases of discrimination and sees some of the problems of institutional systemic sexist and racist oppression, he insists on a definition of individuals' essential interests that limits justifiable state intervention to social changes people could endorse, if adequately informed, within current social structures.

The first explanation for the appeal of this account of essential individual interests is the apparent difficulty of justifying a commitment to "working behind the backs of individuals." The crux of liberalism as Kymlicka presents it, it would seem, is the answer it offers to questions about *how* state actions are ultimately justified—namely, in terms of considerations of what is required for individuals to pursue their essential interests (in living life from the inside, with true beliefs). Any departure from *this* conception would apparently require quite different sorts of arguments, ones not primarily about the centrality of individuals' choices but rather about the merits of some particular social order.

But there is another, deeper reason for Kymlicka's view of individual essential interests, one that has to do with a certain conception of justification and a related issue about individuality. The appeal of Kymlicka's conception of essential individual interests has to do with an apparent problem of indeterminacy that arises if, contrary to the liberal view, an individual's essential interests are defined in terms of large-scale social considerations— considerations, for instance, about what kinds of goods someone would choose and value if, say, her society were of a different sort. If an individual's essential interests were defined in terms of beliefs, desires, and interests someone would hold if both the society and she were radically transformed, it would look as though there would be no way to say of some particular person at a time that some options are better for her than others. For there are any number of ways in which the society could be transformed so individuals would hold quite different sets of beliefs and commitments. If the best options for a person are indeterminate, it would not make sense to say, as we often do, that individuals *get better* in their deliberations about how they should live their lives.

The indeterminacy problem upon which the possibility of justifying claims about essential interests is presumed to rest is a problem about the indeterminacy of ends for a particular individual at a time. It is, of course, true that it is always difficult in practice to say that some one set of options is best for some particular person. This is usually because there are some things—such as the consequences of certain courses of action—that are unknown. But we often assume that some story could be told about what the best end or project or set of ends or projects would be for a particular person if we just had enough information about the person, her situation and history, the effects of certain changes, and so on. As I mentioned in Chapter 3, idealizations tell us what sorts of stories we ought to be telling, if we could, in rationalizing judgments about interests. If an individual's settled preferences are not taken as a starting point—if we assume, for instance, that the initial motivational system of the individual is problematic—there would not be the possibility of coming up with a determinate answer to the question of better or worse ends for that person in particular, even in theory.

There is, however, another indeterminacy problem that is also relevant to the question of justifying claims about better or worse choices for an individual in particular, and it has implications for how the first question might be better expressed. This is the question about what people *are* and can be under certain kinds of conditions: We might wonder whether there is an answer, in theory at least, not to the question of what set of ends is best for an individual in particular but rather to the question of what kind of state a person should be in for her basic aims at a time to be taken to define her real ends and interests. On the liberal view, as we have seen, there is an assumption that a person's secure sense of self is taken for granted, at least in the defining of essential interests. If, though, we take someone's initial personal state to be problematic, there is a question about the determinacy of an answer, even in theory, to questions about adequate conditions for determining individuality. Kymlicka's view disregards this possible problem of indeterminacy and hence involves relevant, unacknowledged arbitrariness: On the assumption that a person acts individually when she leads her life "from the inside" (with true beliefs), there is the risk that almost anything could count as actions reflecting essential individual interests depending on the structure of the society in which a person happens to find herself embedded.

It is not surprising that the first question of indeterminacy is taken to be the one that is relevant to defining individuals' real interests, and what an individual *is* as a person at a time is taken for granted in such accounts. As mentioned in Chapter 3, there is something unappealing about questions about the personal, as opposed to moral, adequacy of what people are and what they take themselves to be. We might feel justified in saying someone should be more kind, generous, honest, and so on, but we don't usually think we can say someone should be differently inclined, with different sorts of personal interests and commitments. It is generally assumed that the answer to questions about personal adequacy and individuality would have to be the defense of some sort of ideal of what persons in general ought to be. And neither liberals nor anyone else, for that matter, wants to be committed to saying that some sorts of people are to be preferred in general, at least on nonmoral grounds, over others.

But this sort of reasoning is mistaken. It assumes that questions about justification are indeed questions about the specification of a particular ideal—that, for instance, to make nonarbitrary judgments about the adequacy of an individual's state, one has to have available some one particular general ideal of personal adequacy. In practice, justification of personal choices is often not a question about specifying ideals at all but rather a question about the relation of a choice to a certain path of development. As I suggested at the end of Chapter 3, it is common for people to undertake certain choices not primarily because the choices lead somewhere in particular but rather because the conditions that will be brought about by such choices will enhance the person's possibilities for making proper choices in the future. And I suggested that there are facts about the matter of what conditions are of this sort.

It is not necessary that there be an answer to the question of what would constitute an adequate sense of self for there to be an answer to the question of which paths of development are more likely than others to express someone's real interest in human flourishing. Not only is it not necessary to appeal to some particular moral ideal to be able to say that some transformative actions are to be preferred over others, but doing so would be undesirable. The appropriate moral alternative—the alternative social vision that makes possible and plausible effective criticism of a current social order—*comes* to be articulatable only as a result of deliberative, transformative action in a certain direction, transformative action that makes possible understanding of the social order that was not possible previously; it cannot, therefore, be assumed that such an ideal should be able to be appealed to in advance to completely *justify* such action. On the contrary, such an assumption involves a fundamental misconception about the nature of self- and social understanding.

There may be a worry, of course, that this kind of response involves circularity. What I have suggested is that certain personal and social transformations bring about cognitive and political possibilities that would not have been possible previously and that, in part, it is the ongoing development of such possibilities that provides reasons for thinking such transformations are to be preferred over others. Even if one accepts the idea that transformations can be justified by the kind of conceptual and political unity they promote or, as suggested by Cornell and cited in Chapter 1, by the kinds of storytelling, with their political consequences, that become possible, there is still the question of *adequacy* or, to put it more strongly, of correctness. One could object that both epistemic and moral constraints are justified in terms of the kind of process of development involved and that such constraints cannot therefore constitute objective constraints.

There is a line of thought developed recently by naturalistic epistemologists such as Richard Boyd and Philip Kitcher according to which we acquire knowledge as a result of the development of cognitive and experimental practices that attempt to incorporate true statements (as much as possible) and to articulate the best unification of them.[26] According to this view, what it means for theories to be "cutting the world at its joints," as Plato said, is not for there to exist some special sort of theory-independent access to the world but rather for such theories to make reference to similarities and differences that are causally relevant to what is being studied.

Defining theoretical adequacy is not a matter of specifying epistemic standards a priori but rather of finding out, as the result of ongoing empirical investigation, whether the process of investigation in terms of which adequacy is understood is one involving actual interaction with the physical and social worlds. As Boyd suggests, what it means for theories to be reliable is for there to exist causal mechanisms that bring it about over time that what is predicated by the theory is true of what the theory is about. There is no vicious circularity in defining adequacy in terms of ongoing theoretical and practical traditions if the reliability of such traditions, when they are reliable, is defined in terms of the contingent relationship between those traditions and actual causal mechanisms of the world.

The problem with Kymlicka's model of individual interests and the corresponding picture of the justification of state policies is not that it is too individualistic; rather, it is that it is individualistic in the wrong way. It gives the wrong account of individuality and hence gets it wrong about what it means for state policies to be justified in terms of individuals' essential interests as opposed to an arbitrarily derived external ideal. The liberal view Kymlicka expresses ignores the fact that individuals are already defined in terms of an arbitrarily imposed moral ideal that legislates the arbitrary privileging of some kinds of people and their goods over others and that this needs to be discovered. It ignores the fact that appropriate criticism of such arbitrariness, criticism often presupposing social and political change, is required for the pursuit of genuine autonomy for at least some groups of people. To the extent that the possibility of such criticism depends on the possibility of ranking particular conceptions of the good life, at least tentatively, the liberal view, at least as defined by Kymlicka, leaves such arbitrariness in place. Thus, it ends up promoting, rather than avoiding, the arbitrary imposing by the state upon individuals of particular moral ideals of what sorts of lives people should lead.

Again, it looks as though the standard (liberal) formulation of the question of essential individual interests gets the issues backward, as argued in Chapter 3, particularly but not only as regards the situation of oppressed social groups: To the extent that individuality and autonomy often need to be discovered as a result of the pursuit of the right sorts of transformative actions and engagements, *individuality* is defined in terms of an individual's real interests (in self-respect, dignity, genuine autonomy, and so on); it is not the case that individual *interests* can be defined primarily in terms of individuality. Moreover, to the extent that possibilities for pursuing self-respect and dignity must be questions about the nature of the social order, in particular its moral nature, questions about individuality must also be questions about the *kind* of society that exists and about the sorts of standards of morality it makes possible. I have not defended in this chapter a particular conception of individual adequacy or human flourishing. I do not think such a defense desirable. But I have suggested that it is a mistake to think, first, that ideals of adequacy cannot be defended in particular cases, at least tentatively, as a result of the right sorts of transformative political actions and, second, that there are not plenty of reasons for thinking that some paths of transformative political action are more likely than others to represent individuals' real interests in the bringing about of a more humane society.

Conclusion

In conclusion, the worry about possibly justifying arbitrarily coercive social policies cannot be addressed by a conception of social justification that is rooted in the centrality of individuals' capacities to live their lives "from the inside," with true beliefs. This is because, first, what some individuals choose "from the inside," with true beliefs, is already a result of arbitrarily coercive state interventions, and second, relevant true beliefs, if they are made available, can often not be made proper use of without the right kinds of socially transformative—on some understandings, coercive—state interventions. Kymlicka and other liberals are right to worry about justifying the use of arbitrary state coercion against individuals. But to the extent that unjustified state coercion is already expressed in deep-seated social norms and values, the proper transformation of which may also require state intervention, liberal neutrality, at least as defended by Kymlicka, is not an adequate response to this worry. In advance of the existence of a thoroughly just society, whatever this turns out to be, if it's even possible, there is no reason to think state neutrality is compatible with the kinds of social changes required to provide adequate resources for all, or even any, social members to be able to choose autonomously. A more appropriate conception of political justification would have to be one that took seriously, first, the dependence of individuals' adequate understanding of their options upon the bringing about of the *right* sorts of contexts of choice and hence the question about what these right sorts would be, and second, the need for an account of the central role of general social and moral considerations in defining adequate individuality.

I have suggested that such considerations require metaphysical and epistemological work. In the next two chapters, I deal with questions of integrity, first of the individual and then of social groups. I intend to demonstrate the need for such accounts and, in particular, to suggest that there is nothing threatening or implausible about the idea that normative questions about integrity—about what constitutes a more adequate sense of self or about what groups *ought* to constitute contexts of choice—are objectively constrained.

5

Personal Integrity, Politics, and Moral Imagination

THERE IS A POPULAR conception of individuality according to which the autonomous individual is one who possesses the capacity to reflect on her preferences and to alter them in light of information. As an autonomous being, an individual is aware of the reflective process by which her later selves emerge from her present self so that her preferences are modified not in a random or an uncontrolled way but in light of her own experience and understanding.[1] Thus, as we have seen, we could say of Thomas Hill's example of the Deferential Wife[2] that she is not really acting autonomously when she happily subordinates herself to her husband because we could argue that she would not choose to act in this way if she were more adequately informed about her moral rights and so on.

But this conception of what it means to be acting as an individual has struck some as too simple. The idea is that autonomy is defined in terms of the individual's self-awareness, of her understanding of her experience, and of her strongly held preferences, desires, and commitments. Yet as we have seen, in some cases, in particular those in which individuals are degraded by social conditioning, there is a question about whether an individual's sense of herself (even suitably corrected for false beliefs) provides the right sort of starting place for questions about autonomy and individual interests and responsibilities.

In discussing the Clarence Thomas hearings, Toni Morrison made the following comment about the way both Thomas and Anita Hill were represented in the media:

In a society with a history of trying to accommodate both slavery and freedom, and a present that wishes both to exploit and deny the pervasiveness of racism, black people are rarely individualized. Even when his supporters were extolling the fierce independence and the "his own man" line about Clarence Thomas, their block and blocked thinking of racial stereotype prevailed.

> Without individuation, without non-racial perception, black people, as a group, are used to signify the polar opposites of love and repulsion.[3]

What does it mean for people not to be able to be individuated by others? If some people cannot be individuated by others because of systemic injustice, what is involved in a claim to individuality by such people? Is such a claim even possible? And if self-awareness provides grounds for individuality, what are people in such situations to be aware of themselves *as*?

In some recent discussions, the centrality of self-awareness in questions of personal integrity has been displaced. The question of personal integrity has been taken to be a question in some sense about what kind of person someone *ought* to be to be able to choose autonomously. Whereas in the past metaphysicians have been concerned about the respects of similarity between a self at one time and a self at another or about how we judge that someone is the same person she was before, there have recently been questions about what constitutes an *appropriate* self for a person at a time, about whether what a person is at a time, or even what she is over a period of time, can properly be taken to define her real individual interests and responsibilities.

In what follows I first consider two accounts of personal integrity. I understand the term "personal integrity" to refer to the adequacy of identity, where by "identity" I mean the sense of self presupposed in an individual's deliberations and actions. Identity consists in those traits that are central to capacities for agency, those that figure into a person's deliberations about herself. Thus, identity is not the same as individuation: People can be individuated by features of their appearance, for instance, but these features may not explain the course of their lives. They may not define a person's self-concept.

It may turn out that the set of traits that explains a person's actions and reactions does not, in fact, provide grounds for autonomous action; that is, it may turn out that a person's self-concept is inadequate as regards possibilities for controlling her life in a way that expresses moral considerations usually assumed in a notion of autonomy, considerations such as self-respect. Traits that are presupposed in an individual's deliberations and actions may not, after all, constitute those traits that are central to effective agency. Thus, there is often a question about the sense of identity that has to do with whether one's self-concept—the way one conceives of oneself—is appropriate, whether, given one's self-concept, one actually does possess a genuine sense of agency. And it is often the case that people have to *discover* that conception of themselves that provides a more adequate basis for deliberation and action in their interests. I take it, therefore, that the more substantive notion of identity that is the object of quests for self-knowledge, and in relation to which we make judgments about character and worth, is a normative notion—referring to the kind of self-concept people try to discover and develop to act autonomously, to be in control of their lives, where control is the realization of real interests. And personal integrity, therefore, might be understood as the achievement and presupposition of such a self-concept—a distinct identity—or of an adequate sense of individuality.

If someone acts out of personal integrity, she is understood to have acted on the basis of commitments and principles that are central to her sense of herself as a person, where the notion of person here is, at least in part, a moral notion. That is, it is not just a matter of what commitments people *think* are central to their sense of themselves as a person. As Lynne McFall points out, we wouldn't think someone was acting out of integrity if she acted on her preference for Mountain Dew over fine wine, no matter how strong her commitment to such a preference might be.[4] To the extent that questions about individuality and personal identity are often normative questions—questions about what defines an *adequate* sense of self—I take the terms "individuality," "identity," and "personal integrity" to be occasionally interchangeable, depending on the concerns addressed. The first article I discuss here examines agency and identity, the second integrity. However, to the extent that each has to do with questions about the kind of self required for a certain kind of action, I take the subject matter to be shared.

I argue that whereas the two accounts to be discussed here depart from the liberal view described just above, they are committed to the idea that individual identity or integrity is defined primarily in terms of facts about the individual herself, her constitution, history, interests, circumstances, and prospects—something like Railton's modification of the liberal view of individual interests but with different intentions. I will try to show that this is a mistaken approach to the notion of personal integrity. In particular, I suggest that on such an account, some important examples of sincere and courageous personal choice can only be understood as crazy. My more positive suggestion will be that personal integrity be defined in terms of paths of development, where the determination of the right sorts of paths of development depends on moral imagination, on general beliefs about what *ought* to be possible for human beings in terms of autonomy, self-respect, and dignity. In the final sections, I consider the implications of such a conception of personal integrity for two somewhat difficult, related issues in moral psychology—the occasional moral appropriateness of bitterness and revenge.

Individual Identity: Rorty and Wong

There is a picture of individuality according to which individuals are defined in terms of intrinsic characteristics—physical, psychological, and intellectual—that distinguish them from other individuals. This picture is, of course, misleading. For one thing, people have an enormous number of intrinsic characteristics, and only some of those characteristics are *distinguishing* characteristics—ones that both distinguish the person from other people and also provide some basis for action and deliberation. We don't usually think hair color constitutes part of a person's identity, but we might think skin color does or at least nonwhite skin color. Certainly, it is true that people possess identities in terms of intrinsic characteristics, but *which* of a person's characteristics turn out to be identifying ones depends on the nature of the society in general, as well as on what the individual is committed to in that society.

Amelie Rorty and David Wong attempt to provide an account of individual identity that both acknowledges the contingency of individual identity on particular social roles, customs, circumstances, and so on, and yet preserves a conception of responsibility and agency.[5] They point out that philosophers have dealt with issues about criteria for personal identity over time (Shoemaker, Parfit) or about the social and cultural dimensions of identity (Sandel, MacIntyre) or about the processes of self-definition (Frankfurt, Taylor).[6] But they suggest that philosophers concerned with personal identity have not attempted to answer the question, central to some ethical discussions, of what sort of person one should be—the more robust sense of identity that is at issue when we aim at self-understanding, seek to understand and engage others, and seek to make judgments about character, worth, and responsibility.[7]

Rorty and Wong suggest that a person's identity is constituted by the configuration of central traits—that is, those that make a difference to the course of a person's life, to the habit-forming and action-guiding social categories in which she is placed, to the way she acts, reacts, and interacts. In aiming to provide an account of identity, they want to avoid being either what they call "objective"—that is, depending on the specification of some fixed set of properties—or "relativistic"—that is, denying the specificity of identity altogether. They divide traits into several sorts according to the different ways in which traits enter into the formation of someone's identity and the way they affect a person's values, beliefs, and motivations. Some traits—such as being deft or awkward, weak or strong—are, in their view, somatic, or prelinguistic. Then there are central temperamental or psychological traits, such as shyness, friendliness, and so on; traits a person acquires as a result of a social role, such as by being a tomboy or a daredevil; socially defined group identity traits, such as gender- and class-specific traits and habits; and ideal identity traits, such as traits a person acquires through the pursuit of some (sometimes unrecognized) social ideal.

One might wonder, though, to what extent there really are the kinds of traits Rorty and Wong identify. Consider somatic, or prelinguistic, traits. It is clear that people have bodily traits that are prelinguistic. It is not clear, though, that there are any bodily *identifying* traits—that is, traits that are individually identifying simply by virtue of being traits of someone's body. For instance, possessing two legs is a bodily trait. Yet it is not usually considered an identity trait. However, although having two legs does not figure as an identity trait because most people have two legs, it would become an identity trait if some set of circumstances were to bring it about that it was unusual for people to have two legs. To the extent that bodily traits are identity traits only relative to the existence of certain social norms and values, there may be no identity traits at all that can be said to be merely traits of the body as opposed to traits acquired through social roles, group membership, and so on.

There is a question about the extent to which an account of identity in terms of configurations of traits can capture the radical contingency of individual identities on the nature of social situations generally. Certainly, Rorty and Wong are aware of the contingency of bodily traits on social structures and circumstances and of the overlap between different categories of traits. Their concern is to demonstrate that whereas indeed identity traits are contingent upon social structures, we can nonetheless distinguish some traits as being identifying ones for some particular individual. That is, the fact that identifying traits are identifying relative to social situations does not mean we cannot talk about individuality at all. And they acknowledge that how traits become identifying has to do not with an assumption of a fixed individual essence but with the individual's contingent commitments and actions. The difficulty, though, is not the overlap of categories or the problem of defining traits, as they propose; rather, it is that traits become defined as identifying traits not always by the individual and her commitments but instead by the society—in particular, by the kind of society it is. And in some cases, the integrity defined by such traits may not be *personal* integrity—that is, it may not represent the integrity of a person in the moral sense. If we were to understand "person," for instance, as Rawls does, as "someone who can be a fully cooperating member of a society over a complete life,"[8] personal integrity so defined, to the extent that it defines a person as less than a full social member, does not define the integrity of a person. Depending upon the nature of the society in terms of which the individual acquires an identity to begin with, defining some traits as individually identifying traits at all sometimes serves the purpose not of defining individual identity but of denying its very possibility.

For instance, Rorty and Wong distinguish what they call "socially defined group identity" traits as one sort of individually identifying trait.[9] Socially defined group identity traits are those traits a person acquires as a result of class, age, race, ethnicity, gender, or occupation. So, for example, an elderly person may become passive and dependent because of treatment influenced by ageist stereotypes. It is misleading, though, to speak, as Rorty and Wong do, of socially defined group identity traits conflicting with other aspects of a person's identity: Socially defined group identity traits are often such that they make other significant aspects of a person's identity—those that actually explain the person's choices and aspirations—entirely invisible. The idea that socially defined group identity traits are just one among a number of different sorts of individual traits is misleading to the extent that when some people become identified, by themselves or others, in terms of certain socially defined group identity traits, they cannot possess some other sorts of significant individual traits as identifying traits at all. In other words, group identity traits, depending upon what group it is, can work to *define* other identity traits, to determine which of a person's traits are *individually* identifying and which are not.

Consider Eleanor Bumpurs.[10] On October 29, 1984, Eleanor Bumpurs, a 270-pound arthritic sixty-seven-year-old woman, was shot to death while resisting eviction from her apartment in the Bronx. New York City Mayor Ed Koch and Police Commissioner Benjamin Ward described the struggle that preceded her death as involving two officers with large plastic shields, one with a restraining hook, one with a shotgun, and at least one other supervising. During the course of the attempted eviction, Mrs. Bumpurs wielded a knife that Commissioner Ward said was "bent" on one of the plastic shields and twice escaped the constraint of the restraining hook. At some point, Stephen Sullivan—the officer with the shotgun—fired at her, hitting her hand (making it anatomically impossible for her to hold the knife), then shot again and killed her.

Now, what explains the perception on the part of the officers involved and the judgment of the New York Supreme Court justice that the shooting was justified? It is difficult to say that the obvious existence of real threat to the officers is what explains the perception. For one thing, only certain people could appreciate the threat, so it could not have been obvious: Officer Sullivan's lawyer, Bruce A. Smiry, requested a nonjury trial because, as he said, "the average lay person might find it difficult to understand why the police were there in the first place, and why a shot was employed."[11] For another, Commissioner Ward himself admitted that there were a number of available alternative approaches to the "threat," such as waiting until she had calmed down.

An alternative explanation of the perception that the officers were under threat is that whereas there was indeed no real threat to them from Eleanor

Bumpurs, they were not perceiving Eleanor Bumpurs. In fact, they did not encounter Eleanor Bumpurs, at least not as an individual woman. Instead, as Patricia Williams puts it,

> The animus that inspired such fear and impatient contempt in a police officer that six other well-armed men could not allay his need to kill a sick old lady fighting off hallucinations with a knife. . . . [was] a fear embellished by something beyond Mrs. Bumpurs herself; something about her that filled the void between her physical limited, presence and the "immediate threat and endangerment of life" in the beholding eyes of the officer. Why was the sight of a knife-wielding woman so fearful to a shotgun-wielding policeman that he had to blow her to pieces as the only recourse, the only way to preserve his physical integrity? What offensive spirit of his past experience raised her presence to the level of a physical menace beyond what it in fact was; what spirit of prejudgment, of prejudice, provided him such a powerful hallucinogen?[12]

There is no adequate explanation for the act or the court's evaluation of it in terms of Eleanor Bumpurs herself: She was sick, she was old, she had only a knife. But it is not clear that this story is about Eleanor Bumpurs as an individual or that it could be. For Eleanor Bumpurs is encountered by the officers in the story as a *black woman*—not as a person—and as a black woman she does not possess certain other features, such as humanity, as individual identifying features: Her identification as a *kind* of person—black—disallows the recognition of other features—her humanity—as particular features of her identity as an individual. The official explanation—that the officers' lives were under threat—does not make sense except insofar as what they saw and encountered was determined by historical traditions, practices, and a racist conceptual background that makes black people not understandable *as* people at all.

There are other examples of the difficulty some people have of being understood as individuals. Morrison points out that in the Clarence Thomas hearings, the two main characters were portrayed in terms of two principal social fictions about black people: "On the one hand, they signify benevolence, harmless and servile guardianship, and endless love. On the other hand, they have come to represent insanity, illicit sexuality, and chaos."[13] Thomas was presented as loyal and loving—as loyal to party and to country, as loving God. One of his "most fundamental points," according to his sponsor, was his laughter, the stereotypical expression of black servitude.[14] Hill, on the other hand, "was dressed in the oppositional costume of madness, anarchic sexuality, and explosive verbal violence."[15] No explanation could be found for her charges except in terms of her sexual fantasies. As Morrison says, no other story would fit: "No other narrative context could be found for her charges, no motive except fantasy, wanton and destructive, or a jealousy that destabilized her."[16] Moreover, her charges did not ignite a search for the truth, only a change of stereotypes: "Now it was he, the nominee, who was in danger of moving from 'natural servant' to 'savage demon,' and the force of the balance of the confirmation process was to reorder these signifying fictions."[17]

It would appear that one problem with an account of identity and agency that depends on characterizations of individual traits is that in certain important cases the attribution of individual traits as *individual* traits concedes the validity of a social order that, in fact, disallows individuality to some sorts of people. That is, it disallows a sense of individuality that could explain effective agency. Such an account risks defining the normative sense of identity, that which explains a person's rational deliberations and actions, in terms of individuation—how people are *perceived* as individuals according to social norms and values. And in some cases more than others, these are importantly distinct. In Eleanor Bumpurs's case, the characteristics that distinguish her in the officers' view make her into a physical menace, which she is, in fact, not. Her age and sickness are not appreciable in light of such a characterization; nor, of course, are her intentions and aspirations. The conceptual background in terms of which some traits become identifying as individual traits by others is one in which some sorts of people are not understandable, by others and hence often by themselves, as real persons to begin with. Wanda Coleman describes how, as a young black girl, she became aggressive as a matter of personal survival, survival issues that came about because of her physical appearance: "Darker and larger than my schoolmates, I quickly learned the advantage (when it comes to intimidation), but mainly the disadvantages, of being a big-boned, heavy-set 'mama.' . . . The price black girls pay for not conforming to white standards of physical beauty is extracted in monumental amounts, from breath to death. We bend our personalities, and sometimes mutilate our bodies in defense."[18] Should Wanda Coleman's size be considered an individual identifying trait? In Wanda Coleman's case, she comes to understand herself as she is individuated by others. Her size is certainly a trait she *possesses* as an individual. Yet she becomes identified as an individual in these terms as a result of racist, sexist stereotyping. As she describes her youth, it would appear that to the extent to which her size is individually identifying, her acquiring of an *adequate* sense of individuality becomes increasingly unlikely.

Individual identity and agency are not adequately accounted for primarily in terms of configurations of traits, at least not if by individual identity is meant the kind of self-concept that explains autonomous action. In some important cases, traits *become* individually identifying not primarily as a result of the individual's character but rather because the society possesses a certain character. Moreover, the character a society possesses may be such that for some individuals—whatever their individual commitments, projects, and ideals happen to be—they are understood and treated as stereotypically black or old or disabled. In such cases, an explanation of identity, as opposed to individuation, in terms of configurations of traits may end up endorsing the subordinate social status some people possess as a result of an unjust social order.

Integrity: McFall and Davion

Victoria Davion's account of integrity goes further in acknowledging the radical contingency of individual identity upon social structures than does the account of identity and agency offered by Rorty and Wong.[19] Davion criticizes Lynne McFall's claim that personal integrity has to do significantly with unconditional commitments. McFall argues that it is a conceptual truth that integrity has to do with unconditional commitments: Murder and torture, for instance, are things we *could not do* and survive as the persons we are.[20] In Davion's view, whereas it is clear that there are things people believe they would never do under any circumstances, these are not very interesting. Someone may not be able to imagine herself committing mass murder as a way of expressing anger, but this probably does not distinguish her from most people. It does not *identify* her.[21] Even in cases in which people do have interesting unconditional commitments, Davion points out, these are conditional on the person's understanding of reality. And of course, such understanding will change and ought to change.[22] Instead, Davion suggests that integrity has to do with "being true to oneself," and being true to oneself has to involve exploring commitments and changing them if necessary.[23]

In Davion's view, the unconditional commitment that is required for integrity is one to personal growth and change: She agrees with Sarah Hoagland that integrity has to do with paying attention to who we are becoming.[24] In particular, Davion emphasizes that an unconditional commitment of this sort does not involve the assumption of some particular ideal of personal adequacy: It does not require that someone be committed to performing some particular action in some particular situation. Instead, it requires commitment to considering contingent circumstances and conditions and to a principle about the importance of growth and change.

This seems right. It suggests that personal integrity has to do not primarily with any deeply held core beliefs or commitments but with possibilities for certain kinds of growth within a specific situation. And this has to do, as Davion suggests, with careful attention to the contingent values and circumstances upon which identities depend.

It is difficult to see, though, exactly what this amounts to in practice. Davion suggests that people have to discover what their personal commitments are at a deep level, perhaps through figuring out what general principles their particular beliefs imply and examining whether these are principles they can believe in. The examination of principles and beliefs, in her view, is part of the defining of the appropriate process of growth and development. But people are often not able to identify or properly analyze their deep commitments, beliefs, and principles because of their current situation. Some sorts of commitments and beliefs are difficult to identify and to make explicit without acquiring more adequate conceptual resources. And the resources required for such examination may have to do with the person's social and political position. Thus, it may turn out that people sometimes have to grow and develop *first* before they are able to properly examine their beliefs and principles—indeed, even to recognize them. And to the extent that acquiring the right sorts of conceptual resources itself often requires personal change and growth, it looks as though a commitment to growth and change is, at least sometimes, what *explains* the possibility of properly examining beliefs and principles rather than, as Davion seems to suggest, the reverse.

Consider the film *A Question of Silence* (Marleen Gorris, the Netherlands, 1983). The movie tells the story of three women—a secretary, a waitress, and a housewife—who come together in a dress shop and (gruesomely) murder the dress-shop owner, a man they have never seen before. The focus of the movie is on the female psychiatrist who is called in to discover whether these three women are sane, specifically on her efforts to try to understand the women and their action. Now, the *moral* legitimacy of the act of murder is not at issue in the film: We can all agree that the act itself is wrong and still wonder whether the women had reasons for what they did. Indeed, what the film explores is the possibility that the act is *individually* rational, that it makes sense in terms of each woman's ends. Certainly, there is nothing material to be gained by the act, and there is no evidence that any of the women involved has a deep inclination toward violent acts in general. Yet the women show no remorse, and it appears, in fact, that each is to some extent liberated by the performance of the act—that although she ends up losing her liberty in one sense, she gains in some other sense.

Indeed, it looks as though the act has just the kinds of consequences in terms of growth and awareness that one might see, following Davion's concerns about being true to oneself, as relevant to the pursuit of personal integrity. Each of the women comes to understand and, importantly, to be able to make others (e.g., the psychiatrist) understand that she possesses, first, a commitment to her own self-worth and dignity and, second, an understanding of the (lack of) possibilities for realizing that commitment in current circumstances.

Now, how do we explain the apparent personally liberating consequences of an act that is clearly immoral? In particular, how do we explain the fact that an act that is immoral, according to society's and the individuals' standards, may be significant as regards the individuals' moral responsibilities to maintain their own sense of self-respect and dignity?

One possibility is that it is precisely because the act is immoral in terms of accepted conceptions of morality that it turns out to be morally significant in terms of personal integrity: No real sense of personal integrity is possible for the women under current conditions. And the action, whatever its consequences for the agents, represents a rejection of those conditions. Understood one way, what the women do is resist a system of behaviors and ways of thinking that presumes their inferiority—in fact, their subhumanity. Understood another way, of course, what they do is crazy and self-destructive. The act may be morally significant precisely to the extent that the meaninglessness of morality for the agents—agents we have every reason to think care about morality—reflects the inadequacy of some fundamental moral presuppositions. That is, the women commit the murder not because they do not care about morality—for there is no evidence that they do not—but rather because they do, and they act to resist the system that denies their status as moral agents. The tragedy of the movie may be not the murder and its consequences but the fact that the women are motivated to commit the murder and to willingly take on its consequences. It may be that for these women being true to themselves, or attempting to be true to themselves, *is* the committing of the murder, for they commit the murder to resist a system that denies such a possibility.

Now, of course, many will worry about such an interpretation. I have suggested that there is a story to be told according to which the women are crazy. The movie demonstrates this through the viewpoint of the "progressive" lawyer, husband of the psychiatrist, among others. The lawyer possesses all of the information about the case and thinks it is quite clear that these women are insane. But there is another story that can be told, that to which the psychiatrist refers when she tells her husband that this case is not about *them,* the women. The psychiatrist begins to understand that this case is not about the individual women but rather about the way women are hated and feared in society in general and about how the conditions of these women's lives are an expression of such hatred. If one ignores society's hatred and fear of women, or if one assumes, perhaps, that such hatred is just how things are and ought to be, there can be, of course, no reasons for the women to have done what they did. Yet if one tells a story about systemic injustice, including that it is wrong, there *are* reasons for the women to have done what they did, even though the act is certainly morally wrong.

Still, some will object that any number of stories could be told with any number of differing results about reasons. And some will think that because our assessment of whether these women had reasons depends on what *story* we tell about their situation and we could tell all sorts of different stories, we ought not to say anything at all about good and bad reasons. This kind of response is too easy. In practice, we do in fact assess people's actions and choices, and we even presume that we can do so nonarbitrarily. In theory, there may be an enormous number of stories that can be told about the women in the film, each implying something different about the status of their reasons. But such stories are not all equally plausible. In practice, we don't go on searching for more and different stories for the simple reason that some stories are not worth pursuing. Only some stories are plausible, given general beliefs about the situation and what such stories can and do explain. In other words, we don't start from nowhere when we look for explanatory stories. We have other, well-confirmed stories to rely on, as well as constraints provided by consideration of the likely and actual consequences of taking any particular story seriously. I have tried to show how this is so in discussing Cornell's remarks about *Beloved* in Chapter 1.

Now, the suggestion is not that the women possess reasons for their act merely by virtue of the fact that the act constitutes a kind of resistance. For acts of resistance can be quite unreasonable. Someone can resist her cultural conditioning by refusing to wear clothes, but it's not clear what this would accomplish. It is possible that such an act *could* be epistemically significant if the practice of wearing clothes had some interesting relevance to a person's or a group of person's possibilities for self-determination. But it is not immediately obvious how this could be so. If the women possess reasons for their choice, it is by virtue of the significance of the choice within a life-defining process described in a certain way. However, one reason for preferring a particular description of the process, if it is preferable, is that it can be shown that there do indeed exist the kinds of oppressive mechanisms to which the women's act *could* be understood as resistance, if indeed it is.

A notion of being "true to oneself" cannot by itself explain intuitions about personal integrity for people who are not individuated as people at all. For the available notion of "oneself" is inadequate for such a definition. What is the secretary in the film to do, for instance, when her ideas are repeated by the male chairperson of a meeting, who is then congratulated on them? What would it mean for her to be true to herself? If she points out to everyone that, in fact, the suggestion in question was hers, she will be called bitter and ungrateful at best and be on the way to losing her job at worst. The prudent thing to do, given the context, is to let it pass. But letting it pass has costs: If she articulates to herself what has happened and then lives with it, she accepts humiliation; if she tells herself some other story, such as that the male chair *deserves* greater attention, she denies her own perceptions.

It is hard to see what being true to oneself could mean in such a situation. Or consider Christina, the housewife. Is she being true to herself by not speaking to the psychiatrist? Or is she not conceding the validity of social stereotypes according to which she, the housewife, is *supposed* to be silent? Yet what could Christina say? Would what she really thinks about the incident be understood even if she were able to articulate it? It is hard to see what it would mean for the women in the film to be true to themselves if being true to themselves means acting in a way that expresses a sense of genuine self-worth. For it is not clear that a genuine sense of self-worth would be possible; it is not even clear what it would mean. As I suggested in discussing the example of Sethe, the question of whether the women acted reasonably in some sense is not as interesting as the difficulty of raising the question in the first place. The impossibility, even in imagination, of realizing their most important interests—human dignity and self-respect—makes it difficult to see how they *could* act reasonably as individuals in a nonmoral sense.

Examination of beliefs and principles cannot be what defines personal integrity when for some people the very possibility of belief in oneself *as* a person is itself, on current terms, unavailable. In *A Question of Silence,* it is possible to understand the women's choice as having to do with personal integrity if one understands, first, that the society is not what it ought to be—that it is, in fact, misogynist—and, second, that it could be otherwise.

Certainly, as Davion's account suggests, there is a sense in which the significance of the women's choice for the pursuit of integrity, if it is significant in terms of personal integrity, has to do with what the women *become* or even *could become*. Indeed, it seems right that personal integrity is also defined in terms, in some sense, of what people *understand* as a result of a process of becoming. What I have tried to point out is that the right sorts of processes of development—personal and cognitive—presuppose moral judgments about the nature of the society as a whole. For not only is there a question here about the standards according to which something like "being true to oneself" is to be defined; there is also, in some cases, a question about the standards according to which the *self* to which one hopes to be true is to be defined.

Individuality and Moral Imagination

Personal integrity is defined, at least in part, in terms of moral facts—facts about what would and what would not, in fact, bring about an individual's greater human flourishing. And there *are* facts about this matter, even if they are not unambiguous or immediately accessible. I have suggested in earlier chapters of this book that individual rationality is in the first instance a property of paths of development, not of particular ends. It is true that there are often questions about the rationality of particular choices or plans, but it is paths of development and not ends that are fundamentally definitive of individual rational choices. Now I want to suggest that appropriate paths of development—those providing grounds for individually rational choices and actions—are those that permit the bringing about or claiming of genuine individuality, those that, in fact, constitute resistance to systems of behavior and meanings that preclude such a possibility.

In discussing Rawls and Railton, I made the point that in important cases, the individual for whom the realization of an objective end, as they defined it, would be a realization of *her* best interests—where by *her* we understand an individual—needs to be brought about, often through radical personal and political transformation. Thus, it turns out that the question of individuality is a prior issue to the question of what a person's objective good or best interest is. As mentioned, I was not making the existentialist-type point that people need to undertake a project of self-discovery before it makes sense to ask questions about their objective good. Rather, I argued that appropriate kinds of individual development often *constitute* the acquiring of epistemic resources required for the very identification of relevant available choices. If autonomy is understood, roughly, as the capacity to act in one's interests, to choose from options that are meaningful as regards pursuit of self-worth and dignity, then appropriate resources for autonomous choice must include changes to personal and social conditions that constitute the nonpropositional understanding required for such choice.

The point I want to make now is that individuality must, in turn, be defined in terms of possibilities for the making of rational choices or, in other words, in terms of possibilities for making choices and taking actions that do, in fact, bring about conditions for the pursuit of one's real human interests—interests, say, in dignity and self-worth. Thus, questions about individuality or personal integrity and rational choice turn out to be intertwined. For the kinds of choices that make it possible for someone to possess and care about interests and desires reflecting human flourishing—individually rational choices—are choices that constitute individual development, both personal and cognitive. And what distinguishes choices and actions representing the pursuit of personal integrity from those that really are just crazy are the kinds of developmental possibilities, especially cognitive ones, that are brought about as a result.

Personal integrity, then, depends on moral imagination. Indeed, in significant cases, personal integrity is defined, in important part, in terms of imagined possibilities for pursuing human flourishing, even though these possibilities may not be imaginable by the people in question at the time. In Chapter 1, I suggested that this was the case with Sethe. When we read Sethe's story, we do not, as readers, experience Sethe as crazy. At least, I suggest that most readers do not. Yet there could be reasons for thinking she is crazy. I argued that intuitions that she is not crazy rest on presuppositions about what Sethe *ought* to be able to dream, what *ought* to be available for her to choose but that, under conditions of slavery, is considered crazy.

Yet it is not clear that Sethe herself is motivated primarily by moral judgments about the wrongness of slavery; instead, she seems to be motivated by love for her children, by strong personal emotions and attachments. Moreover, readers' intuitions that she acts reasonably, or, to put it less strongly, not unreasonably, suggest that there are moral constraints on the reasonableness of individual choices that are not explained by socially defined norms and values. For it is evident that antiracist norms and values do not define *her* society, and there is not much reason to think that they define current societies. Thus, intuitions that Sethe's choice is other than a whim of the moment, that it is not without reason, would appear to presuppose the possibility of moral truths.

The problem with the accounts of integrity discussed so far has not been a failure to recognize the contingency of individual identities upon social structures or the compatibility of radical contingency with a notion of adequate selfhood; rather, it is a failure to recognize that some social structures are of the wrong sort altogether for some individuals to be able to pursue personal integrity and that questions about the moral nature of society often need to be asked *first* before questions about personal integrity can properly be raised. Indeed, questions about integrity may turn out to be not ones about the relationship between individual characteristics, interests, choices, and so on, and a society but rather about what kind of society it is in terms of which an individual comes to possess certain interests, characteristics, and so on. This does not imply that questions about personal integrity are entirely moral, not having to do with the idiosyncratic characteristics of individuals; rather, it suggests that the very meaning of personal integrity in particular cases sometimes depends on more general considerations about the nature of the society that makes some idiosyncratic properties identifying and others not.

The pursuit of adequate personal integrity often depends not so much on understanding who one is and what one believes and is committed to but rather on understanding what one's society is and imagining what it could be. People who chose to "drop out" during the Vietnam War era were not necessarily trying to "find themselves," as the cliché goes; rather, it seems more likely that many were trying to lose themselves, to lose or at least transform an identity acquired in terms of a society that turned out to be founded not on values of freedom and democracy after all but rather on greed and imperialism. People often choose to act in ways that are radically self-transformative—to engage in radical politics or alternative lifestyles—when they discover that their *society* is deeply skewed. Are such choices to be explained in terms other than the pursuit of personal integrity, as in the pursuit of some abstract ideal, perhaps, or even as irrational? Or is personal integrity more adequately defined in terms *not* derived primarily from consideration of the person as she is at a time?

Mab Segrest describes how, as a young white girl in the South, she could not *not* question her own identity and upbringing when she came to perceive racism in her surroundings:

> As racial conflict increased in Alabama in the 1960s, I also knew deep inside me that what I heard people saying about Black people had somehow to do with me. This knowledge crystallizes around one image: I am thirteen, lying beneath some bushes across from the public high school that was to have been integrated that morning. It is ringed with two hundred Alabama Highway Patrol troopers at two-yard intervals, their hips slung with pistols. Inside that terrible circle are twelve Black children, the only students allowed in. There is a stir in the crowd as two of the children walk across the breezeway where I usually play. I have a tremendous flash of empathy, of identification, with their vulnerability and their aloneness within that circle of force. Their separation is mine. And I know from now on that everything people have told me is "right" has to be reexamined. I am on my own.[25]

Surely, we are inclined to think Segrest's choice is morally admirable, as expressing integrity. Yet it is hard to see how the morally admirable character of Segrest's commitment can be explained entirely in terms of abstract moral principles or at least her adherence to them. For one thing, at thirteen, she is unlikely to possess such a worked-out moral ideal. For another, it does not look as though conceptual ideals play the primary explanatory role in this case. If they did, it would be hard to see why Segrest takes her experience under the bush to provide reason to question her entire set of moral beliefs rather than, as would be much easier, taking her system of moral beliefs to provide reason to reject her perceptions under the bush. The moral reasonableness of Segrest's deliberations would not appear to be explained by *her* commitment to general moral principles and beliefs. Instead, her choice appears to be motivated by her feeling of empathy and her conviction that her feeling *is* one of empathy and not something else— for instance, not crazy. The reason her choice strikes us as reasonable, individually as well as morally, is that there are reasons for thinking the relationships she wants to pursue really *are* right, even if Segrest herself may not fully possess them.

The reasonableness of Segrest's choice of direction, for herself personally, does not depend primarily on consideration of who she is as an individual at the time. Rather, it depends on a judgment about what her society is— racist—and consideration of the implications of this for what she could be, even if she herself is not explicitly committed to any such long-term end. It is hard to account for her choice to question her entire set of moral beliefs in terms of who she currently is as an individual. For it looks as though she comes to make her choice precisely because she comes to distrust who she is as an individual. Instead, her choice is more adequately accounted for in terms of *possibilities* for future development—in particular, in terms of possibilities for acquiring greater understanding of her situation and developing more adequate personal relations. Thus, the appropriateness of her choice of direction depends not just or even primarily on facts about her—her beliefs, interests, and so on—but on facts about the nature of the society in which she makes her choice.

What is particularly difficult for an account of personal integrity is that it is not at all clear that the women in the movie *A Question of Silence* or Mab Segrest under the bush could themselves articulate the moral ideal according to which what they choose to do is what it is and not crazy. To the extent that we might think the three women and Mab Segrest are motivated to some extent, as I think we should, by the pursuit of personal integrity, the moral vision in terms of which it makes sense to think of their choices in this way may not be one they themselves possess. Indeed, it may not be one anyone possesses, at least not fully. The notion of self presupposed in such judgments is defined in terms not primarily of what the individuals concerned believe and desire but of facts about what they *could be* in a more adequate society.

Thus, it looks as though judgments about personal integrity, in some important cases, presuppose the existence of truths about human possibilities, of moral truths regarding human flourishing generally. In assuming the possibility of moral truths, I again rely, as I mentioned doing in Chapter 4, on a line of thinking developed most recently by naturalistic epistemologists. The idea of moral facts, or moral truths, need not presuppose direct, theory-independent access to some sort of queer entities.[26] Instead, moral facts can be thought of as those beliefs about morality that are adequately supported by reason and argument, beliefs that are reliable on grounds of their plausibility in light of background beliefs and their role in ongoing theoretical and practical development. As Nicholas Sturgeon argues, there is no reason, other than ill-founded assumptions about foundationalism, to think that moral theories cannot be justified simply by appealing to what we know about the natural and social world through empirical investigation.[27] Indeed, in practice, it is common to assume the existence of moral facts. We make assumptions about what is and what is not likely to promote human well-being in specific situations, and we design research programs on the assumptions that we can *discover* more about the actual nature of injustice and what sorts of strategies should be adopted to combat it.

In earlier chapters, I tried to demonstrate that it is often thought, in moral and political philosophy, that individual interests and individual autonomy are defined in terms of individuality, in terms of who the person really is. We start with a conception of who the person is—usually defined in terms of deep-seated commitments—and define interests, responsibilities, and autonomy in these terms. In some cases, however, who a person is at a time does not provide an appropriate basis for answering such questions. In some cases, for instance, what an individual is is, in fact, degraded and dehumanized. In such cases, integrity is not primarily a question about deep-seated commitments; rather, it has to do with what a person *could* be and *would* be in more adequate conditions. As I have already suggested, instead of defining individual interests in terms of individuality, it might be more appropriate to define individuality in terms of individual interests, of the choices an individual makes that, in fact, turn out to constitute choices in the direction of greater human flourishing. Individuality turns out to be best defined in terms of paths of development, where the right sorts of paths of development are constrained, at least in part, by general moral considerations and, in particular, by facts about general human possibilities in specific social arrangements.

Thus, individual identity is radically contingent upon social structures and moral values. Indeed, I have suggested that in some cases, and perhaps in general, the pursuit of personal integrity requires the radical disruption of one's secure sense of self to challenge such structures and values. I take it that this is true in Mab Segrest's case and perhaps in any case in which someone acquires a sense of self within a profoundly inhuman society. But this may be worrying to some. We want to think there is some starting place for defining personal integrity—some specific features of or facts about the individual in particular that define her as a unique individual. And if it sometimes turns out that what is most fundamental to a person's sense of self at a time is irrelevant to the pursuit or preservation of personal integrity, it might look as though there is no *person* at any particular time about whom we can say questions of personal integrity are especially *about*. It may look as though personal integrity becomes entirely a moral question, a question about defining an abstract ideal. And this would make it look as though any kind of intervention in individuals' affairs—undesirable forms of paternalism as well as arbitrarily coercive state policies—could be justified in terms of individuals' interests.

But the assumption that social dependency implies a denial of individuality rests on a mistake: Such a view depends on the mistaken assumption that individuality, whatever it is, must be something that is *not* contingent upon social circumstances and conditions. The conflation of social dependency and social determination is often useful in resistance to claims about, and appeals for investigation of, systemic discrimination. It is thought that if it is claimed that an institution or a society is systemically unjust, individuals cannot be held responsible for racist or sexist actions carried out, unintentionally, by generally well-meaning agents: If the *society* is profoundly skewed and the individual's actions reflect society's values, harm inflicted is not the individual's fault but rather is society's. It is convenient in such cases to think there is no normative sense of personal identity, no way to distinguish between the self-concept a person possesses as a result of social and historical conditioning and a more adequate sense of self. For then we can say that if someone is well-intentioned and acts and thinks ignorantly according to the racist, sexist norms endorsed by her or his society, the *society* fails morally, but the individual cannot be held *personally* responsible.[28]

Individuals can, however, find out about the kinds of social relations and structures they allow to determine their identity. At least, we can find out some things or can choose to accept or reject that which has already been found out. Of course, not everyone is in the same position with respect to resources. But there is enough information about systemic discrimination available to make it reasonable to think that quite often the interesting question about responsibility is not that of availability of information. One of the points I tried to make about nonpropositional understanding in Chapter 1 is that it is not just the oppressed whose understanding of their social situations depends on personal transformation; people who are more favorably situated also need to undergo personal change if they are to understand the ways in which their actions and thoughts presume their privileged social position, working to damage the prospects of others. And personal change is not always appealing. The argument that claims about systemic discrimination and charges of individual responsibility are incompatible is untenable and, even worse, obscures important issues about what kinds of responsibilities educated people possess to identify, resist, and challenge the deep-seated injustices of the institutions that make them what they are.

The reason the women's choice to murder the dress-store owner is not an instance of insanity, if it is not, is not primarily something about *them* as individuals with idiosyncratic commitments. What makes such an action—understood as part of an individual path of development—reasonable is the fact that the society is indeed profoundly sexist and that the dress-shop owner's behavior and attitude are, in fact, an expression of this sexism. In other words, the act makes sense in individual terms because of its role in a process of development taking place in a society of a certain sort. Whether it is an act related to the pursuit of personal integrity will depend in part on facts about that society and the possibilities for such a pursuit within it. Personal integrity—the adequacy of a sense of individuality—is defined in terms of paths of development, in terms of possibilities for developing capacities and understanding, but which paths of development constitute adequate constraints on individual choices and actions depends on facts about the nature of the actual society and what structures do and could exist.

Bitterness

I want to make a few remarks here about the moral significance of emotions, a topic I discuss further in Chapter 7. The idea that personal integrity is defined not primarily in terms of facts about individuals themselves but in terms of paths of development and moral imagination can make sense of the moral value of apparently immoral, or at least undesirable, behavior. In "What's Wrong with Bitterness?" Lynne McFall argues that bitterness, generally understood as an entirely demeaning emotion that is not conducive to the pursuit of integrity, is "a move away from self-deception and moral slavery in the direction of truth, a refusal to defer, and is therefore moral progress."[29] McFall points out that there are clearly some cases in which bitterness is morally inappropriate. Few would fail to be annoyed by someone who continues to repeat the minor or even major injustices of her or his unhappy life.[30] Bitterness does not seem to be justified as a response to the inevitable misfortunes of life, such as failing to achieve a goal, losing a friend or lover, approaching death.[31] But if an individual's legitimate expectations are disappointed for the wrong reasons—as a result of "wickedness, moral stupidity, weakness or indifference"[32]—there would be something odd about an absence of bitterness. Such a person would have to be saintly to avoid becoming bitter, and as McFall suggests, we might wonder whether saintliness is really something that should always be aimed for.[33]

Some will say that whereas there may be some situations in which something like bitterness is appropriate, it is anger rather than bitterness that is desirable. Why is anger morally acceptable, even admirable, and bitterness not? In McFall's view, "Unforgiving anger or deep sadness can lack vindictiveness, be 'clean,' and so can grief; bitterness cannot."[34] McFall suggests that bitterness and grudges, and not grief and rage, involve something like meanness or self-righteousness.

Now, this suggests that the "cleanness" of grief and rage has to do with the fact that bitterness, as opposed to grief or rage, has a particular kind of personal character. Grief and rage, although certainly personal, can be accounted for in terms of general human needs and values—love for a child, desire for justice, and so on. We expect that grief and rage can be given a rationale that can be understood by most other human beings, whatever their personal situations. Bitterness and grudges, on the other hand, arise from experiences of insults, humiliation, put-downs. And often these cannot be understood by any other human being, whatever her situation. They can only be understood by some other people—those who are in relevantly similar circumstances. For instance, we often hear people say in response to accusations of bitterness, "you can't know what it is like to . . . " whereas such a response would presumably be unnecessary in cases of grief and rage.

But it may be *precisely* the occasional moral appropriateness of bitterness that explains its apparently personal character. McFall argues that bitterness is especially understandable in cases in which degradation and humiliation are permitted by norms of systemic bias. And in such cases, anger about such norms and values, at least if expressed by someone who is discriminated against because of such norms and values, would be understood as bitterness. For it would be understood as personal. Ronald de Sousa points out, for instance, that an angry man is a "manly man" but an angry woman is "hysterical."[35] Women who express anger at departmental meetings are usually considered to be bitter; men are angry. This usually has to do not with the fact that male reactions are generally more explainable in moral terms but rather with the fact that what is explainable in moral terms is often interestingly restricted by the behavior of male persons. To the extent that "bitterness" is often anger that is expressed at genuinely unjust discriminatory norms and values, it will be understood as personal. For the fact that those norms and values are indeed systemically discriminatory will likely have as one of its consequences the exclusion as genuine participants in moral discourse precisely those persons who are most affected by them.

Sue Campbell argues that whether someone can be angry rather than bitter depends on whether their emotional expression receives uptake: "Whether the members of subordinate groups can reclaim anger, whether in particular they can get angry at the right time to the right people, does not depend solely on the actions of these people."[36] Instead, it depends upon whether the truth of what such people are saying can be understood and accepted. When Audre Lorde speaks about the situation of women of color, she is angry, not bitter. But Campbell points out that Lorde's communication of anger is an achievement—indeed, a politically fragile one—marking the struggle of women of color to be taken seriously as moral and political agents. Campbell warns that "anyone who speaks from and for an oppressed group can expect to encounter the criticism [of bitterness] at its most brutally political,"[37] for if someone is bitter rather than angry, their concerns can be dismissed.

It is because emotional expression is so dependent upon uptake that Campbell thinks McFall is wrong to distinguish among the different sorts of bitterness on grounds of rationality. Campbell argues that McFall considers bitterness a rational response to the frustration of important and legitimate hopes, where a hope is not legitimate if it is unlikely to be realized.[38] But many quite legitimate hopes will never be realized. And moreover, it is quite legitimate for members of subordinate groups to hope for treatment they will probably never receive. Campbell argues that to think of one's emotions in terms of legitimacy so defined can be highly debilitating.

But perhaps it is precisely because the hopes of members of subordinate groups cannot be legitimate in such terms that the expression of bitterness is rational and needs to be understood as such. At least, such hopes need to be understood as rational in the sense in which the pursuit of ends such as self-respect and dignity can be rational, even when these may not be fully imaginable. If we consider unimaginable goals such as genuine autonomy to be appropriate ends for an individual in an unjust society, then the expression of bitterness is rational to the extent that such expression constitutes the acquiring of epistemic resources needed for such pursuits. To the extent that bitterness, in the interesting cases, is characterized, as Campbell says, by the fact that the people who express it are not heard or understood—indeed, that it is the fact that such people are not heard that *makes* the emotion bitterness in the first place—its expression constitutes an epistemic achievement, one that also constitutes individual development. Campbell is right that the rationality of emotions ought not to be defined in terms of the legitimacy of hopes, where legitimacy is defined in terms of likelihood that such hopes will be realized. But perhaps it is the legitimacy of hopes, defined in terms of moral considerations about human flourishing, about human *being,* that defines rationality.

In Dorothy Allison's wonderful novel *Bastard Out of Carolina,* the young protagonist, Bone, is taken by her working-class mother to the manager of Woolworth's to return stolen Tootsie Rolls.[39] The manager's condescending response does nothing to reinforce the mother's efforts to encourage her daughter's feelings of remorse, at least not about this particular act of theft. Quite the contrary, his response instills a desire in her, later realized, to steal from Woolworth's again:

> I understood. I understood that I was barred from the Woolworth counters. I could feel the heat from my mama's hand through my blouse, and I knew she was never going to come near this place again, was never going to let herself stand in the same room with that honey-greased bastard. I looked around at the bright hairbrushes, ribbons, trays of panties and socks, notebooks, dolls and balloons. It was hunger I felt then, raw and terrible, a shaking deep down inside me, as if my rage had used up everything I had ever eaten.
>
> After that, when I passed the Woolworth's windows, it would come back— that dizzy desperate hunger edged with hatred and an aching lust to hurt somebody back. . . . It was a hunger in the back of the throat, not the belly, an echoing emptiness that ached for the release of screaming. Whenever we went to visit Daddy Glen's [middle-class] people, that hunger would throb and swell behind my tongue until I found myself standing silent and hungry in the middle of a family gathering full of noise and food.[40]

Bone's desire for better treatment is, of course, unlikely to be realized in a classist society. But her experience of such emotions constitutes an initial expression of class consciousness, the identification of the object of some of her own and her mother's frustrations. Bone doesn't articulate her anger toward the manager of Woolworth's, but if she did she would be understood, presumably, as expressing bitterness. For her anger would not receive uptake. What makes her emotions morally significant is certainly not the likelihood of realization, as Campbell suggests. Instead, it would appear to be the fact that her experience of such emotions and, more important, the significance she gives to them constitute a specific sort of individual development, one in which she acquires capacities to identify and to act in resistance to actually existing mechanisms of economic oppression. It is the individual development through expression of emotion that explains the possibility of acting rationally, of acting in one's best interests as a human being; it cannot be, as Campbell rightly argues, the rationality of emotions, defined in terms of current standards, that defines individuals' claims to legitimacy and appropriateness of expression.

Elster and the Rationality of Vindictiveness

Similarly, consider what might be said about the rationality, and in some sense the morality, of revenge behavior. Jon Elster argues that no rational account of vindictiveness can be given.[41] He notes that at first glance it may seem obvious that revenge behavior is not rational: Revenge is "the attempt, at some cost to oneself, to impose suffering upon those who have made one suffer, because they have made one suffer."[42] Since revenge behavior involves costs and risks, people who act in a rational, outcome-oriented manner, choosing the best means to achieve their ends, should not engage in acts of revenge. Nonetheless, Elster points out that norms of revenge are part of a great many cultures. Societies that have had social norms regulating feuds or vendettas include medieval Iceland, the Balkans, and other Mediterranean countries, as well as South American tribes.[43] Elster notes that revenge behavior is a universal human phenomenon and that social norms of revenge seem to have cropped up with some regularity in premodern cultures.

So what arguments might be made for the individual rationality of revenge behavior? Elster restricts himself to arguments to the effect that revenge can be rational in terms of the selfish, material interests of the agent, not, say, in terms of broader motivations like the concern to uphold one's honor: If it can be argued that an action is rational because it allows someone to uphold his self-image and honor as a norm follower, claims to rationality become uninformative. For the alternative choices will also be regulated in some sense by social norms. The possible arguments, therefore, in his view, are three: First, in a society with norms of revenge, an individual may be worse off if he fails to avenge an affront because of the external sanctions to which he then exposes himself. Second, a person who demonstrates that he cares about revenge will often have an edge in dealing with people who do not. Last, revenge can be viewed as tit-for-tat in iterated games.

Briefly, Elster's response to these arguments is that if we accept the first answer, we have to ask what motivates people to sanction someone who fails to avenge himself. If the answer is the fear of being sanctioned by others, then the argument falters. For it is unlikely that people frown on others who fail to sanction people who fail to sanction people who fail to sanction people who do not conform to a norm. It is more likely that some other factors such as emotional forces explain revenge behavior in Elster's view. The second argument fails because, among other reasons, it requires that there be some people in the population who are genuinely vengeful: For it to be rational to appear vengeful, there must be people who really are vengeful, and again it is hard to see how for those who really are vengeful the material benefits gained from such behavior offer a better explanation than emotional forces. The third argument asserts that threats of vengeance can be part of a cooperative equilibrium because the knowledge that defectors will be punished keeps everyone in line. This fails in Elster's view because, for one thing, it cannot explain why people would actually carry out revenge since actually carrying it out would have quite severe results.

More generally, Elster suggests that such arguments fail because rational-choice arguments cannot capture the phenomenon of honor that figures so prominently in all accounts of revenge. The pursuit of honor, rather than any particular material gains, seems to offer the best explanation of revenge behavior. In his view, whereas the phenomenon of revenge is universal, forms of norms of revenge can be quite diverse. But what is common among norms of revenge is the "devastating feeling of shame experienced by the man who fails to avenge an insult and who is constantly reminded that he is less than a man."[44] The key to understanding revenge behavior is that "asserting one's honor . . . is an aspect of a deep-rooted urge to show oneself to be superior to others."[45]

We might wonder, though, whether the failure of rational-choice arguments to capture the significance of the pursuit of honor is a problem not for the rationality of revenge behavior but instead for a notion of rationality that cannot properly accommodate such pursuits. Elster's reason for not accepting the argument that revenge behavior is rational because it upholds one's honor as a social norm follower is that such statements can provide no guide to how an agent could rationally choose among alternative means to the stipulated end: One can say of almost any means available that it allows a person to uphold his self-image and reputation as a norm follower.[46] In Elster's view, a norm is "the propensity to feel shame and to anticipate sanctions at the thought of behaving in a certain way."[47] So, for instance, "eat pie with a small fork" and "wear black at funerals" are social norms: One feels shame and the fear of sanctions if one fails to conform to such directives. If we were to say that eating with a fork is rational because it results in the benefit of not being sanctioned in some way, then it would look as though any kind of such socially motivated behavior is just as rational as any other.

But it is not at all clear that maintaining personal honor is a matter of upholding social norms or that even when it is it is just such a matter. For one thing, the motivation to maintain honor is not always an anticipation of shame and sanctions at the failure to measure up to social norms. Indeed, maintaining one's personal honor is occasionally something one does at great *risk* of being sanctioned, even severely. People sometimes go against social norms, at great material and personal risk, just to maintain or to gain a sense of personal honor. Indeed, revenge is sometimes motivated not by shame at being "less than a man" or less than whatever else it is that people are supposed to be according to social norms and values; rather, it is motivated by anger and frustration at being constantly reminded that one is not expected to be anything more than less than a man. Elster thinks "asserting one's honor . . . is an aspect of a deep-rooted urge to show oneself to be superior to others."[48] But sometimes asserting one's honor is also an aspect of a deep-rooted urge just to be equal or perhaps to *be* at all. And if pursuing honor can be something one does against social norms or at least in spite of social norms, there must be more to an explanation for the motivation for such pursuits than what can be derived from consideration of social norms.

After all, racism and sexism are often, in fact, social norms: In some social arrangements and institutions people who resist practicing racist, sexist behavior—who fail to uphold, or who engage in challenging, racist, sexist norms—are, in fact, severely sanctioned. It looks as though rather than being potentially explainable in terms of the rationality of conforming to social norms, seeking honor—sometimes through revenge behavior—is at least sometimes a motivation for going against the norms at great risk. The question of the rationality of revenge behavior is, then, at least sometimes not so much a question about the rationality of seeking honor through revenge but rather a question about the consequences for one's personal honor of seeking to be rational in Elster's sense.

Now, what could explain the significance of honor as a motivation for going against the norms, conformity to which is required for the realization of many of one's other preferences and desires? Elster's concern about the possible rationality of revenge behavior is a concern to know whether an explanation can be given for revenge behavior in terms of personal material benefits. Rationality, in his view, has to do with the appropriateness of actions relative to individual ends—ends defined in terms of the individual's ordered preferences and desires. But honor, as Elster himself notes, has to do with personal worth.[49] And personal worth is not just one of a number of human goods; it is that without which people do not—indeed, sometimes cannot—*care* about certain other human goods. Someone who lacks a sense of self-worth is often not able to take advantage of goods and opportunities that may be available to her, sometimes because she is not able even to identify them. If personal honor is a condition for acquiring the right sorts of ends, it may be that whereas revenge behavior cannot be explained rationally in terms of material benefits, the role of the acquiring of honor in the identification of the right sorts of material benefits explains the possibility of rationality. To the extent that acquiring personal honor is, in some cases, a prerequisite for possessing the right sorts of ends, its acquisition is the acquiring of the very possibility of individual rationality; to ask about the extent to which seeking honor plays a role in the realizing of presupposed ends would appear to misunderstand altogether the rational significance of honor itself.

Elster concludes that vindictiveness cannot be explained rationally but instead that it can only be explained in terms of "psychological tendencies and urges."[50] But to the extent that some tendencies and urges are directly related to individuals' possibilities for acquiring self-respect and dignity, such tendencies and urges are sometimes directly related to possibilities for *individual* rationality. Vindictiveness is often clearly unjustified and despicable. But sometimes it is the seeking of honor required for the possibility of other goods. If we take questions about individual rationality to have to do with individuals—with questions, at least in part, about individuality—then revenge behavior may sometimes be rational on a less narrow, more plausible conception of individual rationality than the one Elster presumes.

Conclusion

There are some cases in which individual choices would appear to be best explained by the pursuit of personal integrity and in which the choices involved are radically disruptive of both the individuals' and, occasionally, a society's existing fundamental commitments. I have argued that defining personal integrity in terms derived primarily from consideration of facts about the individual herself is inadequate in particular for such cases. On such accounts, important sorts of sincere and courageous choices may well turn out to be crazy. Thus, I have suggested that personal integrity be defined in terms, in part at least, of facts about the prospects of developing a more just and equitable social arrangement, one making more adequate sorts of choices and actions meaningful and understandable. To the extent that I think there is always a need for individuals to try to understand the values and norms of the society of which they are a product, I take this point to be entirely general, not restricted to the particular kinds of cases I have discussed. I suggest that in general, personal integrity should be understood to depend not necessarily on the realization of important fundamental values and commitments but often precisely on their disruption.

Much recent social criticism rightly focuses on the overly individualistic nature of Western societies. But it is not clear that a rejection of the kind of individualism that characterizes North American and European societies is a rejection of individualism per se. It may be that the deep problem of Western societies—that which distorts people's thinking about their own interests and about what is good for a society in general—is a problem about what constitutes personal integrity, the virtue of individuality. If personal integrity is ultimately defined in terms of individuals' intrinsic traits and characteristics and their fundamental beliefs and commitments, then there are many reasons to worry about the primacy of individuals in social and political theorizing. But if individuality is defined in terms, at least in part, of general beliefs about what ought to be possible for human beings—in particular in terms of possibilities for genuine autonomy, self-respect, and dignity—then the primacy of individuals, rather than undermining possibilities for effective radical change, is, in fact, required for such change.

6

Feminists and Nature:
A Defense of Essentialism

In CHAPTER 1, I introduced the problem of identifying real similarities and differences, a problem about unifying experience that I suggested, following Cornell, is central to feminist political theory. In Chapter 4, I suggested in criticism of Kymlicka's treatment of the role of cultural identities in autonomous choice that discussions about political identities are sometimes just discussions about relevant similarities and differences, in particular about the way unrecognized arbitrary assumptions about relevant similarities and differences between groups can affect political theorizing and strategizing. In this chapter, I argue that influential debates about essentialism and constructivism are, in fact, debates about the nature of justification for actions and policies on behalf of a group—indeed, about the dependence of social rationality, of questions about group interests, on judgments about social unity. Some political theorists have pointed out that to take for granted the unity of a social group is to concede the validity of arbitrarily dominant norms and values defining that group.[1] I suggest that the force and persistence of essentialist-constructionist debates, even though I think such debates are sometimes incorrectly represented, are an expression of the significance to issues of social rationality, and of political theory generally, of questions about how social unity gets defined to begin with.

As I suggested in Chapter 1, the concern about essentialism in discussions in feminist politics is a concern, in practice, not primarily about metaphysical questions about the individuation of entities but, more important, about the political consequences of assuming that what unifies a group such as women can be defined a priori. Elizabeth Spelman, for instance, in her influential book *Inessential Woman*, is concerned with a subtle sort of racism that pervades contemporary feminist theory because general claims about "women" are based on assumptions about the interests and experiences of the most dominant and visible groups of women in society, a tendency she explains in terms of the appeal of essentialist conceptions of classification.[2] I argue that there is nothing threatening as regards the appreciation of differences about the idea that social kinds can be objectively defined and that transcultural, lawlike generalizations can be made about the nature and origins of social kinds. And if these views constitute essentialism, feminists—and anyone else for that matter—should endorse essentialism.

I focus here on an argument by Donna Haraway primarily because I find Haraway's work particularly interesting and sophisticated. I do not presume that hers is the best or the most representative of the arguments regarding these issues; I discuss her work because her concerns somewhat overlap with those of this book and because the example she employs in the article discussed here provides an appropriate vehicle for the examination of the issues I intend to develop. I suggest that claims about real similarities and differences are made and ought to be made in political theory sensitive to the interests and experiences of subordinated groups—that is, that such theory presupposes and should presuppose knowledge of real essences. Moreover, I suggest that the effectiveness of such theory requires acknowledgment and defense of the larger metaphysical and epistemological picture—one including the existence and knowledge of real essences—that would justify such claims. I do not claim to completely develop such a picture but rather to argue for its plausibility and importance.

Haraway argues that the only route to a nonracist, nonimperialist conception of humanity is through radical nominalism, or the idea that systems of classifications are merely linguistic.[3] She acknowledges that we need to give content to general concepts such as "women" and "humanity," but she suggests that we should not think of these concepts as things we can "name and possess." Instead, as she puts it, "the only route to wholeness is through the radical dis-membering ... of our names and our bodies."[4] Unlike many antiessentialist theorists, Haraway has attempted to set out the epistemological issues that have been (mostly implicitly) connected with antiessentialist views. (I use the term "essentialism" to refer to the doctrine that there exist *real* essences, or essences discoverable through empirical investigation; the commitment to the existence of *nominal* or linguistic essences I refer to as "nominalism.") In what follows, I argue first that the political analysis Haraway carries out in "Ecce Homo, Ain't (Arn't) I a Woman, and Inappropriate/d Others: The Human in a Post-Humanist Landscape" is not, after all, an example of radical nominalism. Moreover, I suggest that if the epistemological picture she offers as an account of the possibility of radical criticism were to be more fully spelled out, her resistance to essentialism would turn out to lack proper motivation. A more fully developed picture of the radical contingency of knowledge claims indicates that essentialism may be *required* for the proper appreciation of difference rather than being, as is generally assumed, responsible for its denial.

I will try to demonstrate that some recently developed analytic philosophy of science and naturalistic epistemology provides resources for rethinking issues about concept development, in particular about what it means to think that general concepts and standards "cut the world at its joints."

Essentialism

It is important, first, to see what essentialism is and why it has become a political issue. In biology, essentialism was the view, ultimately based on Plato's concept of *eidos* (type), that each species is characterized by its unchanging essence and is separated from all other species by a sharp discontinuity. According to essentialists, variability in nature is explained by the existence of a finite number of permanent essences, of which individual members of a kind are merely the expressions.[5] Nominalism, the position taken to be opposed to essentialism, is the view that it is individuals, rather than types, that exist and that the classification of individuals into groups is entirely arbitrary. Nominalists hold that classifying individual entities into groups is a matter not of the existence of shared essences but rather of arbitrary definitional conventions. The only thing uniting classes of similar things, according to nominalists, is a name.

Arguments against the idea of real essences in philosophy have been largely epistemological: Since we cannot observe real essences, we cannot know whether our classificatory categories correspond to the actual causal structures of the physical world. John Locke, for instance, argued that we should think of natural kinds as defined by nominal essences—that is, in terms of arbitrary sets of observable properties—because we cannot observe the microstructure of things.[6] But Locke thought the factors that govern the behavior of substances are their unobservable real essences. In Locke's view, since we cannot know the real essences of things, we cannot expect that our classificatory systems will lead us to systematic general knowledge of the physical world.[7]

Feminists and other theorists interested in questions of social change have opposed essentialism for different sorts of reasons. There is, on the one hand, resistance to the notion that there is some thing, some essence, some fixed set of properties that defines members of a group. Elizabeth Grosz points out that essentialism in feminist theory can be biologistic—defining "women" in terms of biological capacities like reproduction—or can involve psychological characteristics—nurturance, empathy, supportiveness, and so on.[8] Sometimes, she adds, essentialism can even be theological or ontological, claiming that women's nature is derived from God-given attributes or, following Sartrean existentialism or Freudian pschoanalysis, is defined in terms of human freedom or the function of genital morphology.

Essentialism in feminist theory is taken to be the view that those characteristics defined as women's essence—whether biological, social, psychological, or more broadly human—are shared by all women at all times and are immutable, a doctrine that turns out to be false. There is a line of argument against essentialism, then, that is largely ontological: There *are* no fixed sets of properties, no unchanging essences, that individual members of a group express.

Feminists have also made epistemological arguments against essentialism, albeit of a somewhat different sort than those offered by Locke. Locke argued that we cannot know the real essences of things, so we ought to accept that our classifications are largely arbitrary and that, therefore, they cannot lead to objective knowledge of the physical world. Feminists have insisted that if we take categories such as "women," "lesbians," "blacks," and so on, to be defined in terms of some entity, some thing, some fixed set of properties, we become committed to rigidly and arbitrarily defined political possibilities—ones in particular that preclude the proper understanding of the situations and interests of less visible and powerful members of a particular group. Spelman, for instance, argues that the concept of "women as women," the attempt to define women as a group and to formulate some notion of "sisterhood across boundaries," has been the "trojan horse of western feminist ethnocentrism."[9] In her view, an emphasis by feminists on attempts to find the shared ground that would make the political identity of women as a group possible—on essentialist terms—leads to the reassertion of economic and racial privilege. For the experience and interests that will be taken to characterize women as a political group are likely to be the experience and interests of the most dominant groups of women.

Thus, essentialism in feminist theory appears to be a view both about what defines a thing or a person, and, perhaps more important, about the nature of the process of categorization required for political theory and strategizing. There is a claim, first, that it is a mistake to think that there exist "real essences," that is, that there exist sets of properties—biological, psychological, or whatever—that are shared by all members of a group. But there is also the perhaps more important claim that if we proceed as if there are real essences that define individuals as members of groups, we will be tempted to overlook the role of contingent social and political factors in proper political theory development. Diana Fuss, for instance, points out that "what is at stake for [nonessentialists] are systems of representations, social and material practices, laws of discourse, and ideological effects. In short, constructionists are concerned above all with the *production* and *organization* of differences, and they therefore reject the idea that any essential or 'natural pregivens' precede the processes of social determination."[10] So whereas Locke's epistemological argument was that we cannot *know* the real essences of things and cannot, therefore, have general knowledge of the world, the current arguments often seem to be that we ought not to accept the idea of real essences because such an idea undermines the possibility of acquiring more adequate understanding of the (social and political) world.

Haraway's Radical Nominalism

Let us return to Donna Haraway's claim about radical nominalism and the possibilities for effective feminist criticism. Haraway's work is significant in that she has tried to spell out the details of an epistemological picture that recognizes "situatedness," or contingency. Her notion of "situated knowledges" is intended to take seriously the "radical historical contingency of all knowledge claims and knowing subjects."[11] In her view, objectivity consists in "partial, locatable, critical knowledges sustaining the possibility of webs of connections called solidarity in politics and shared conversations in epistemology."[12] Now, Haraway's epistemological picture is complex, but two points are immediately significant. First, her emphasis on the epistemic significance of oppression, or the "view from below," is not a romanticization of oppression. It is not the view that *all* oppressed people possess special insight into the nature of social reality. On the contrary, Haraway claims that "*how* to see from below is a problem requiring at least as much skill with bodies and language, with the mediation of vision, as the 'highest' techno-scientific visualizations."[13]

Second, Haraway does attempt to provide some indication of what it is that allows us to distinguish between better and worse views from below. The temptation in acknowledging the epistemic significance of "situatedness" is either, on the one hand, to deny the possibility of any kind of privileged critical perspective and embrace some kind of relativism or, on the other, to (often implicitly) take some particular oppressed position to be epistemically privileged. Haraway claims that much feminist work has been of the first sort, resulting in a kind of radical relativism. She suggests, importantly, that the issue of objectivity as it arises in feminist theory needs to be reformulated. The question, in her view, is not one about whether it is possible to specify some kind of "transcendent" position, some critical perspective that is not affected by biases. Rather, she suggests that the question of objectivity is one about "the possibility of webs of connections called solidarity in politics and shared conversations in epistemology."[14] In other words, she suggests that questions about objectivity, if objectivity is claimed, ought not to be questions about how to define *a particular* critical perspective; instead, they are complex ethical, political, and epistemic issues about the kinds of connections, solidarity, and interactions that need to be emphasized and developed to envision and bring about a better world.

Consider how this epistemological picture might work in Haraway's "Ecce Homo." Like many feminist theorists, Haraway recognizes that questions about women's oppression cannot simply be addressed intellectually through analysis: Questions also need to be raised about the kinds of practical traditions in which intellectual activity is carried out. Feminists have insisted upon the danger of taking the meaning of certain general terms, such as "self-respect" and "dignity," for granted. For the accepted understanding of such terms is often such that the pursuit, even the understanding, of self-respect and dignity for women is precluded. As Claudia Card points out in a citation noted at the beginning of this book: "If oppressive institutions stifle and stunt the moral development of the oppressed, how is it possible, what does it *mean,* for the oppressed to be liberated? What is *there* to liberate? What does it mean to resist, to make morally responsible choices, to become moral agents, to develop character?"[15]

To answer these sorts of questions, Haraway says, feminists need to look for new, more appropriate representations, not representations of man or woman but representations that point the way to what she calls a "nongeneric humanity." In this she appears to share some of the concerns in Drucilla Cornell's work I identified in Chapter 1—the political importance of challenging and retelling relevant social myths and fantasies upon which people's conceptions of themselves and their interests always depend. In Haraway's view we must have feminist figures of humanity, but these must, she says, "resist representation, resist literal figuration, and still erupt in powerful new tropes, new figures of speech, new turns of historical possibility."[16]

Sojourner Truth is one of these figures. Why is it, Haraway asks, that Sojourner Truth's question, "Ain't I a woman?" stands for something that unifies women: "Why does her *question* have more power for feminist theory 150 years later than any number of affirmative and declarative sentences?"[17] The answer, she suggests, has something to do with Sojourner Truth's "power to figure a collective humanity without constructing the cosmic closure of the unmarked category."[18] Indeed, her "body, names, and speech . . . may be read to hold promise for a never settled universal, a common language that makes compelling claims on each of us collectively and personally, precisely through their radical specificity, in other words, through the displacements and resistances to unmarked identity precisely as the means to claiming the status of 'the human.'"[19] The power of Sojourner Truth's question, for Haraway, is that it displaces and resists the "unmarked universal"—"woman." It serves to disrupt the accepted system of classifications in, as she puts it, "the service of a newly articulated humanity."[20]

Now, this is somewhat vague. Perhaps part of the point Haraway is making is that if we take knowledge to depend on the possibility of what she calls "transcendent" categories and principles, we will either be misled into taking for granted general concepts whose content depends on the dominance of certain groups in society and precludes the proper appreciation of difference—that is, the appreciation of those experiences and interests not properly represented by existing general theories and concepts—or we will give up the possibility of knowledge altogether. But we need not give up the possibility of knowledge altogether if we give up the assumption that knowledge, when we do have it, depends on the possibility of transcendent categories and principles. In Haraway's view, Sojourner Truth's question disrupts dominant assumptions about who is represented by the concept "women," leading us to a greater appreciation of the ways in which this concept has been arbitrarily constructed. This appreciation of arbitrariness points, presumably, in the direction of more adequate understanding of humanity.

But why does Sojourner Truth's question point in this direction? Haraway rejects the idea that the alternative to the notion that there are no transcendent concepts and principles is the radically constructivist, relativistic view that all there is to knowledge claims is a working out of power relations. So it is useful to ask why *this* question amounts to an acquiring of understanding rather than the mere assertion of some particular opinion. Perhaps this can be understood by asking not why Sojourner Truth's *question* was so powerful but why *Sojourner Truth's* question was so powerful. For the claim here is not just that Sojourner Truth's question disrupts and displaces the unmarked universality of the category "human" or "women" but that it does so in a way that gives content to the "we" of humanity. And surely not just any woman who stands up and asks "Ain't I a Woman?" manages to disrupt the relevant assumed universals in this way. Christina Sommers, for instance, likes to point out that many women swoon when Rhett Butler carries Scarlet O'Hara up the stairs to rape her.[21] If Sommers asked, "And ain't they women?" would this disrupt the category "women" in appropriate ways? It might, after all, disrupt the feminist category "women." Or when Judy Wubnig says at a debate about hiring policies in Canada that she doesn't see any serious problem of gender discrimination in Canadian philosophy departments,[22] could she not also ask, "And ain't I a woman?" thereby disrupting assumptions about the deeply sexist nature of Canadian academic institutions?

One might think Sommers and Wubnig don't point the way to the bringing about of a more appropriate "we" because the categories they disrupt are not dominant ones. But if the context is relevantly individuated, they are indeed dominant. In any case, Haraway's suggestion about the need to disrupt categories is directed specifically toward the development of feminist theory: The categories of feminist thought and politics are the ones that need to be "shifting and multiply organized across variable axes of difference."[23]

So what, then, are these "axes of difference"? What is it that makes the specificity of Sojourner Truth a relevant vehicle for the articulation of the concept "we" and not, say, a woman who swoons when Rhett Butler disappears up the staircase? The features Haraway lists in her characterization of Sojourner Truth as sign, as figuration, include the facts that Sojourner Truth has been "forcibly transported, without a name, without a proper home, unincorporated into the discourses of (white) womanhood, raped by her owner, forcibly married with another slave, robbed of her children, and doubted even in the anatomy of her body."[24] Haraway specifically does not include other features of Sojourner Truth's person in the list of differences that matter, features, for instance, such as that she is from the state of New York or that her master was Dutch. She also does not include reference to Sojourner Truth's height or weight or the kind of art she appreciated. What distinguishes Sojourner Truth as a relevant figuration for the "reconstruction of founding stories, of any possible home"[25] is, it turns out, quite specific. What distinguishes her is the oppression she suffers as a black woman in North America at the time, which is different from the sexist oppression suffered by white women.

But how does Haraway pick out these specific features as the ones that characterize the differences between the way white women and black women suffered sexist oppression in North America at that time? Why are these facts—namely, that Sojourner Truth was "forcibly transported, without a name, without a proper home, unincorporated into the discourses of (white) womanhood, raped by her owner, forcibly married with another slave, robbed of her children, and doubted even in the anatomy of her body"—*relevant* differences, ones, in particular, that show how the category "women" privileges white women? Why are these facts not evidence of something else, say, that Sojourner Truth has fallen short of the ideal of womanhood? The features Haraway lists as differences are not *just* differences. They are differences between what a particular concept—"Women"—represents according to the current system of meanings and practices and what it *ought* to represent. Her claim about "differences that matter" would not make sense except on the assumption, first, that slavery is wrong and that black women ought to be treated as full human beings and, second, that being treated as a full human being has at least some identifiable, essential features, such as *not* being forcibly transported, without a name, and so on.

Realism

But these are assumptions about how the world really divides up, not just about how the world is represented given the current linguistic systems. These are definite assertions about what is and is not right, about what does and does not reflect real humanness. They are not judgments that can be explained entirely by currently existing linguistic patterns because they are judgments precisely about the *difference* between the social-political reality, as it is determined by currently existing patterns of language and behavior, and what is really going on. Haraway's claim about radical nominalism is a claim that systems of classification are not determined by facts about how the world really is; they do not reflect the real nature of things. Instead, they depend on "systems of representations, social and material practices, laws of discourses and ideological effects."[26] Yet it would not be correct to say either in 1851 or in 1995 that it is current linguistic and behavioral patterns that identify society as deeply racist. People who struggle to be able to identify racist patterns of thinking and acting usually discover that it is current linguistic and behavioral patterns that need to be challenged and transformed. Judgments about racism and sexism, it would appear, are often the result of discovering how what appears to be the case, given dominant conceptual and linguistic patterns, is not really the case. The question that, as Haraway claims, has served to unify "women" over the past 150 years is not just any question. It is a question the political effectiveness of which depends not on the recognition of difference in some general sense but rather on the recognition of quite specific differences between a socially determined usage and what really is the case.

Moreover, whereas Haraway claims that the kinds of "never settled universal[s]" made possible by the disruption of accepted categories are not ones we can ever "name and possess," it does seem that Sojourner Truth certainly names and possesses certain concepts. Sojourner Truth asks the question in the first place, it would seem, because her struggle against a specific—*named*—form of oppression has allowed her to demonstrate the wrongness of certain racist, sexist assumptions. And she has been able to accomplish this, it would appear, because she *possesses* a concept of herself as a full human being in a quite definite (nonracist, nonsexist) sense of the term. Why does Haraway take Sojourner Truth to be an example of the "radical dismembering . . . of our names and our bodies"?[27] The names and bodies that are "radically dismembered" are the names and bodies that constitute a racist, sexist social structure. But that dismembering, as she herself describes it, appears to depend heavily on the struggle of people like Sojourner Truth precisely *to* name these structures *as* racist and sexist and, in doing so, to *become* the bodies that contradict the viability of those structures and assumptions.

There are some good reasons for Haraway's taking the disrupting of categories to be of primary importance to feminist theory and politics. The assumption is that proper political understanding depends importantly on disrupting those arbitrarily defined concepts that operate in analyses of political situations so as to preclude the proper appreciation of differences. In some cases, it seems, we cannot even get started on the project of properly understanding social situations until some quite fundamental concepts are challenged and, to some degree at least, reformulated, as I've pointed out in previous chapters.

Still, the disruption of categories is only politically effective in some cases and, more important, when that disruption is of a certain sort. Indeed, there are plenty of examples of cases in which political progress toward equality depends on the *imposition* of certain conceptions of how a society or a group is defined. Often in practice, it seems, effective political change depends primarily not, as Haraway's defense of nominalism suggests, on asking questions and disrupting categories but on bringing about quite definite changes according to a specific conception of unity.

For instance, many have suggested that one reason Castro's Cuba has been relatively successful in addressing racism and sexism in that society has been an explicit effort by leadership to confront the task of redefining national identity. Raquel Mendieta Costa argues that in the decades following the revolution, artists, historians, and writers worked to bring about certain social values—values such as universal health care and education, low rent, and so on.[28] Mendieta points out that such values, in a sense, had to be imposed on the society for people to be able to understand possibilities that could not be understood previously, possibilities that were, in fact, disallowed by capitalist values.

Now, Haraway might want to describe the work of Cuban writers and artists as an asking of the kinds of questions that resist what she calls "cosmic closure" on the question of "humanness" and lead in the direction of a "never settled universal." But it is important to note that on another interpretation of the "reconstruction of founding stories," the questions that are being asked here presuppose a particular conception of humanity, and it is this presupposition that explains the relevance of the questions, not primarily the fact that they lead in a certain direction. In other words, an alternative account to Haraway's of the effectiveness of Cuban writers' and artists' questions is that they express a conception of real humanness, one in particular that reflects the fact that human beings ought not to be racially and sexually divided. This would suggest that it is not resisting closure that leads to the right sorts of unsettled universals but rather the assertion of the right sorts of (contingently defined) universals that leads to the possibility of appropriate resistance.

Haideh Moghissi's excellent book *Populism and Feminism in Iran* describes another example of revolutionary struggle the analysis of which does not easily fit Haraway's antiessentialist metaphysics.[29] In examining women's experience in the 1979 revolution in Iran and attempting to explain why the extraordinary upsurge of gender awareness and political development among women in postrevolutionary Iran did not develop into a strong women's movement, part of Moghissi's argument is that Shiite and

Iranian concepts and perceptions of female sexuality determined the nature
and scope of the roles women assume in Iran. Patriarchal values and moral-
istic visions of female sexuality and sex roles "were shared by and had a determining influence in the ideological formation, political culture and practical activities of secular nationalist and socialist organizations."[30]
Moghissi argues that had there been a cohesive ideology—an appropriate
alternative picture—activist women's groups that existed in Iran in the late
1970s might have been able to organize and channel the spontaneous
women's protests in defense of their rights. But the left in general and
women's organizations in particular failed to challenge, in theory as well as
in practice, patriarchal norms and values that limited the choices and actions of Iranian women.

Now, it is not at all obvious that an emphasis on "axes of difference"
and "displacements and resistances" primarily explains what was required
in the struggle for liberation in this case. Haraway might suggest that this
example fits a postmodernist reading because there appears to have been a
refusal to ask the kinds of questions that would have disrupted dominant
assumptions about how leftist struggle was organized. But this does not
seem to properly accommodate Moghissi's main point. She suggests that it
was *not* a mistake, for instance, to name and define the enemy—U.S. imperialism; she argues, however, that other enemies needed to be named as
well. What seems to be suggested by Moghissi's analysis is that *more,* not
less, naming (of patriarchal norms and values, for instance) was required. It
is not clear that the *questions* and *disruptions* themselves are as significant
in this example as the bringing about of the kind of (theoretical and political) unity that would have made the *right* sorts of disruptions possible.

It might look as though I have just missed the point about what Haraway
means when she suggests that the postmodernist character of feminist theory consists in resisting closure. What she means is that feminist theorists
should resist any *absolute* definitions, definitions that preclude any appreciation of difference. Of course, some kinds of tentative, more fluid assertions of identity and unity are required for the purposes of political solidarity and direction. But the rejection of essentialism by many feminist
theorists is not just a rejection of rigid, absolute assertions of identity; nominalism is also the view that it is a mistake to think that proper systems of
classification reflect how the world really is, that they are determined by nature. As Diana Fuss suggests, "Locke's category of nominal essences is especially useful for anti-essentialist feminists who want to hold onto the notion
of women as a group without submitting to the idea that it is 'nature'
which categorizes them as such."[31] Antiessentialism, as expressed in radical
nominalism, is not just a rejection of certain sorts of definitions; it is also a
rejection of a metaphysical position about what explains general definitions, about what those definitions represent. Specifically, antiessentialism

is a rejection of the view that appropriate systems of classification correspond to "nature" or at least to facts about (social or physical) reality. And
this rejection is motivated, it appears, by the assumption that realism about
classifications precludes proper appreciation of the role of contingent linguistic and social practices in the development of political theory and practice.

But this is a mistake. Moreover, Haraway in effect *argues* that it is a mistake. According to her, a certain dichotomy—between what she calls "transcendent" concepts and relativism—should be rejected. What exactly is implied by this rejection? Feminist theorists have almost always expressed a
well-motivated concern about the epistemological assumption that we can
find foundational standards—foundational beliefs or principles upon which
to build knowledge.[32] Many have explicitly resisted the idea—developed in
a tradition deriving from Descartes and Hume and adhered to in this century by positivists—that some kind of "pure" knowledge, unaffected by the
contingencies of particular positions, provides appropriate foundations for
the acquiring of further knowledge. Instead, the argument has been that *all*
epistemic standards and concepts are dependent for their content upon particular historical traditions and social and political circumstances.

Now, one response to the recognition that all epistemic judgments are
relative to specific traditions and circumstances is to take a constructivist
approach to knowledge. One might take, as many feminist theorists appear
to,[33] some version of a Kuhnian approach, arguing that knowledge is simply a social construction, that scientists, for instance, are merely engaged in
constructing the world out of paradigms.[34] Thomas Kuhn suggests that *all*
aspects of scientific judgments and practice are dependent upon scientists'
particular traditions and values and that the only way we can make sense
of the theory-laden character of scientific practice is to assume that scientists are constructing the world, not discovering it after all.[35] The foundationalist notion of objective knowledge is that such knowledge requires getting free of the limitations imposed on inquiry by one's particular
attachment to some specific set of circumstances and values. Positivists ini-
tially thought it was possible to be free of particular circumstances because
we can appeal directly to observation and experiment: Observation and experiment can provide the required foundations for building knowledge.
Constructivists acknowledged that there are no such unmediated perceptions of the world; there can be no "outside point," no neutral beliefs or
judgments. They therefore concluded that there is no possibility for objective knowledge.

But this argument is invalid, as has been pointed out.[36] It rests on the
mistaken assumption that objectivity requires that we be able to have what
Philip Kitcher calls "out of theory" experiences.[37] The profound theory dependence of all judgments does not imply that objectivity is impossible un-

less we accept that objectivity requires theory independence, which is false. And Haraway acknowledges this. At least, she acknowledges that it is mistaken to think that objectivity requires theory independence. She rejects the notion that objectivity requires that knowledge claims be ultimately grounded in foundational beliefs—beliefs that are untainted by social influences, that are incorrigible, and so on. So she should think it is possible to have objectivity—to have beliefs that are made true by facts about the structure of the physical and social world—even though theory independence is both impossible and, more relevantly, undesirable.

On her acceptance of radical contingency, Haraway and others are aligned with naturalistic epistemologists who have argued that foundationalist conceptions of knowledge are fundamentally mistaken.[38] But Haraway's particular treatment of the radical contingency of knowledge claims— particularly her emphasis on the epistemic significance of the view from below"—would appear to be best expressed by an epistemological picture that not only denies foundationalism but that fully acknowledges the epistemic significance of quite particular conceptual and historical traditions, as well as sets of relations and practices. Some philosophers of science have recently argued that the acquiring of more accurate scientific theories is radically contingent upon the coming about of the *right sorts* of traditions—that is, by the epistemically and historically contingent emergence of the right sorts of conceptual and practical traditions, ones the dependence upon which leads to more accurate perceptual and theoretical judgments.[39] Such a view would appear to be consistent both with Haraway's emphasis on "situatedness" and with the general emphasis in feminist theory and politics on the moral and epistemic significance of particular relations and attachments.

But it is often difficult to grasp and to spell out the implications of thoroughgoing acknowledgment of radical contingency. Such a picture of knowledge conflicts with deep-seated epistemological and metaphysical assumptions. It is hard, for instance, to acknowledge that even though knowledge could have developed in enormous numbers of ways—that is, that if history had developed differently, we would tell different sorts of true stories—the stories we do tell about the world can still, nonetheless, be true. They are not arbitrary; they correspond to facts about the world. The radical contingency of knowledge development might be explainable in something like the way Stephen Jay Gould, in a 1989 book, describes the contingency of evolutionary development. He points out that people repeatedly misinterpret evolution, despite evidence to the contrary, as movement in a certain, predictable direction—as a "ladder of progress."[40] Instead, he suggests that if we were able to rewind life's tape—thoroughly erasing everything that has actually happened—to some time in the past, there is no reason at all to think the replay would be anything like the actual history of life.[41] Each replay would demonstrate radically different evolutionary directions. This does not mean, though, that evolution is senseless and without meaningful pattern. It does not imply that in evolutionary processes "anything goes." For "the divergent route of the replay would be just as interpretable, just as explainable *after* the fact, as the actual road. . . . Each step proceeds for cause, but no finale can be specified at the start, and none would ever occur a second time in the same way, because any pathway proceeds through thousands of improbable stages."[42] It is often assumed that claims about realism are something like "ladder of progress" claims—claims about the inevitability of telling some one true story about the world. If the acquiring of knowledge, however, is explained by the radically contingent development of appropriate patterns of engagement with the (physical and social) world, there is no reason to think claims about realism need involve such an unlikely commitment.

Feminists in general, it would appear, have a particular interest in more fully pursuing the implications of the radical historical contingency of meaningfulness and knowledge, particularly as that contingency affects fundamental philosophical and political assumptions and concepts. There are two reasons for this. First, feminist theorists, arguably more than other groups of political theorists, have acknowledged the extent and the implications of the effects of oppressive social structures on what people are and how they understand their lives. Political philosophers, for instance, often discuss the question of the distribution of resources without examining the consequences of, or even acknowledging, the fact that to the extent that a society is deeply racist, homophobic, and so on, there is a question about how resources are *defined* to begin with. In Chapter 4, I argued that this is the case with Will Kymlicka's influential treatment of minority rights in *Liberalism, Community, and Culture.*[43] As I suggested previously, feminist theorists have quite consistently been concerned to show that, given the effects of long-standing and deep-seated oppression, difficult questions need to be raised about how issues are formulated and about what is being assumed in such formulations. Arguably, one of the most significant contributions of feminist theory to political philosophy in general is its recognition of the ways in which the existence of systemic discrimination pervades all aspects of interpretation and analysis to the extent that finding out what actually is going on in a society demands much more complex sorts of investigations than are usually undertaken. As Toni Morrison points out, again in discussing the Clarence Thomas hearings, "To inaugurate any discovery of what happened is to be conscious of the smooth syruplike and glistening oil poured daily to keep the machine of state from screeching too loudly or breaking down entirely as it turns the earth of its own rut, digging itself deeper and deeper into the foundation of private life, burying itself for invisibility, for protection, for secrecy."[44] It would appear, and I have been trying to suggest, that to the extent that feminist theorists have emphasized the significance of processes of investigation and development—for instance, the retelling of social myths and fantasies *in a more appropriate way*—a commitment to a plausible version of realism is the best expression of both theoretical *and* political concerns.

A second reason the picture of objective scientific knowledge developed recently by some philosophers of science might be helpful to feminist theorists interested in the possibility of radical social critique is that such a picture of knowledge and justification indicates not just that the traditional *answers* to questions about the nature of scientific objectivity have been wrong but also how, in fact, the *questions* have been wrong. Certain issues in sometimes abstract metaphysical debates about the nature of knowledge are crucial for the spelling out of the practical consequences of fully rejecting distorting foundationalist assumptions about knowledge. For instance, realists about scientific knowledge have been charged, among other things, with claiming some kind of special dimension of correspondence between true propositions and the world, one that ignores the social and pragmatic dimensions of knowledge claims. Yet there is no reason to think that realists need be committed to the possibility of some particular theory about the relations between true propositions and the world if the foundationalist picture of knowledge and justification is rejected. Instead, what realism demonstrates is that the possibility of understanding what is really going on turns out to require the asking of specific sorts of questions, questions in particular about processes of development, certain consequences and relations, and so on—questions defined not in terms of any preestablished notion of what constitutes knowledge at all but rather in terms of entirely contingent, multifarious developments. Realists are indeed usually committed to some version of a correspondence theory of truth, but only on assumptions of the truth of foundationalism should such a commitment involve denying the role of social and pragmatic considerations in knowledge. Thus, the virtue of a more fully developed alternative to foundationalism—including, as it turns out, the development of questions about realism—is that it becomes possible to identify the extent to which, as many feminists have suspected, some standard epistemological arguments, including feminist arguments, are often a response to the wrong questions.

Essentialism/Nominalism

To return to the more specific topic of this chapter, it turns out that on a more full-blown naturalistic picture of scientific knowledge, there is no reason to think that a commitment to the idea of real essences requires commitment to the idea of fixed, eternal essences that separate one group from another with sharp discontinuity. Indeed, if knowledge claims are contingent upon the emergence or bringing about of the right sorts of theoretical and practical transitions, there is no reason to expect that the identification of real essences should result in precise sets of categories with clear boundaries and fixed content. On the contrary, if knowledge is explained by the contingent development of the right sorts of conceptual and practical traditions, a realistic conception of classificatory schemes *explains* the very fluidity and complexity of categories upon which feminist political theorists, especially postmodernists, have insisted. It is certainly true, as nominalists have been concerned to acknowledge, that judgments about kinds are determined in part by human interests, projects, and practices. But the possibility that human interests, projects, and practices sometimes develop as they do because the real (physical or social) world is as it is suggests that this sort of dependence is not by itself an argument against essentialism.

After all, biologists do think they know how the world really divides up, that our natural kind categories, at least sometimes, are based on more than linguistic conventions. And it is quite clear that this does not have to do with discovering some thing or some entity that defines members of a kind for all times. Ernst Mayr, for instance, advances a notion of species divisions according to which kinds are defined in terms of reproductive relations and isolation mechanisms.[45] Mayr and others assume a notion of real essences in the discussion of species that does not depend on the existence of fixed essences, specifiable a priori. In Mayr's view, the appeal of nominalism as a response to the nonexistence of fixed essences has to do with the mistaken assumption that individuating one thing from another is strictly a matter of the intrinsic properties of the thing. In other words, it has to do with a mistaken conception of what individual identity consists in, that it is a matter primarily about individuals rather than of the relations between individuals and communities, histories, environments, and so on.[46] Sydney Shoemaker argues that the role of relations in determining *which* of a thing's properties are the defining ones does not mean those properties are any less intrinsic.[47] What Shoemaker's account shows of importance, and that accords with Mayr's account of species divisions, is that individuating an entity in terms of relations is not incompatible with the notion that entities are distinguished in terms of their own idiosyncratic properties.

To be sure, classification of nonorganic natural entities—like minerals—involves, at least eventually, considerable precision and fixity. It is still true, however, that the identification of such precision and fixity depends on the emergence of the right sorts of conceptual and practical traditions. Whether the similarities between members of a kind' are fixed, that such similarities count as *relevant* similarities—ones that are causally significant to the entity's behavior—depends on a process of investigation. It is possible that the significance for feminist politics of the reconception of real essences in biology and the philosophy of science is not so much the retrieval of the notion of real essences as a reconsideration of what kinds of questions need to be asked in determining issues of nonarbitrary classification. What appears to be true about the classification of entities in biology is that not much hangs on the possibility of answering the question "What is it to be an x?" for all xs at all times. Rather, what we want to know is what is involved in applying the term "x" nonarbitrarily. As Richard Boyd argues, on a realist, naturalistic view, the establishment of natural definition arises under circumstances in which there are (theoretical) reasons to believe that certain sorts of similarities and differences are causally relevant to the behavior of systems under study.[48] And there are often such reasons available to us in the case of social groups and social systems. The Sojourner Truth case may indeed show that it is a mistake to try to define "women" for all women at all times, but it is not clear that this is very interesting or relevant. The example does *not* show that it is a mistake to think that *real* similarities between women—such as an interest in resisting a sexist social system—can come to be distinguished from apparent ones, such as white skin color.

Consider Edward Stein's interesting analogy to the debate about essentialism and constructionism regarding homosexuality.[49] He imagines a society, Zomnia, much like our current one, in which members are particularly concerned about sleep habits.[50] In particular, Zomnians are concerned about whether people sleep on their backs or their fronts. The former are called "backers," the latter "fronters." The majority of Zomnians are considered to be fronters, and there has existed discrimination against people thought to be backers. Most Zomnians think they can identify a backer on the basis of posture, skin color, and certain personality traits, such as aggressivity. Scientists and psychiatrists in Zomnia are interested in what makes some people backers. Some think whether one is a backer is genetically determined, some that it has to do with one's relationship to parents, others with diet during puberty.

Stein urges us to imagine ourselves as visitors in Zomnia having to respond to such a situation: If he were in such a position, he would argue that the practice of discriminating against people who sleep on their backs is morally wrong and that their scientific theories concerning the "etiology" of "backerhood" are pseudoscientific. The analogy is supposed to demonstrate the appeal of social constructionism. For if such were our reaction, it would be similar to the complaint social constructionists make about categorizing people as homosexuals and heterosexuals. According to social constructionists, the only reason groupings according to sleep position seem silly and groupings according to sexual orientation seem sensible is that we are used to the latter. Now, Stein admits it could turn out that there are some deep properties having to do with sleep positions. But this is an empirical question. The issue between essentialists and constructionists, then, Stein proposes, is an empirical issue about whether there exist objective, transcultural categories (like being color-blind or six feet tall) or whether the categories are merely culturally dependent.

But the empirical issue regarding such a question may not be about deep properties regarding sleep positions, at least not if those deep properties are properties of backers themselves. It may be about the kind of society in which being a backer becomes relevantly significant. Even if there are no "deep properties" having to do with sleep positions, it is not clear that the category "backer" is not objective and that it does not enter into lawlike generalizations. Whereas it is certainly true that the category "backer" is culturally dependent, there may be objective facts about what it means to be a backer in the specific backerphobic society of Zomnia. If Zomnia is a society in which there does exist real discrimination against backers, then there do exist good reasons for distinguishing between real and apparent similarities between backers and fronters. Some people, including backers themselves, will think backers are those people who share the property of sleeping on their backs. Such people may think, then, that backers possess shared interests and have reasons for organizing themselves politically primarily by virtue of their inclination to sleep on their backs. Others, however, will argue that to take bodily sleep positions as grounds for unity is to concede the validity of a way of distinguishing between human beings that is, in fact, backerphobic and that such ways of thinking need to be resisted. Moreover, they could argue that to effectively resist such backerphobia, it is necessary to identify and challenge ways of thinking about human beings in Zomnian society in general that provide grounds for backerphobic behaviors. Indeed, given that this particular society *defines* itself in terms of sleep orientations, backer-liberation struggles must involve a challenge to fundamental, stabilizing beliefs and values, ones about what it means to be a Zomnian generally.

In such cases, what is going on is an argument about real similarities and differences: How we conceive of the similarities and differences between backers and fronters has implications for what kinds of strategies will best advance the real interests of backers in Zomnia in the pursuit of human flourishing. If someone says, for example, that as a backer she is committed to hating and fighting against fronters, there would be good reasons for trying to persuade her that she is wrong about what it means to be a backer, that she is mistaken about what constitutes backer political identity. One would make such an argument by appealing to facts about the nature of backer oppression, including its explanation in terms of broader social features—economic, political, historical, and moral. One would try to persuade such a fronter-hating backer that she is mistaken about the target of backer-liberation struggles. For the proper target of resistance to backer-phobia is not just fronters themselves, although backerphobic fronters are certainly instruments of and are responsible for backerphobia, but broader social practices and institutions generally.

In making such an argument, it would appear, one does assume the objectivity of the category "backer." One assumes that being a backer is not just what the cultural norms and values dictate and that there are indeed facts about social structures, history, and practices on the basis of which it could be argued that what one thinks about backers, even if one is a backer, is mistaken. The category "backer" does not have the same status as, say, the category "silly." It is not clear that there could be reasons to argue that what a Zomnian thinks is silly is not really silly. "Silly" does not appear to be objectively constrained in the way "backer" is, if indeed there does exist systemic discrimination against backers. In the case of "backer," there are facts about the matter of what it means to be a backer, facts about the nature of backers' oppression in Zomnia, facts that provide reasons for thinking some understandings of the term are better than others, even independent of what the majority of Zomnians think. Moreover, it would appear to be possible to make lawlike generalizations about backers. If one were to find out that discrimination against backers has certain social and historical explanations, one would be able to make some generalizations about what societies with similar tendencies and histories might have reason to watch out for.

The issue about essentialism and constructionism as regards homosexuality *is* an empirical issue, as Stein suggests, but it is not clear that it is an empirical issue about deep properties if by "deep properties" is meant properties of homosexuals themselves. Sexual orientation is not a feature of human beings that is relevant to judgments about human worth; it does not provide good reasons for distinguishing between people in terms of character and treatment. But there is certainly something that it means to be homosexual, something that can be argued about. People who are homosexual do possess a shared interest by virtue of the fact that homosexuals do receive unfair treatment in homophobic societies: Simply by virtue of being a homosexual, an individual can expect to face systems of barriers and forces that preclude the realizability of certain important possibilities. The empirical issue is one having to do with the nature of the specific society, with questions about whether such systems of barriers and forces do, in fact, exist, and with questions about their identification. Whether there are deep properties associated with being a homosexual is an interesting question but not necessarily as regards questions about the objective status of "homosexual." The very fact that it is possible to argue that there are *not* such properties and that discrimination against homosexuals is morally wrong and scientifically unfounded suggests that there *are* facts about the matter, facts that can be empirically investigated. Thus, it looks as though the definition of "homosexual" can be guided by nature even though at the same time it is culturally relative.

Boyd points out that it is a mistake to think that the conventionalism of some ways of classifying undermines the plausibility of realism as a general picture of the nature of knowledge.[51] For instance, the term "IQ" is an example of a concept that possesses a nominalist definition: There is good reason to think that the meaning of "IQ" is explained entirely by the existence of social conventions and practices, not by facts (genetic or otherwise) about the phenomenon to which it supposedly refers. Haraway is interested in precisely these kinds of cases. The general concept "women," in the example she discusses, is one that possesses meaning in terms of racist, sexist conventions and practices, not in terms of any deep facts about women and women's interests. Others have made similar arguments about "homosexuality." But the fact that "IQ" has a conventional definition does not mean that nominalism is true in general about such sorts of categories. "IQ" is not the same as "silliness," after all. We know, on the basis of reason and evidence, that "IQ" refers to nothing, whereas "silliness" is a concept to which evidence is not applicable. Silliness is, it seems, a matter of convention. In the case of "IQ," we would not be able to come to *know* that there is no single entity called "intelligence" that can be measured according to a single set of criteria if it were not the case that we are able, *at least in some cases,* to *discover* that what we thought were real similarities between entities or people are, in fact, not.

What the Sojourner Truth case shows is not that general social categories are nominalist and that we ought to think of them as such but rather that people using the term at the time were mistaken about the relevant similarities among women at the time. There need be no commitment to the existence of fixed, underlying natures to think that we are capable, at least in some cases and to some extent, of distinguishing real similarities and differences from apparent ones. And there is no reason, epistemologically or metaphysically, for thinking that real definitions, or at least definitions approximately reflecting facts about the (social or physical) world, involve much more than this.

Why does Haraway, who acknowledges the connection between concern about essences and the possibility for radical critique and who explicitly urges a reconception of standard, foundationalist assumptions about knowledge and justification, insist on radical nominalism? Why does she think the insight that accepted general concepts like "self-respect," "dignity," and "humanness" are problematic is best expressed by the rejection of essentialism, or the view that appropriate systems of classification reflect what is *really* going on in the world? Why does she not extend her picture of the radical contingency of knowledge claims to include the radical contingency of judgments about real essences?

Probably, the answer has to do with a confusion about the implications of accepting a realist view of classification for the possibility of fully acknowledging contingent developments in the acquiring of political understanding. As already mentioned, a significant part of the feminist resistance to essentialism has to do with a well-motivated concern about the dangers of foundationalist epistemological assumptions for the development of radical critique: If we assume that knowledge depends on the identification of neutral, universally applicable concepts and standards, we will either be misled into the arbitrary formulation of fixed, general concepts or we will be tempted toward relativism. The appeal of nominalism appears to depend importantly on assumptions that nominalism and not essentialism allows for the ongoing revisability of general concepts and an appreciation of their multidimensionality. As it turns out, however, whereas Locke was right to think that we cannot see the internal structures of things and that, therefore, our classification of entities into groups depends primarily on judgments about similarity, he was mistaken to think that judgments about similarity cannot be judgments that reflect knowledge of how the world is, at least approximately. When Sojourner Truth asks, "Ain't I a Woman?" she is acting on knowledge of relevant similarities, even if her knowledge may not have been able to have been fully articulated or even to have been fully understood if it were. To the extent that a realistic conception of classification *requires* classification according to particular needs and traditions and according to consideration of ongoing developments within a specific context, it is essentialism and not nominalism that properly expresses feminist insistence upon appreciating complexity and difference.

Undoubtedly, part of the motivation for resisting essentialism in feminist theory is that essentialism is associated with the often arrogant, exclusionary politics of largely white, middle-class North American feminisms. As Diana Fuss notes, essentialism can

> be read in the accounts of universal female oppression, the assumption of a totalizing symbolic system which subjugates all women everywhere, throughout history and across cultures.... Essentialism emerges perhaps most strongly within the very discourse of feminism, a discourse which presumes upon the unity of its object of inquiry (women) *even* when it is at pains to demonstrate the differences within this admittedly generalizing and imprecise category.[52]

But it is important to note here that the exclusionary politics of such "essentialist" feminisms involves exclusions of a particular sort—namely, the exclusion from feminist politics of poor, black, disabled, and other women. It is not clear that exclusionary politics is always undesirable. Indeed, some sorts of exclusions seem to be necessary and desirable for effective politics. Surely, we don't think arrogant and patriarchal the people who praised a small Quebec town for excluding the neo-Nazis?[53] Feminist theorists do not even give epistemic and moral weight to all *women's* views. Some women's views are discounted. For instance, those who argue for more women-oriented approaches to new reproductive technologies tend to discount the views of women who think of embryos as little persons who ought to be given names.[54] These women's views are excluded. And why not? There are good moral, political, and epistemic reasons for excluding some persons and some views from feminist politics. A defense of essentialism involves the commitment not to arbitrarily exclusionary politics that favor the status quo but to the formulation of unifying concepts that allow the possibility of properly distinguishing exclusions that are arbitrary from those that are not.

In conclusion, I have suggested that the opposition to essentialism is at least partly, but perhaps most importantly, an opposition to a particular conception of justification, one according to which standards and concepts are justifiable a priori and that indeed precludes the proper appreciation of difference. But the rejection of this notion of justification, as Haraway herself acknowledges, is not a rejection of the possibility of applying nonarbitrary (objective) epistemic standards. What she doesn't acknowledge is that part of what is involved in the acquiring of nonarbitrary beliefs about what a society consists of and where it is going are quite definite judgments about what is and is not important to the society—in effect, judgments about what norms and values *ought* to define the unity of a society. I have defended essentialism, or at least suggested that it should be defended, because radical feminist politics requires, above all, the bringing about of alternative, more appropriate classifications and norms, and the success of such a task requires the identification of real social structures and relations. Some will say that the concept of essentialism needs to be abandoned by feminists because of its association with imperialistic, oppressive ways of thinking and behaving. I take the reclaiming of essentialism to be necessary for just these same reasons. I have tried to suggest that feminist theorists do indeed make assumptions about real, as opposed to nominal, essences. And precisely because such practices have sometimes, in feminisms of the past, been associated with imperialist tendencies, they should be admitted, spelled out, and properly defended.

7

Reason and the Erotic:
The Moral Significance
of Personal Relations and
Commitments

I HAVE SUGGESTED THAT PERSONAL development and relations sometimes constitute the bringing about of more adequate conditions for knowledge and that some sorts of understanding depend on radical disruption of one's settled sense of self, indeed, even on radical disruption of social structures and institutions. Moreover, I have argued that the epistemic significance of some personal developments and relations is defined in terms of paths of development, where the adequacy of such paths of development depends on facts about the specific nature of the society as a whole, including moral facts about what kinds of injustices exist and need to be resisted in the interests of human flourishing. I now want to examine in more detail the epistemic significance of personal relations and commitments and how it might be accounted for philosophically. Although it is true that such significance is ultimately morally explained, I suggest that appropriate moral principles and concepts often need to be discovered *as a result of* claims for the significance of personal relations and commitments. In other words, I suggest that claims to the significance of personal relations and commitments often have to be made without available moral justification in order that such justification be discovered.

In *Sister Outsider,* Audre Lorde makes an intriguing reference to an erotic relationship with a bookcase or at least to the making of a bookcase as an erotic experience.[1] She speaks about the erotic as a capacity for a certain kind of response, the "physical, emotional and psychic expressions of what is deepest and strongest and richest within each of us, being shared: the passions of love in its deepest meanings."[2] For Lorde, the experience of such passion—listening to music, dancing, building a bookcase, writing a poem, examining an idea—is not only a source for power and energy but is also rooted in what she calls "nonrational knowledge." Indeed, for Lorde it is these sorts of experiences of feeling—of "creative energy empowered"[3]—that constitute the possibility for measuring the value of other experiences, the possibility of standards: "Once we know the extent to which we are capable of feeling that sense of satisfaction and completion, we can then observe which of our various life endeavors bring us closest to that fullness."[4]

Similarly, Dorothy Allison writes that "it is frustrating to me that so many people divide the erotic and the everyday into such stubbornly separated categories."[5] For Allison, as for Lorde, the experience of desire and its realization is a source for a kind of knowledge, constituting the possibility of seeing some things differently, of *naming,* of assessing: "The experience of having our love or desire for women twisted, misused or totally denied seemed to me central and basic to feminism in the same way that our politics itself was supposed to rest in the actual lived experience of women who must name for themselves their needs, hopes and desires."[6] Allison explains the erotic significance for some of science fiction in terms of its capacity to make alternative moral assessments imaginable: "It could be different. You might be able to have sex with plants or intelligent waterfalls or friendly machines—or women—and not have it be a social or moral catastrophe. Once out, that's a secret that could change everything, and has."[7]

Some have worried about the significance of personal relations, including the experience of feelings and emotions, in feminist theory. In an important summary of developments in contemporary ethics, Stephen Darwall, Allan Gibbard, and Peter Railton characterize feminist ethics as maintaining "'fidelity to existing conceptions in all their particularity,'" a commitment they take to consist in emphasizing particular relations *rather than* general ethical principles.[8] For they point out in criticism that it is as a result of appeal to general ethical principles that much moral progress has been made.

Feminists have also criticized other feminists for emphasizing personal relations, especially sexual ones. In "Women's Equality and National Liberation," Angela Gilliam argues that Western feminist concerns about sexual identity, for instance, are narcissistic.[9] Gilliam argues that Western feminists' sexual politics "concentrates on the *individual.* [It] pulls away from the *collective* or shared concerns." In her view, "Sexualism is becoming the new elitism . . . since most of the world's working women—including many poor women of the United States—identify survival issues to be food, housing, health care and employment, not sexuality."[10]

How are we to understand the insights to be drawn for moral and political philosophy in general from recent emphases on personal relations and commitments? To try to situate remarks such as those by Lorde and Allison in relation to analytic philosophical traditions, I consider a recent philosophical account of the moral significance of personal relations and the extent to which such an account can accommodate the kinds of personal experiences suggested by my previous remarks. I suggest that such remarks are neither perniciously particularistic nor narcissistic; rather, they provide, or at least can provide, resources for identifying and understanding subtle and sometimes the most damaging forms of injustice and oppression.

Miller's Account of Partiality

What explains the moral significance of personal commitments and attachments, including feelings and emotions? If someone's close friend tells him she is there to support him primarily because it is her duty as a friend to do so, that person might feel disappointed.[11] He might prefer to think his friend was there because of particular feelings for him as an individual. Or if someone decides not to spend money to visit a friend in trouble because the money would bring about more happiness overall if it were donated to charity, many would think such moral reasoning inadequate. Of course, in many cases it would be morally inappropriate to place concern for one's particular relations over general considerations of duty or consequences.

Richard Miller offers an account of the moral significance of particular relations and commitments that provides a rich example of the kind of philosophical story one might tell in discriminating between those cases in which personal relations and commitments are morally significant and those in which they are not.[12] Regardless of whether Miller's concerns about particular personal relations are the same as those of feminist ethics, his account could well be one those working in feminist ethics could find appealing. Like many feminist ethicists, Miller rejects what he calls the "legislative" or impartialist approach to ethics, according to which ethical conflicts are resolved by general rules defined in some sense a priori.

In Miller's view, an impartialist ethical approach is a type of deliberation in which one's evaluative principles do not by themselves entail that any preference for one's own relationships and projects over the interests of strangers is morally permissible (p. 330). Of course, impartial moral theories can allow for the moral significance of partiality. An impartialist consequentialist theory could say, for instance, that particular relations, feelings, emotions, or whatever are morally significant to the extent that they contribute to some overall good. The significant feature of impartialist views, or of what Miller calls the "legislative approach to morality" (p. 365), is that on such views, ultimate ethical validation is determined by a standpoint everyone ought to adopt.

Miller's alternative to the legislative approach is what he calls a "person-centered" view. He proposes that moral wrongness is not determined by a detached, impartial perspective; rather, it is determined by choices in which morally responsible people respond to the totality of their concerns, concerns involving a variety of concrete norms of character. In Miller's view, "An act is morally wrong just in case it is disallowed under the circumstances by any system of rules for the regulation of one's conduct that no morally responsible person could refuse to impose on herself if she rationally responded to all relevant information but put coercion to one side" (p. 366). In short, an act is wrong if it is not one a similarly situated, similarly morally responsible agent would choose if uncoerced and fully informed (p. 312).

Consider E. M. Forster's claim that if he had to choose between betraying a close friend and betraying his country, he hoped he would choose the latter. Assuming, as Miller urges us to do, that what Forster has in mind are the moral perils of close friendship, Miller considers a case in which George decides to keep silent in light of evidence that his close friend Jim has been spying for the Soviets (sometime in the past). Were it certain that people would die on account of his silence, George would tell. But, of course, no such certainties are available. George's actual assessment of risks and moral responsibilities leads him to think it morally wrong not to report what he has found. Still, he almost certainly wonders whether he should keep his friend's secret nonetheless (p. 310).

Miller suggests it might be rational for George to betray his country for his friend if his commitment to his friend is sufficiently strong: In some cases it is rational for a person to depart from general moral principles because of particular competing attachments. Miller suggests that we can account for the reasonableness of George's choice *not* to tell his secret according to the following three criteria. First, the judgment is universalizable: If the act is not wrong, it would not be wrong for anyone with relevantly similar characteristics in a relevantly similar situation. Second, the universalized judgment must be judged in light of relevant considerations, as a morally insightful person could assess them. A third test permission to go against morality must pass concerns the relation among one's actions, one's assessment of them, and one's assessment of oneself. When a choice would not be wrong and the chooser knows this, self-reproach, once the choice has been made, would not be rational—although it may be unavoidable. In general, Miller suggests that "the proposal that George would not be wrong to do what is morally wrong is, at a minimum, a proposal that features of his situation justify a choice ruled out by moral reasons, so that George and any similarly insightful, similarly situated chooser can rationally avoid self-reproach" (p. 312).

Miller takes his account to preserve "the supreme authority of morality," to express what most find appealing in legislative approaches—namely, that such approaches provide objective constraints on morality: They do not define morality entirely in terms of what people feel is right. George's choice is not morally permissible *just* because George feels a strong attachment to Jim; rather, it is morally permissible because George can claim that any similarly situated, morally responsible person could make the same choice. Whereas Miller's account may sound like a version of contractualism, it differs from contractualism insofar as it appeals not to standards everyone in a given community would accept but rather to standards a certain kind of person within the community would accept, namely, those who are capable of the right sort of self-regulation. The community of people to which one appeals to determine what is and what is not morally reasonable is a community of people who are able to respond to situations and relations in a morally responsible way. The hypothetical community of "relevant self-regulators" would be defined in terms of concrete norms of character such as noncapriciousness, freedom from arrogance and hypocrisy, capacity for self-criticism, and so on (pp. 368–374).

Miller claims that his account reflects the deliberations of morally serious people, that in cases of conflict between personal commitments and moral obligations, morally responsible people ask themselves what similarly situated, morally insightful people might be able to do without having reason to feel remorse. He is careful to say not that it is morally right to act wrongfully because of strong personal commitments but rather that it is sometimes not unreasonable to act wrongfully according to one's usual moral commitments. His account has the virtue of recognizing that personal attachments and projects, insofar as they constitute someone's individuality, must be part of the ultimate standard one employs to validate moral choices (p. 366). Thus, Miller recognizes that moral choice is not impartial and that the moral point of view is not adequately expressed in general principles, but he also argues that partial concerns do not have moral weight just because their satisfaction helps to achieve a further goal.

Problems

Now, let us see what Miller's account could say of a different sort of example, one taken from Toni Morrison's novel *Jazz*:

> I know my mother stole that ring. She said her boss lady gave it to her, but I remember it in Tiffany's that day. A silver ring with a smooth black stone called opal. The salesgirl went to get the package my mother came to pick up. She showed the girl the note from her boss lady so they would give it to her (and even showed it at the door so they would let her in). While the salesgirl was gone, we looked at the velvet tray of rings. Picked some up and tried to try them on, but a man in a beautiful suit came over and shook his head. Very slightly. "I'm waiting for a package for Mrs. Nicolson," my mother said.

The man smiled then and said, "Of course. It's just policy. We have to be careful." When we left my mother said, "Of what? What does he have to be careful about? They put out the tray so people can look at things, don't they? So what does he have to be careful about?"

She frowned and fussed and we waited a long time for a taxi to take us home and she dared my father to say something about it. The next morning, they packed and got ready to take the train back to Tuxedo Junction. She called me over and gave me the ring that she said her boss lady had given her. Maybe they made lots of them but I know my mother took it from the velvet tray. Out of spite I guess but she gave it to me and I love it, and only lent it to Dorcas because she begged so hard and the silver of it did match the bracelets at her elbow.[13]

Now, this is an example of someone choosing to act contrary to her usual moral commitments because of a personal commitment, a personal commitment to her own sense of self-worth and personal dignity. The man's assumption that she is going to steal, when she not only has no intention of stealing but is committed to honesty, is degrading. She steals in defiance of his judgment about her moral status and in defiance as well of the moral system that rationalizes his judgment.

Can such a choice be shown to be not unreasonable on Miller's account? We may not want to say the choice to steal the ring is morally right, but surely as readers we do not think the mother unreasonable either. As readers of the novel, it is hard to see the choice as crazy, and it is also hard to see the choice as simply a choice motivated by a strong desire to accomplish an end—namely, the possession of the ring. Indeed, it is not even clear that the mother strongly desires the ring.

Can we tell a Miller-type story to account for the nonunreasonableness of the mother's act? We can understand the narrator's mother as appealing to a community of morally responsible people if we imagine that any similarly insightful, similarly situated, morally responsible person would understand the threat to her humanity that is embodied in the system of behaviors and ways of thinking of which the store manager's "very slightly" shaking his head is an instance. The mother's lack of feeling of remorse might be accounted for by the fact that similarly situated, relevantly self-regulating, morally responsible people would understand that general concepts and principles of morality are often not as general as they appear but rather are expressions of the dominant interests of arbitrarily privileged groups. People like the store manager, who might be *considered* morally responsible, would not, of course, see things this way. But then, the store manager's perceptions would be irrelevant according to Miller's criteria. For the store manager's views are the result of racist ignorance, and Miller says people whose views are the result of ignorance are not people whose moral values are of the right sort to be appealed to in such deliberations.

The community of relevantly self-regulating, morally responsible agents in this case, of course, would be rather small. Whereas it is possible to argue that the choice is reasonable or at least that it is not crazy, such a choice would not generally be regarded as reasonable, perhaps even by members of the woman's own community. For instance, one could think the mother could get into trouble, that her stealing will reinforce racist stereotypes, that the act does not accomplish anything, and so on. Described from a number of perspectives, the act could be understood as criminal, as crazy. Nonetheless, it is possible that there *are* "person-centred" standards of Miller's sort according to which the mother's choice can be understood as reasonable, even though, at the same time, as wrong.

Consider a second example. Dick Gregory, in his autobiography, *Nigger*, recounts how, as the eldest child of a large, poor family, he had to do the grocery shopping at the corner store.[14] Since the family was very poor, most of the shopping was done on credit. The store owner, benevolently, always gave Gregory free food, but he always gave him stale or bad food—three-day-old bread, rotten peaches, and so on. Gregory resented this. And he resented it when his mother said of the old bread, "Oh that Mister Ben, he knew I was fixin' to make toast." Once, three days in a row, Gregory asked the store owner for a piece of penny candy in the store window. The store owner shooed him off, saying he would tell his mother he was begging. Gregory describes how on the night of the third rejection he threw a brick through the store window and stole the piece of candy.

Dick Gregory's act is not obviously unreasonable, even though wrong. The choice will strike many as reasonable, or at least as not being crazy, because it is understood as a choice to resist a certain kind of dehumanizing treatment, as an attempt to claim—even just for himself—some kind of human status. It looks like an example of the sort of moral conflict Miller is interested in—one in which a strong personal commitment, in this case a commitment to oneself, provides reason to go against general moral principles. Indeed, if the young Dick had not been committed to morality and if he had not possessed a strong sense of self-respect, the act would not have been particularly interesting. The choice is interesting because we know Gregory is sincere about morality, that he cares enormously about how he is perceived by others and about how he is able to perceive himself. As in Morrison's story, the choice is not easily understood as simply one in which the desire to attain an immediate goal overrides someone's usual moral commitment.

Again, this example can be shown to fit Miller's account. Certainly, it is one that demonstrates the inadequacies of impartialist views. If we were to try to apply some impartialist standards—consequentialist, perhaps—to Dick Gregory's choice, we might fail to identify the personal significance of the choice. We would be led to assess the significance of the act in relationship to various sorts of possible results. But the results of the act in this case are not as interesting as the meaning of the act in terms of Dick Gregory's personal projects and commitments. For one thing, when considered in terms of Gregory's personal projects and commitments, the choice *becomes* a choice expressing self-respect, whereas it might not be so easily understood this way from a more general perspective. Miller is concerned to accommodate the moral significance of personal projects and commitments, the fact that these constitute a person's individuality and must figure into evaluations of moral appropriateness. And his analysis of choices and acts in terms of life processes, it would seem, aims to allow for the attribution of moral meaningfulness to choices that might not otherwise have been considered morally meaningful. Considered not as an isolated act directed at a particular goal but as a choice with a role in a process of development, of what Miller calls "self-regulation," Dick Gregory's choice can be shown to be one expressing self-respect and hence to be noncrazy. And the kind of process of justification Dick Gregory might go through in his mind, if he were to try to articulate a justification for his choice, might be something like what Miller describes. He might argue that any similarly situated, similarly morally insightful, morally responsible person would have done the same thing or at least could have done the same thing without remorse.

But there is a problem. The moral community to which the mother in *Jazz* and Dick Gregory might appeal is not just small. It is one that becomes imaginable largely because of the narrative skills of people like Morrison and Gregory. Many people, including members of oppressed groups, might not find such choices reasonable if confronted by them in their own neighborhoods. For they might not see such choices as ones expressing self-respect. The norms and values according to which it becomes possible to understand such choices as reasonable are made plausible by skillful storytelling—storytelling, importantly, that goes against the grain of dominant social norms and values. In other words, the choices are able to be understood as reasonable because they are choices that are described in a certain way. And it is not clear that they would or could be described that way by most members of the society in which they take place, even those who share the chooser's background.

It is true that there could be a community of morally responsible people to which one could appeal to demonstrate the meaningfulness in terms of self-respect of acts like that of the mother in *Jazz*, acts that might otherwise be classified as crazy. But it is not clear that there actually *is* that community. And even if there is, there could well not be. If readers find the mother's choice to steal the ring reasonable, it seems unlikely that they do so because of considerations of what members of an appropriately defined community of morally responsible choosers could choose while rationally avoiding self-reproach. For readers can find the choice reasonable while not possessing the capacity to envisage or even identify such a community. Instead, it seems more likely that readers sympathize with the choice, if they do, because they know what it is like to experience condescension. And Morrison's storytelling permits the reader to experience this particular incident as an instance of this sort—as degrading condescension. Unless a story is told according to which the incident *can* be seen as an instance of condescension and as a *serious* offense rather than as a small thing the mother should have dismissed, it is hard to see how the mother can be understood to possess reasons. And to the extent that the description Morrison provides—the description according to which the mother does possess reasons—goes against at least some grains, it is not clear that the moral community that justifies a judgment of reasonableness in this case is or needs to be one that exists.

But if the relevantly defined moral community does not exist, what would justify an appeal to it? If the reasonableness of the mother's choice depends on an appeal to norms and values that could be, but are not, accepted by those currently considered morally responsible, especially if those norms and values contradict norms and values of the current society, what makes this a moral community?

Miller offers criteria for determining who the morally responsible members of a community are. But depending on who applies them, they could give quite different results. From the perspective of the mother in *Jazz*, the store manager should be discounted because his moral views stem from (racist) ignorance. But so do the views of most members of a racist society. And what about the store owner in Dick Gregory's case? His benevolence can also be said to be explained by racist ignorance. But such benevolence is morally respected in the society at large.

Miller claims his view presupposes that people have reason to care about avoiding harm to others, and to be seen to be avoiding harm to others, because they have reason to care about the "protection of one's self" (p. 315). But this is only true for some members of a society. On the contrary, for some people, to be and to be seen to be conforming to what is considered reasonable human behavior *is* precisely to accept the denial of their sense of self. This would have been true in Sethe's case. Miller thinks people care about avoiding wrongdoing because "covert doing, if intentional, will almost certainly have a great cost to a rational product of this social world" (p. 315). He seems to overlook the fact, though, that some people need to try, above all, to avoid becoming "rational products of this social world" to begin to have a self at all.

Consider again the passage from Patricia Williams cited in Chapter 4:

My parents were always telling me to look up at the world; to look straight at people, particularly white people; not to let them stare me down; to hold my

ground; to insist on the right to my presence no matter what. They told me
that in this culture you have to look people in the eye because that's how you
tell them you're their equal. My friend's story also reminded me how very difficult I had found that looking back to be. What was hardest was not just that
white people saw me, as my friend's client put it, but that they looked through
me, as if I were transparent.

By itself, seeing into me would be to see my substance, my anger, my vulner-
ability and my raging despair—and that alone is hard enough to show. But to
uncover it and have it devalued by ignore—ance, to hold it up bravely in the
organ of my eyes and have it greeted by an impassive stare that passes right
through all that which is me, an impassive stare that moves on and attaches itself to my left earlobe or to the dust caught in the rusty vertical geysers of my
wiry hair or to the breadth of my freckled brown nose—this is deeply humiliating. It rewounds, relives the early childhood anguish of uncensored seeing,
the fullness of vision that is the permanent turning-away point for most blacks.

The cold game of equality staring makes me feel like a thin sheet of glass:
white people see all the worlds beyond me but not me. They come trotting at
me with force and speed; they do not see me. I could force my presence, the
real me contained in those eyes, upon them, but I would be smashed in the
process. If I deflect, if I move out of the way, they will never know I existed.[15]

Certainly it is true, as Miller suggests, that everyone wants and needs to be
respected by other people. But in some sorts of social relations, and in the
face of the ideological forces that sustain them, genuine self-respect is not a
viable possibility for some people within the system as it exists. If this is the
case, then it is at best insufficient but perhaps seriously distorting to define
moral reasonableness primarily in terms of what similarly situated, similarly insightful, morally responsible reasoners would do, at least in the first
instance. Something needs to be said about how the *relevant* respects of
similarity are defined, in particular about the kind of society that determines what "morally responsible" means.

In ignoring the possibility that something needs to be said about what
moral view determines what *sort* of society should be assumed in defining
who the relevantly self-regulating agents are, Miller can be understood as
taking the "morally responsible" to be those who are morally responsible
by current standards. In assuming, for instance, that "for most of us, undetectable stealing from strangers would not be a reasonable choice" and that
"possessions gained by wrongdoing would not be worth the reduction of
the security in one's self on which one's enjoyment of possessions depends"
(p. 316), he suggests that by "most of us" he means people for whom "security in one's self" is guaranteed by conformity to current social and moral
standards. In Morrison's story, undetectable stealing is reasonable: It is reasonable, in the first place, because the very imaginability of a world in
which African Americans can be respected as human beings depends heavily on the rejection—indeed, sometimes the militant opposition to—a sys-

tem the standards of which presume that such a possibility is crazy. And it is reasonable, in the second place, because such a possibility is *not* crazy. For people for whom security in oneself is not a possibility within current relations, at least not if we understand "self" normatively, enjoyment of possessions may depend precisely on disrupting the security of self offered by conformity to accepted conventions, including, sometimes, moral conventions.

The reasonableness of the choices discussed here, if they are reasonable, suggests that Miller's account may be getting things backward. We understand the reasonableness of such choices only if we understand them as choices of a certain sort, as, for instance, choices having to do with the pursuit of self-respect. But often we can only understand such choices as having to do with something like self-respect if we understand something about the real nature of the society in which the choices are made—for instance, that it is such that the pursuit of (real) self-respect is precluded by dominant standards of both reasonableness and morality.

This sort of understanding, at least in the more interesting examples, requires storytelling—that is, it requires a conscious effort to discover the sorts of conceptual resources that can allow particular events and relations to be understood in a certain way. If this is so, the reasonableness of the narrator's mother's choice is not explained *in the first instance* by general standards of reasonableness since the appropriate sorts of standards of reasonableness may not be available; rather, it is explained by judgments about what the personal experience is, about how it should be described. That is, it is explained by experience of particular events and relations *as* events and relations of a certain sort and the development, in theory and practice, of the conceptual framework in terms of which such events and relations can be understood as such. This suggests that it is not judgments about reasonableness that make sense of the moral significance of personal relations and commitments; rather, it is the experience of certain personal relations and commitments as morally significant in a relevant sense that helps explain in general the possibility of more adequate conceptions of reasonableness.

Particularism in Feminist Discussions

I would like to look now at the sense in which personal relations and commitments have been significant in feminist discussions, or at least how they might be significant if more fully explicated. The issue in the most interesting examples of such significance is not about *conflict* between personal commitments and general moral commitments, as is the concern of Miller's account; rather, it often turns out that personal commitments are *all* there is. Particularly in situations in which it is difficult to know how to talk about justice, when there are relations that *cannot* be talked about in terms of justice because they cannot be talked about at all, personal relations are significant in a way not capable of being addressed in the kind of analysis Miller offers.

Consider Mab Segrest's account of how she came to understand, in part, the racism of her grandmother's benevolence toward blacks in the southern United States:

> What am I to do with the knowledge that now jumps at me from her Bible: she did not see the terrible irony in her words, "the dear and faithful dead who make Heaven a home for us"; she expected Carrie to be her maid in Heaven too. In my grandmother's imagination, could this "beloved" friend never be free?
>
> It scares me to death to realize this whole level of reality to which my grandmother was oblivious. Taking this new look at her is hard. I don't think she would like me for what I am seeing. But I feel, whether accurately or not, that in knowing myself I knew things about her she was never conscious of, and in dealing with her I come back around to myself. . . . I have to ask, what accounts for her—for my, for our—failure of love, of moral imagination?[16]

Segrest's understanding, like her grandmother's failure to understand, is explained in terms of moral imagination. And the explanation for Segrest's imagination lies in a personal experience, one I made reference to in Chapter 5:

> As racial conflict increased in Alabama in the 1960s, I also knew deep inside me that what I heard people saying about Black people had somehow to do with me. This knowledge crystallizes around one image: I am thirteen, lying beneath some bushes across from the public high school that was to have been integrated that morning. It is ringed with two hundred Alabama Highway Patrol troopers at two yard intervals, their hips slung with pistols. Inside that terrible circle are twelve Black children, the only students allowed in. There is a stir in the crowd as two of the children walk across the breezeway where I usually play. I have a tremendous flash of empathy, of identification, with their vulnerability and their aloneness within that circle of force. Their separation is mine. And I know from now on that everything people have told me is "right" has to be reexamined. I am on my own.[17]

As with the story in *Jazz*, Segrest's choice here is not best explained as an appeal to standards of reasonableness. For one thing, it is not clear that she has available to her the kinds of standards of reasonableness that could give her experience the significance it has as regards her moral beliefs. Certainly, she could have given some significance to her experience from within the moral framework available to her. But Segrest takes her experience to provide reason to question that moral framework—*all of it*. She takes the experience to be significant—perhaps as a result of tacit knowledge. She then has to discover the standards and meanings that can accommodate such significance.

It is mistaken to suggest, as Darwall, Gibbard, and Railton do, that feminist emphases on personal relations and commitments are emphases on "existing relations in all their particularity"; instead, such emphases are quite often emphases on relations that, according to the dominant conceptual and moral framework, *do not* exist. The mother in *Jazz*, the young Dick Gregory, and Mab Segrest take as morally significant relations and commitments that are not supposed to exist at all. These people go against the grain not in taking their personal relations and commitments to be morally significant but in possessing such commitments in the first place.

Darwall, Gibbard, and Railton claim that feminist theorists have ignored the fact that generality in ethics has succeeded in eliminating "entrenched particularistic moral conceptions."[18] But the point of the examples given here is that it is often attention to particular relations that explains how entrenched particularisms became identifiable in the first place. Experience of particular relations *as* relations of a certain sort, as possessing a certain kind of significance, explains the development of conceptual resources according to which relevant sorts of particularisms can be identified. For instance, Segrest's experience of relatedness to the black children requires that she question her entire moral framework. She has to do this if she is to preserve the significance of her experience since, according to her general background beliefs, her experience of relatedness is crazy. Thus, it is precisely Segrest's commitment to *preserving* the significance of her experience and the kinds of explanations she must discover *in order to* preserve such significance that explain her eventual understanding of the racism of benevolence. Emphasis on particularism is not necessarily opposed to emphasis on generalizations: Such emphasis is sometimes required for the identification of *false* generalizations.

When Darwall, Gibbard, and Railton credit the generality of ethics with explaining how it is we have come to root out entrenched particularisms—theories and concepts that are understood to be general but that, in fact, represent the experience and interests of only some—they have in mind, presumably, the generality of concepts such as human flourishing, equality, and justice. But the problem is that it is often (unacknowledged) particularistic ethical traditions that *define* general concepts like human flourishing, equality, and justice. Charles Mills, for instance, demonstrates how the fact that the history of philosophy is, as he says, "a bunch of white guys talking to each other" has had implications for the concepts and questions that have been central to ethical and political philosophy.[19] If it is true as Miller, Darwall, Gibbard, and Railton urge, and I believe it is, that we need to appeal to general moral principles and values to root out *arbitrary* particularistic conceptions, then there is also a question about how we discover the right sorts of general moral principles—in particular, about how we come to see as morally significant relations that according to current understanding of the "supreme authority of morality" might not count as relations at all.

Consider Sarah Hoagland's arguments in *Lesbian Ethics*.[20] Hoagland is concerned with the fact that given the extensiveness and the force of misogynist practices and ways of thinking, certain possibilities—such as genuine autonomy—are not even thinkable, let alone realizable, for women whose lives and identities are defined by such practices. She recognizes, as Miller, for instance, does not seem to, that the conceivability of certain relevant possibilities is ruled out from the start by social norms and values that make only some ways of being a person possible. Hoagland argues that lesbian separatist communities provide the possibility for the *bringing about* of more adequate ways of being and acting.

It is true that Hoagland does not adequately explain why not just any kind of personal relations is a candidate for liberatory community. One might worry, for instance, that it would follow from Hoagland's arguments about the importance of bringing communities about to make certain kinds of relations and commitments meaningful that the development of just any kind of community could become justifiable. As I have suggested previously, some relations and commitments sometimes need to be claimed as significant precisely because their significance is denied by a general conceptual framework. Indeed, as was suggested in the remarks of Lorde and Allison at the beginning of this chapter, certain experiences of desire, of passion, of involvement provide *standards* for assessing significance. Lorde even says that such experiences arise out of "nonrational" knowledge or out of chaos. To the extent that not only are general standards inadequate for assessing such experiences but that such experiences are significant in constituting the basis for effective opposition to such standards, one might think any kinds of relations could become justifiable.

But these sorts of worries depend on an assumption I discussed at the end of Chapter 4 and in Chapter 6—namely, that if there are no rational standards defensible a priori, there are no rational standards at all. In the case of Hoagland's argument, the answer to the question, Why lesbian relations? is fairly obvious. Lesbian community is ethically significant because the current society is deeply misogynist. The significance of lesbian relations has to do not primarily with the significance of lesbian relations per se but with a general concern for liberation in relation to which some personal states and relations more than others become morally, politically, and epistemically significant. The reason it does not follow from Hoagland's claims that neo-Nazi communities, for instance, should be permitted to flourish is that neo-Nazis are just wrong in their beliefs about who is being unjustly treated.

Nigerian sociologist Ifi Amadiume, for instance, suggests that lesbian relationships do not have the political significance for Nigerian women that they do for North American women. She argues that the suggestion by American feminist Audre Lorde that West African women's associations are lesbian associations constitutes another example of the imposition of Western prejudices and assumptions on liberatory struggles of women in developing countries.[21] Are we to understand Amadiume's reluctance to acknowledge and embrace lesbian identity, as students of mine once thought, as a kind of failure of political sensitivity?

We can explain the insignificance of lesbian identity for Nigerian feminists, just as we can explain its significance for North American feminists, in terms of facts about the nature of the sociohistorical situation in which political struggle for specific goals occurs. In Nkiru Nzegwu's work on Igbo women's associations, Nzegwu describes the traditional political power base Igbo women have through a variety of women's associations and the weakening of women's political power that has followed the acceptance of certain colonialist conceptions of women's social roles.[22] According to the traditional organizational patterns, Igbo women meet regularly in kinship groups according to lineage and in village-wide meetings, called *mikiri*. Although Igbo women also participate with men in village meetings, the influence and strength they have in society are derived largely from the solidarity expressed in regular meetings and from their capacity to use strikes, boycotts, and force to carry out their decisions.

Thus, Igbo women have power over certain areas of the community life entirely independent of men. If it happens that decisions made at women's gatherings are ignored, Igbo women have a variety of ways of enforcing them, one of which has been the practice of "sitting on a man."[23] To "sit on," or make war on, a man involved gathering at his compound—sometimes late at night—dancing, singing scurrilous songs that detailed the women's grievances against him, banging on his hut with the pestles used for pounding yams, and perhaps demolishing the hut and plastering it with mud and roughing him up a bit. To tackle men as a group, the women used boycotts and strikes. For instance, if after repeated requests to clear the paths they were still uncleared, the women would all refuse to cook for their husbands until the task was carried out. In more serious issues, women could agree to close down the whole market for a matter of weeks. If the *Omu* (the leader) and her councilors made the decision, word would go out in a matter of hours, and the entire market would quickly close down. Indeed, it was as a result of this organized solidarity that Igbo women were able to wage the "Women's War" against British colonialists in 1929. They organized across several provinces to demonstrate at District Offices and eventually forced the British to make at least some reforms in the corrupt Native Administration Centers.

Now, if we consider the situation of Igbo women in light of these considerations, it becomes clear that the insignificance of lesbian relations for Nigerian feminists can be explained other than by the failure of political awareness of compulsory heterosexuality: Whatever emancipation is about or requires for Igbo women, it is not about developing a conception or practice of women-orientedness that could shift the relations of power between men and women. If the question of equality is taken to be the question about the *terms* according to which it would become possible for women to be full persons in a more just society, there is not an obvious political role for the development of lesbian community: The existence of women-oriented social relations and the power such relations bring about are already part of the social fabric. What is primarily striking about the Igbo political system from a Western point of view is that women have power that does not depend on their singular connections to men. One need not interpret the resistance to the notion of lesbian identity as an instance of homophobia or insensitivity if one recognizes that to the extent that the mechanisms of oppressing women are quite different in Igbo society, the relations that need to be developed to further understand and challenge such oppression will also be quite different.

The significance of lesbian relations in Hoagland's work is no expression of concern for "existing relations in all their particularity." On the contrary, it is on the basis of judgments about what the *whole* is morally that some particular relations come to be given priority, practically and theoretically, in the first place. As I argued in Chapter 5, whether there exist good reasons for certain choices and practices depends on how we understand the situation as a whole, on what story is told about the *kind* of society it is in which choices are made and practices undertaken. The fact that the development of lesbian community is politically and morally significant presupposes a certain story about the whole, even though this may not be made explicit; for without this story about the nature of the whole and what is required for certain people to live well within it, there would be no good reason to care about these relations in particular.

Of course, some would worry that this means that any choices or practices could be reasonable as long as we can make up an appropriate story. But, as I pointed out, this sort of worry assumes an endless generation of stories and the absence of any grounds for taking some to be more plausible than others. And, in fact, we do have such grounds. In Hoagland's case, for instance, there is plenty of evidence for the existence of the kinds of unjust structures and practices to which the development of lesbian community might be thought to constitute resistance. Moreover, there are ways to discover whether the development of such communities does, in fact, constitute effective resistance to such structures and practices. As I suggested in Chapters 1 and 6, judgments about the relative merits of theories and practices as regards the pursuit of human flourishing depend on general beliefs about human flourishing, as well as on consideration of the consequences of applying and executing such theories and practices *for* human flourishing. If we reject foundationalist views about knowledge and justification, as we should, the appearance of circularity here is not damaging; rather, it simply expresses the dialectical relationship between the development of theories and concepts and interaction with the physical and social world. What is being suggested by Hoagland's arguments is *that* and *how* personal relations and commitments are sometimes a significant part of such a dialectic.

I am not suggesting that Hoagland herself makes this suggestion. Indeed, I believe she would not do so. My aim here is to try to situate her remarks to show that questions that may be raised by her proposals are not unanswerable regardless of whether she herself would agree with the particular answers I am offering.

Ways of Being

As I argued in Chapters 2 and 3, individual rationality is not best understood as a question about what can be done or chosen but rather as a question about what the individual can be. And emotional experiences—of relation or commitment—are often experiences of ontological significance, of the bringing to be of certain states and conditions. Thus, the moral significance of certain personal relations and commitments is sometimes constitutive of rationality.

Consider again *Thelma and Louise* (Ridley Scott, U.S.A., 1991). Some people find the movie depressing because it might be thought to suggest that women's liberation is hopeless, that the real pursuit of autonomy in the current social and moral order is best expressed in death. Indeed, the story is depressing if one considers it in terms of ends or projects. It is true that Thelma and Louise do not, and indeed we see that they cannot, accomplish their end of being independent women. As Louise suggests, the world is not able to accommodate such a pursuit. But it is hard to see Thelma and Louise themselves as depressing. What is interesting to many about Thelma and Louise is not so much what they do or do not accomplish; rather, it is what they *become*.

We do not have to ascribe any special moral significance to violent behavior to admire what Thelma and Louise become. In a sense, the violence is incidental. It happens that the women's resistance to misogyny has to involve, or at least ends up involving, violence. But we could imagine them being treated as they are and choosing death as the only way to continue their pursuit of autonomy if they had resisted in nonviolent ways. Thelma could have been considered dangerous and crazy without using a gun to tell the state trooper what to do. And the women would have been in trouble because of their treatment of the truck driver even if they hadn't shot his tires out. What is notable is that Thelma and Louise choose to act in ways that go against the grain of sexist social conventions. They are dangerous and crazy not because they use violence but because they assume power and authority in a society defined in terms of their lack of power and authority. What explains the craziness of Thelma and Louise—the fact that they are called and call themselves "crazy"—is that what they become is not understandable according to current standards of what is and is not reasonable. And what makes them dangerous is that their becoming what they do proves the realizability, at least in part, of a possibility that is not supposed to exist.

Morality is not sufficient, at least not in the first instance, as an account of reasonableness in such cases. We might be able to say that considered in terms of a sexist social system that degrades and dehumanizes women—in terms of the degradation and violence Thelma and Louise had experienced themselves—Thelma and Louise's choices were not morally unreasonable. But this is not what is most interesting about Thelma and Louise. What some will ask about Thelma and Louise is not how explainable their actions are in terms of general moral conceptions but rather how explainable *they* are—what standards of reasonableness can account for the noncraziness of desires and interests Thelma and Louise come to possess as individuals, desires and interests that end up being in conflict with general standards of both reasonableness and morality.

On the contrary, consideration of what Thelma and Louise are, or at least of what they become, can imply serious criticism of existing general standards of morality. In light of the two women's fundamental desires and interests, what they do in taking their lives—given their options—is reasonable. But in light of the nature of the existing social order, their fundamental desires and interests are, of course, not reasonable. If we accept and admire what Thelma and Louise *are,* we cannot also accept the reasonableness of current social (moral and nonmoral) standards. As with the previous examples, one either has to deny a particular description of what is, in fact, experienced or perceived by them or raise questions about the general political and moral situation in which that experience comes to acquire the particular significance it does acquire in practical human terms.

Radical Critique and Moral Imagination

We might think the significance of personal relations and feelings is primarily epistemic. Hoagland's arguments are sometimes arguments for the bringing about of relations that make understandable possibilities that would not be understandable otherwise. But the significance of personal relations is also ontological and political and, in fact, is epistemically significant for this reason. Suppose, for instance, we consider personal relations and commitments in terms of the development of Hacking's notion of "human kinds," discussed in Chapter 4.[24] As we have seen, Hacking argues that the development of new ways of classifying people and behavior can transform the way people see themselves, the way people understand the world, and, as well, their possibilities for acting. A category such as "sexual harassment" would be an example. It sorts human behavior and is made relevant by the existence of certain social interests and expectations. The category "sexual harassment" does not bring the practice of sexual harassment into being, but it makes it possible for people to understand human behavior as such and to pursue understanding that could not otherwise have been pursued.

Sexual harassment becomes identifiable as a form of human behavior in part because people look for ways to understand their personal feelings of discomfort and disgust as noncrazy: They construct *personal* stories that can more adequately account for feelings that would, according to a dominant conceptual framework, be meaningless or even crazy. Indeed, Susan Franzosa argues that feminist interest in autobiography is not interest in the possibility of telling the story of a life but is rather about the possibility of telling a particular kind of story about a life, one that makes sense of an identity that might not otherwise make sense.[25] One might say it is not an interest primarily in describing what people are and what they have done; rather, it is in telling stories that make it possible for people to better understand what they are and what they have done and hence to be able to act in a certain direction.

But as we have seen, Hacking thinks human kinds are different from natural kinds in involving a certain impossibility. For instance, Hacking says God could not have made George Washington a pervert. God could have delayed his birth or changed the times, but God could not make this change in George Washington.[26] Hacking notes, and others have noted, that it was not possible to *be* a homosexual before the nineteenth century. Certainly there existed homosexual behavior, but it wasn't possible to choose to be a homosexual: There wasn't that way of being to be chosen.[27] In advance of the coming about of a certain kind of society, one couldn't be understood as a homosexual, be treated as one, and deliberate about one's life as one.

But it is not clear that in advance of the coming about of a concept, there isn't or cannot be an awareness of that to which the concept comes to refer. Arnold Davidson argues that before the second half of the nineteenth century, sexual identity could not be detached from facts about anatomy.[28] Before the development of what he calls a "psychiatric style of reasoning," "anatomical sex exhausted one's sexual identity."[29] Yet this is surely false. It may be true that there existed no concept for what we now think of as gender traits, those psychological, emotional, and intellectual traits associated with possessing a certain kind of genitalia. But people would have understood themselves in such terms. If there had been no gender differences prominently assumed by people in deliberations about themselves and their relations with others, it would have been a remarkable society—a rather sexually liberated one. And it seems clear that it was not. The reason we now distinguish between sex and gender traits is not that there now *exists* a way of identifying oneself sexually that did not exist before but rather that there now exists an interest in *understanding* such identification that did not exist before. As John Boswell argues, the nonexistence of a concept does not indicate the nonexistence of a way of being to be chosen and deliberated about; it simply demonstrates a difference in the ethical and social significance of that way of being.[30]

Of course, Hacking's point is that the concept comes about because of certain interests in understanding. And he acknowledges that *activities* exist before concepts. They just don't exist as ways of being to be chosen. His point is that it would have been impossible to choose to be what was not there to be chosen. It would seem, however, that whereas the concept comes about because of certain interests in understanding, it is not clear that the way of being comes about because of the *same* interest. Hacking's view is that in the case of human kinds as opposed to natural kinds, there is a dynamic relationship between the development of the concept and the development of that to which it refers. So, for instance, the concept "glove" has the meaning it does because gloves were developed in dynamic relationship to the concept.[31]

Yet in some cases, it looks as though it is the *choice* of those ways of being that are not supposed to be there to be chosen that explains the social and political interests that determine the need for the concept. Hacking and Davidson seem to want to deny that the *kind* exists before the concept comes about that allows us to *understand* an activity or a way of being *as* an instance of that kind. Thus, we ought not to apply the term "homosexual" to those who engaged in same-sex activity before the nineteenth century. This means human-kind terms have a different epistemological status than natural-kind terms. For in the case of natural kinds, for instance, if all of the instances of a certain kind disappeared, we would be able to say there *is* something of which there now happen to be no instances. But we cannot say there were no homosexuals before there was that way of being for people to be. The idea is that human kinds are dependent for their existence upon the emergence of certain kinds of societies and interests in a way natural kinds are not.

But as Boswell points out, we need to be able to see the activities and ways of being of people in different sociohistorical circumstances as instances of a same sort if we are to be able to see how they are different and hence to increase our understanding of the socialhistorical contingencies of such categories. And we do identify relevant sociohistorical contingencies. For instance, Boswell points out that there are very few commonalities among the experiences of Catholics in fourth-, fifteenth-, and twentieth-century Italy.[32] But we have to see these as instances of a kind to see that there *are* few commonalities. In identifying differences, we have to see events and phenomena as instances of some (changeable) sort: If we assume that they are different *things* altogether, we have no basis for identifying relevant *sorts* of differences between them. Identification of relevant sorts of differences presumes the possibility of saying that certain behaviors and ways of being are of a same sort, even if they are not understood as such at particular times. Boswell's point seems to suggest that appreciation of the contingency of human behavior and human identity on social and historical factors—an appreciation Hacking and Davidson acknowledge and want to capture—presumes that, with social kinds as with natural kinds, it is sometimes appropriate to say there are *sorts* of things of which there were no existing instances at a certain time and place.

The significance people sometimes give to personal relations and commitments would seem to require that one can sometimes choose what is not there to be chosen in a particular society at a time. That is, one can choose to understand one's actions as ones of a certain sort before there is that sort within the general social understanding. The reasonableness of the narrator's mother's choice in *Jazz* would appear to have to do with the fact that she does, in fact, choose to be what is not there to be chosen: In resisting racist condescension, she *is* choosing to be what is not there to be chosen for her as a black woman—a fully self-respecting human being. Moreover, when we understand her act, we understand it as one of a sort, even though, in important respects, there may not have been that sort available in the public understanding for it to be. We think her choice to act as she does is reasonable not because it is understandable but because it is a choice of a certain *kind,* a choice based on her commitment to self-respect and dignity, even if—in her society or this one—there were not that way of being for her, as a black woman, to choose.

Now, one might say that in the case of the story from *Jazz,* we can explain the reasonableness of the woman's choice because there does exist a category of reasonableness and humanity that applies to black women; it is not the most dominant one, but there does exist such understanding among a struggling minority of the population and in antiracist political theory. In other words, we might think her choice is reasonable because there is a way of being there for her to choose. This is probably true. But it need not be true. Suppose there had not been such struggles. Suppose it really was not possible to choose to *be* a reasonable black person. If someone were to conceive of the possibility, assume it in imagination, and act on it, would it make sense to say that this is not an instance of the sort that would come about at some later, less racist time? To say it is not would appear to be not just an unnecessary multiplication of categories but also an obfuscation of the nature of radical critical thought.

Although Hacking says God could not have made George Washington a pervert in his society as it then existed, suppose God had been able to make it possible for George Washington to *imagine* a system in which he could have been a pervert. Then George Washington would have been able to deliberate about his life as if he *could* have been one. He would have been able to discriminate in his deliberations between right and wrong ways of being a pervert and to figure this information into his practical reasoning. The possibility of such imagining, if it were possible, need not imply that the entity pervert is "out there" waiting to be discovered; rather, what it implies is that there are facts about human behavior, needs, and tendencies according to which being a pervert can be explicated and made understandable. And the same is true of some other social kinds. As I tried to point out in Chapter 6, the idea that there exist real similarities and differences between sorts of humans and human behavior need imply nothing about the existence of fixed sets of identifying properties or even about the existence of deep properties at all. Instead, it implies that nonarbitrary judgments can be made about the application of such general kind terms and even that by looking at differences in its instances we can discover that what we thought was meant by a kind is mistaken.

The reasonableness of what Thelma and Louise *become*, like the reasonableness of what the narrator's mother, Dick Gregory, and Mab Segrest choose, presupposes the possibility not of certain nonmoral ideals of personhood, some abstract conceptions of what individuals ought to be, but rather of discovering relevant respects of similarity and difference—relevant, that is, in terms of the pursuit of human flourishing. It presupposes the possibility of choosing to be a sort of person and of understanding one's life and choices in these terms, even if one's being that sort of person cannot be understood as such. And in important cases, such choices possess ontological significance, significance in terms of the bringing about of the conditions according to which appropriate conceptual representation of such choices can be discovered.

Personal relations and commitments are sometimes significant in explaining the *bringing about* of possibilities that are not imaginable in current terms but that make sense in terms of a more humane social vision. Whatever one thinks about the reasonableness of the narrator's mother's choice, there do seem to exist such sorts of choices, choices that lack any possibility of being shown to be reasonable according to current concepts and practices but that nonetheless strike us as reasonable in some sense. Choices leading to effective social change are often of this sort. If an individual chooses to go against the grain, to defy social conventions as Thelma and Louise do, even if she does so legally she is likely to suffer. Considered in terms of her total system of fundamental desires and interests—including especially interests in material well-being, security, health, and chances for success—it is unreasonable for an individual to choose not to conform. Yet it is sometimes the case that people take it to be more important to bring about certain states—personal or political—to *identify* what is really reasonable than to consider what is reasonable according to current standards—moral or nonmoral—before deciding what to do.

The reason many will worry about the possibility that the narrator's mother's choice could be reasonable in moral terms is that it would then look as though any kind of lawlessness might become morally permissible. The reason such a worry is unfounded is that it is not true that just any kind of lawlessness *is* reasonable in terms of what individuals require, epistemically or politically, to pursue genuine autonomy: Not just any kind of act of defiance does indeed bring about conditions that make possible more effective pursuits of personal integrity and autonomy.

Moreover, to say that some sorts of defiance and immorality are, in fact, morally significant is not to say that the acts themselves are morally significant. Rather, it is to say that pursuing genuine self-respect is morally reasonable. The fact that pursuing self-respect sometimes involves immoral acts implies not endorsement of immoral acts but criticism of the society in which the pursuit of self-respect has sometimes to be of that sort. Thus, to say that Dick Gregory's choice is morally reasonable, if it is, is not to say that it is morally appropriate in general to throw bricks through windows even if one is oppressed. But to deny that his choice *can be* morally reasonable is to beg the question of what defines the standards of reasonableness according to which his action is to be described, interpreted, and assessed to begin with.

As it turns out, moral justifiability possesses explanatory priority in judgments about reasonableness. In this, Miller is right. But he is wrong about how he takes this to be expressed. Miller takes this to be expressed in terms of judgments of moral similarity, where the relevant respects of similarity appear to be defined in terms of social norms. Instead, it looks as though, at least in some cases, moral justifiability depends on moral imagination, where such imagination is contingent upon the developing or at least the valuing of certain sorts of personal relations and commitments. To the extent that personal relations sometimes *explain* the possibility of (a more adequate conception of) reasonableness, it is a mistake to assume that we need to be able to *appeal* to some conception of reasonableness to explain the moral significance of personal relations. What makes some choices reasonable is that they affirm the possibility of pursuing certain states of being, even if what the full realization of such states would mean cannot at the time be entirely clear.

The Erotic Again

So how should we understand the remarks of Lorde and Allison about the erotic? How are we to understand, for instance, Lorde's remark that certain kinds of experiences of passion, of "creative energy empowered," constitute epistemically significant experiences? A few years ago on Whistler Mountain, British Columbia, when I succeeded in connecting a whole series of turns down a steep slope covered with untouched deep new snow, I heard a spectator yell out, "better than sex!" At the time it struck me that that experience *was* better than sex. But is it just a kind of ecstatic experience Lorde and Allison are referring to? It seems not. Lorde describes the erotic as the personification of creative power and harmony.[33] The erotic, she says, is the "assertion of . . . lifeforce" women are reclaiming through art, language, love.[34] It is not, then, just an experience *of* art or love that is erotic but rather such an experience of passion *in relation to* other life possibilities—indeed, an experience that *creates* such possibilities. Skiing on that mountain, like Lorde's building the bookcase, is not erotic, if it is, simply by virtue of being a creative experience. Rather, it is a creative experience that, by virtue of what it does to the person creating, possesses evaluative significance in relation to other events. Lorde's point seems to be that there is something about certain occurrences at particular instances in a person's life that—depending on what one does with them or, more important, what is done *to* someone *by* them—can constitute, as Lorde suggests, the possibility of measuring the value of anything else.

Virginia Woolf talked about "moments of being"—moments in a person's life when, for whatever reason, individuals are able to "stand outside" their lives and identify what is and what is not important.[35] Such moments may come, as in Woolf's own experience, from something as apparently trivial as seeing a flower and understanding it as part of a greater whole.[36] Woolf referred to "moments of being" as moments of recognition and revelation, the value of which is independent of the object or experience that was the catalyst. For her, such experiences were so personal and so intuitive, so apparently lacking in identifiable causes or relevant consequences, that, according to Jeanne Schulkind, "Virginia Woolf herself wrote in describing her 'philosophy' [that] 'it will not bear arguing about; it is irrational.'"[37]

But such occurrences *are* rational, or at least they can be. They are rational by virtue of their ontological significance, their significance in bringing to be certain personal conditions, ones that constitute conditions for action and knowledge. In Chapter 2, in discussing nonpropositional understanding, I mentioned that people sometimes acquire insight as a result of being engaged with, and indeed transformed by, relations with people of different sorts. For instance, people sometimes acquire certain insight—particularly

insight into their own cultural biases—when they adopt and adapt to values and practices culturally different from their own. In a sense, such experiences constitute a "standing outside" of one's own cultural situation and
values. But I also acknowledged that people can very well have all sorts of
experiences of engagement and interaction and acquire no special insight of
this sort at all. For instance, people can travel all over the world listening to
people, looking, taking in information while continuing to interpret everything from the perspective of an initial, fixed set of standards and values.
They will, then, acquire knowledge—propositional knowledge—but not
the kind of knowledge that explains radical criticism, criticism *of* standards
and values. Perhaps what makes some experiences erotic in Lorde's sense is
that some personal experiences—of insight, passion, creation—are, for
whatever reason, experiences of standing outside. Yet it is also true that experiences of feeling love and passion may have no ontological value at all in
a person's life, even though, indeed, they are experienced. One can experience them and then continue on in just the same way as before, epistemically unchanged. Whether such experiences constitute standing outside will
depend on the situation and the role of such experiences in relation to
broader life plans and paths. Contrary to Woolf, there are causes for and
consequences of such special moments of insight—causes and consequences
that constitute rational significance—but she is nonetheless right that such
instances of insight are highly personal and intuitive.

Perhaps an implication to be drawn from Lorde's and Allison's remarks
is that the interesting question as regards human well-being has to do not
with the pursuit of happiness, as often thought, but rather with the experience of ecstacy—*ex-stasia*, or standing outside. To the extent, at least, that
some experiences of ecstasy do have causal consequences, such experiences
can explain and, according to Lorde's and Woolf's account, presuppose the
discoverability of well-being. This would be especially significant, as
Lorde's, Allison's, and Woolf's remarks also suggest, in accounting for the
pursuit of well-being by people who are not typically *expected* to pursue
it.[38]

Conclusion

I have suggested that it is a fundamental misunderstanding of much important feminist work to think of feminist emphases on personal relations as
emphases on "existing conceptions in all their particularity" or to claim, as
some have, that they are narcissistic. Not only are such emphases often not
particularistic and narcissistic, but in many cases they are an attempt to address problems that arise precisely because of the deep-seated narcissism
that characterizes current capitalist societies. Some remarks about lesbian

separatism, for instance, acknowledge that unless there is radical resistance to some deep-rooted assumptions about reasonableness, especially through the bringing about of ways of being, there is little possibility of being anything *but* narcissistic.

To the extent that a general system is recognized as unreasonable, as being characterized by norms and values that are, by many accounts, inhumane, questions about reasonableness *must* also be questions about what it is possible for people to be. The point of this chapter is that to understand personal stories and relations as particularistic because they are not justifiable in terms of current conceptions of moral reasonableness begs questions about what the relevant standards of moral reasonableness are. More important, perhaps, it denies the significance of personal, political, and theoretical developments in terms of which relations and commitments relevant to understanding morality, particularly human flourishing, become identifiable and understandable at all.

8

Philosophy and Literature:
Recalling the Archangel

In *Love's Knowledge,* Martha Nussbaum defends Aristotle's view that it is a mistake to try to understand rationality on a "scientific" model. For Aristotle, in Nussbaum's view "the content of rational choice must be supplied by nothing less messy than experience and stories of experience. Among stories of conduct, the most true and informative are works of literature, biography and history; the more abstract the story gets, the less rational it is to use it as one's only guide."[1] Nussbaum points out that for Aristotle, good deliberation is something like "theatrical or musical improvisation, where what counts is flexibility, responsiveness, and openness to the external" (p. 74). To expect a "scientific" account or something like an algorithm, she suggests, would be a sign of immaturity and weakness.

I consider Nussbaum's remarks on rationality here, first, because her treatment of the role of literature in deliberation does indeed challenge traditional conceptions of rationality. She argues that good literature can constitute a moral achievement: The style and form of writing can bring about possibilities that could not have been imagined otherwise. Second, the answer Nussbaum offers to the question of arbitrariness, or of why some experiences and stories are relevant to considerations of rationality and others are not, employs the Aristotelian and (Henry) Jamesian metaphor of theatrical improvisation to argue that emphasis on experience and stories can be more, not less, rigorous than adherence to general rules and formulae (p. 94).

My main intention in this chapter, though, is to suggest that the role of personal stories in rational deliberation cannot be accounted for without something very *like* the "scientific" account or the "transcendent" position. Nussbaum's reference to R. M. Hare's Archangel-Prole metaphor for moral deliberation suggests an interesting and fundamental problem with her discussion of individual rationality. I argue that whereas Nussbaum's discussion of rational deliberation acknowledges and helps to explicate the moral and epistemic significance of personal relations, she does not take seriously enough the extent to which such significance is often defined in terms of moral systems that themselves preclude the imaginability of the full humanity of some sorts of people.

Aristotle and Rationality

Recent approaches to practical reasoning—particularly, perhaps, the emphasis on game theory—presume that rationality is or ought to be "scientific," that is, that it should be formulatable in terms of general rules or models specifiable in advance. Aristotle thought such a view mistaken. In his view, according to Nussbaum, "discernment" of the right choice rests on "perception," or complex responsiveness to the salient features of one's concrete situation.

Nussbaum identifies three components of Aristotle's attack on "scientific" rationality: (1) his attack on the notion that all valuable things are commensurable, (2) an argument for the priority of particular judgments over universals, (3) a defense of the emotions and the imagination as essential to rational choice (p. 55).

Aristotle's attack on the "science of measurement" rejected the idea that some one value, common to all alternatives, can provide a suitable basis for weighing the chooser's options. In Aristotle's view, it is a mistake to think that choices and actions have value not in themselves but only as instrumental means to the good ends they produce. Instead, he defended "a picture of choice as a quality-based selection among goods that are plural and heterogeneous, each being chosen for its own distinctive value" (pp. 56–57).

But Aristotle's attack on metricity and singleness, of course, invites worries about arbitrariness and indeterminacy (p. 59). Nussbaum responds correctly that the objection about arbitrariness presumes that deliberation must be either quantitative or a mere shot in the dark. Experience, however, shows an alternative: Deliberation is qualitative and is rational *because* it is qualitative, because it is based on a grasp of the special nature of each of the items (p. 61).

The second component of Aristotle's attack on the "scientific" model of rationality, closely related to his attack on commensurability, was his insistence that rational choice cannot be captured in a system of general rules and principles that can then simply be applied to each new case. Instead, he defended the priority of concrete, situational judgments of a more informal, intuitive kind (pp. 66–74). For Aristotle, there could be no definite answers in advance about what constitutes rationality; indeed, according to Nussbaum, Aristotle said it is a mistake to look for a definite answer:

Good deliberation is like theatrical or musical improvisation, where what counts is flexibility, responsiveness, and openness to the external; to rely on an algorithm here is not only insufficient, it is a sign of immaturity and weakness. It is possible to play a jazz solo from a score, making minor alterations for the particular nature of one's instrument. The question is, who would do this, and why? (p. 74)

Nussbaum argues that this rejection of general rules, defined a priori, does not involve arbitrariness. No indeterminacy is necessarily implied by the replacement of general rules, justifiable a priori, by the notion of good improvisation:

The salient difference between acting from a script and improvising is that one has to be not less but far more keenly attentive to what is given by the other actors and by the situation. You cannot get away with doing anything by rote; you must be actively aware and responsive at every moment, ready for surprises so as not to let the others down. An improvising actress, if she is improvising well, does not feel that she can say just anything at all. She must suit her choice to the evolving story, which has its own form and continuity. Above all, she must preserve the commitments of her character to the other characters (of herself as actress to the other actors). More not less attentive fidelity is required. (p. 94)

In other words, to say that contingent relations are more important than general rules in rational deliberation does not imply that just any relations can define rational deliberation. The deliberator, according to Nussbaum, "does not feel that she can say just anything at all. She must suit her choice to the evolving story, which has its own form and continuity." Elsewhere Nussbaum quotes Henry James who says stories are like plants, causing an idea "to flower before me ... " (p. 4). Thus, like metaphors, stories are constrained by the conditions under which a process of development or investigation is taking place. Background conditions and beliefs, as well as the intentions and aspirations of people involved in the process, make it the case that not just any story could cause ideas "to flower before me."

And of course, it needn't be the case that a story causes ideas to flower in anyone and everyone. Just as metaphors work to make connections only if one is familiar with the tradition within which such metaphors are introduced, stories will cause ideas to flower only in those who are relevantly involved with the "evolving story." The fact that the improvising actress must be responsive to contingent conditions does not mean she must conform to whatever it is the other members of the group think she should do. Often, it is assumed that if rationality is not defined in terms of general rules and formulae, it will just be a matter of conforming to the norms and values of the group. Yet the claim is that the improvising actress must "preserve the commitments of her character to the other characters," not just *any* characters but those characters, presumably, who also hold commitments to the "evolving story." This need not be an appeal to the norms and values of the majority. For not everyone holds commitments to the relevant process of (social, moral, or political) development, the particular evolving story. Indeed, in some cases, there may be few people who hold such commitments. I suggested in Chapter 7 that this would be the case if we tried to account for the rationality of the mother's choice in *Jazz*. In that case, there was a story that was unfolding, one possessing explanatory power and causing "ideas to flower." And it is still a story, even if it might have been heard and understood by very few.

The third component of Aristotle's attack was his defense of the role of emotions and imagination in rationality (pp. 75–82). Nussbaum points out that the idea that rational deliberation might draw on and even be guided by the emotions and imagination might be taken by some to be a conceptual impossibility, the "rational" being defined by opposition to these "irrational" parts of the soul (p. 76). But Aristotle saw rationality as involving the ability to grasp particulars in all of their richness and concreteness. And emotions and imagination are required for such an ability. Imagination, or the capacity to go beyond interpretations and evidence that are readily available, is required to identify a particular *as* something and to link particulars together without disregarding their rich and vivid concreteness. As for emotions, Aristotle did not just think emotions are helpful for rational deliberation, that the appropriate emotional response has *instrumental* value; rather, he thought that if a person fails to respond to a situation with appropriate sympathy or grief, this person doesn't really *see* what is happening. Aristotle thought the emotions are themselves modes of vision or recognition. According to Nussbaum, "Their responses are part of what knowing, that is truly recognizing or acknowledging, *consists in*" (p. 79).

Literature and Moral Imagination

Consider now one example of the relationship between literary stories and rational deliberation—in this case, moral deliberation. Henry James stresses an analogy between the ethical task and the artistic task, one Nussbaum takes seriously: The work of moral imagination is in some manner like the work of the creative imagination, especially that of novelists. She claims novels can be a paradigm for moral activity (p. 148).

In *The Golden Bowl*, Adam must give up his daughter, let her go so she can live with her husband as a real wife.[2] The daughter must also let her father go, knowing that for him life without her will be empty and like death. She is passionately in love with her husband, but she feels pain and guilt at giving up the man who has raised her, protected her, truly loved her.

Nussbaum points out that the general sacrificial idea—that the father will go to America—is not in itself a solution (p. 150): "For it to become a solution it has to be offered in the right way at the right time in the right tone, in such a way that she can take it; offered without pressing any of the hidden springs of guilt and loyalty in her that he knows so clearly how to press; offered so that he gives her up with greatness, with beauty, in a way that she can love and find wonderful" (p. 150).

James resolves the situation by having the father perceive his daughter in a certain way, namely, "as a creature consciously floating and shining in a warm summer sea, some element of dazzling sapphire and silver, a creature cradled upon depths, buoyant among dangers, in which fear or folly or sinking otherwise than in play was impossible" (pp. 150–151). It is this image, according to Nussbaum, that is morally significant. This is not just because of its causal role, its significance in grounding the father's subsequent speeches and acts, but rather because the *picturing* of his daughter in this way—as *beautiful* in freedom, maturity, and sexual playfulness—constitutes "the act of renunciation that moves us to pain and admiration" (p. 151). There could have been other pictures, perhaps involving conflict or a desire to swim alongside her, that would have had different consequences for his actions. This particular picture—representing, as it does, her freedom and maturity as artful, as beautiful—is the achievement of a certain kind of valuing, of interpretation, something that is itself a moral achievement.

It is significant that the image moves us, that it moves the father. It is not flat but is a work of art with detail, tone, and color. And to the extent that it moves us it is action guiding, as moral valuing characteristically is. Nussbaum emphasizes that what is achieved through the picturing of the daughter as a sea creature could not be paraphrased, reduced to a set of propositions. It has to be presented, and it has to be presented properly. Otherwise, it would not possess the action-guiding role it does. According to James, Nussbaum says, "moral knowledge . . . is not simply intellectual grasp of propositions; it is not even simply intellectual grasp of particular facts; it is perception. It is seeing a complex, concrete reality in a highly lucid and richly responsive way; it is taking in what is there, with imagination and feeling" (p. 152).

Nussbaum's discussion of the role of literature in deliberation is significant in several ways. First, her suggestion about the priority of the perception of particular persons and situations acknowledges the moral significance of personal change. In *The Golden Bowl,* the image of the sea creature, and the father's grasp of its intrinsic beauty, constitutes the creation of the possibility for the father's appreciation of his daughter's maturity. Grasping the *beauty* of the image itself makes such a judgment possible in a way that grasping a set of propositions could not. For the recognition of beauty by the father constitutes a change to the father, one that allows him to interpret differently the propositional information available to him. Nussbaum's remarks acknowledge that interpersonal relations and personal commitments ought to be thought of as being, in part, *constitutive* of rational standards rather than requiring a justification in terms of standards that are somehow independently justified.

Now, it is true that in Nussbaum's account, moral significance is defined in terms of responsiveness to what she calls an "evolving story." But this is a different kind of answer to the question of arbitrariness than one that attempts to specify a model for rationality itself, to indicate in advance what sorts of considerations define rationality. On Aristotle's metaphor of the Lesbian Ruler, no real architect would use a straight ruler for curved columns; instead, following the lead of the builders of Lesbos, the architect would measure with a flexible strip of metal, the Lesbian Rule, that, as Aristotle said, "bends to the shape of the stone and is not fixed" (p. 70). The idea is that the *standards* for defining rationality, the ruler itself, must be flexible. And Nussbaum's metaphor of theatrical improvisation tells us something about the nature of this flexibility, that it is contingent upon complex aspects of both a past and a future evolving story.

Thus for Nussbaum, morality does indeed possess explanatory priority: What is morally significant explains, at least in part, what is individually rational. But the morally significant is itself, at least occasionally, the experience of emotions and feelings, the telling of personal stories: It is not emotions and feelings that need to be explained in terms of the morally significant, as if the morally significant were always something other than personal relations and commitments; rather, it is sometimes emotions and feelings themselves that explain the development of the "external" criteria, the relevant evolving story. In Nussbaum's view, that act of deliberation is "an adventure of the personality as a whole" (p. 88). The struggle to picture events and relations in a certain way is itself a moral activity (p. 88).

Objectivity is not lost. Nussbaum talks about a kind of "internal" objectivity (p. 164), one she says is human and does not attempt to approach the world as it is in itself. Whatever else this means, and the notion of objectivity here is somewhat vague, she seems to be suggesting that objective criteria are relative to facts about human possibilities and capacities, including capacities for feeling and imagination. When Nussbaum says the improvising actress "must at every moment—far more than one who goes by an external script—be responsively alive and committed to the other actors, to the evolving narrative, to the laws and constraints of the genre and its history" (p. 155), she adds that an important part of the commitment is to direction of thought and imagination (p. 167). That is, the process of development that both constitutes and constrains the evolving story is also a process of cognitive development. Whereas for Miller the moral constraints on rationality are largely social, Nussbaum is concerned to emphasize the dependency of moral standards on *possibilities* for development, including emotional and imaginative development, where the right sort of development would be defined by the constraints of continuing the developmental process itself.

A second point of significance in Nussbaum's treatment of the question of arbitrariness is her use of the notion of nonpropositional knowledge. Nussbaum identifies the experience of literature, or even just the experience of beauty, as, at least in some cases, the acquiring of a kind of nonpropositional understanding. The moral force of the image of the sea creature cannot be conveyed in propositions because that force *is,* in important part, its constitution as a work of art, its capacity to move, to elicit responses (p. 162). The father's imagining his daughter as a sea creature, playing about, *is* an acquiring of understanding, understanding that goes beyond what he could have acquired through intellectual acceptance of the fact of her maturity and sexuality: "If he had grasped the same general facts without these responses and these images, in all their specificity, he would not really have known her" (p. 152).

The Archangel and the Prole

In *Moral Thinking,* Hare introduces the image of the Archangel and the Prole.[3] The Archangel is one who uses *only* critical thinking, whereas the Prole uses *only* intuition. We are to consider the Archangel a being with "superhuman powers of thought, superhuman knowledge and no human weaknesses."[4] This "ideal observer," when faced with a new situation, "will be able at once to scan all its properties, including the consequences of alternative actions, and frame a universal principle . . . which he can accept for action in that situation, no matter what role he himself were to occupy in it."[5] The Archangel excludes such human "weaknesses" as partiality to self or partiality to one's own friends and relations from critical thinking. Since the Archangel would be able to scan the situation from a distance, he would not need to rely on sound general principles, good dispositions, or the intuitions that guide the rest of us.[6]

The Prole, on the other hand (after George Orwell's *1984*), is incapable of the kind of critical thinking typical of the Archangel. The Prole possesses all of the human weaknesses and relies on prima facie principles, dispositions, and intuitions. Not possessing the clarity and distance the Archangel is capable of, the Prole sees moral dilemmas as real and indissoluble. Hare's intention here is not to say that when it comes to moral deliberation, human beings fall into one or the other group. He acknowledges that all people share the characteristics of both to different degrees and at different times. His concern is to examine the relationship between these two levels of moral deliberation and to determine the priority of one over the other. His conclusion is that the Archangel's superior clarity and simplicity, his ability to rise above human problems, is preferable to the Prole's rootedness in human relations.

In Nussbaum's view, however,

> We want more Proles and fewer Archangels, not only in daily choice, but as leaders and models. Angels, Thomas Aquinas held, cannot perceive what is there for perceiving in the world of contingency. And thus they are, as Aquinas concluded, poor guides indeed for getting around in this world, however well off they may be in heaven. It is, said Aristotle, the human good that we are seeking, and not the good of some other being. (p. 66)

Nussbaum is right to suggest that morality is better thought of as concern for the contingencies of an evolving story—at least better thought of this way than as an "ideal perspective," defined somehow in terms of general rules justifiable a priori. For it seems true, as Aristotle argued, that rationality is much too messy, much too dependent upon particular perceptions and stories, to be defined by a unique set of standards. If the Archangel represents the notion of a single standard of value to be simply applied to each new case as opposed to a notion of rationality that acknowledges concrete particularities, then the Prole would appear to be preferable since rationality does seem to involve attention to particularities. But the Archangel's *distance,* the capacity to see the situation as a whole, is often preferable to reliance on human partialities and relations. For if we accept the usefulness of Aristotle's metaphor of theatrical improvisation, with its emphasis on the constraints of an evolving story—if, that is, we accept the idea that *objective* standards can be defined in terms of ongoing relations—we may not want to give up the "transcendence" or removedness that might provide grounds for assessing those relations themselves. Precisely to the extent that rational deliberation does depend on storytelling, that *rational* standards depend on evolving relations, the Archangel may turn out to be important, especially if the notion of rational deliberation is to allow a distinction between the pursuit of real human interests and what people think they should do, often as a result of unfair social pressures.

To put this differently, Nussbaum's defense of Aristotle's conception of rationality is, most interestingly, an argument that the rejection of a "science of measurement," with its emphasis on a priori standards and insistence on the significance of feeling and imagination, does not imply arbitrariness. However, if objectivity is defined by relations, as Nussbaum suggests, there must be some grounds for thinking that not just any set of relations, or any evolving story, is as good as any other. In processes involving *scientific* rationality, for instance, objective standards are defined, in important part, by processes of investigation. Yet it is not just any process of investigation that defines rational standards. For not just any process of investigation is one involving causal interaction with the physical world. Whether scientific standards *are* rational depends on facts about the relationship between an ongoing process of investigation—an evolving story, so to speak—and causal structures of the world. In defining individual rational standards, it would seem, there would appear to have to be some similar kind of explanation for judgments that some processes are better than others. The idea of objective rational standards suggests that there are grounds for saying that what appears to us to be rational, given social norms and standards, is not *really* rational.

Consider the following story. In *Kindred*, Octavia Butler tells the story of Dana, an African-American woman, who is snatched from her home in southern California and transported back in time to the antebellum South.[7] Rufus, the white son of a plantation owner, is drowning, and Dana has been summoned across the years to save him. After the first short summons, Dana returns again and again to the plantation, for increasing lengths of time, to protect Rufus and ensure that he will grow to manhood and father the daughter who will become Dana's ancestor. As Rufus grows older, he becomes more insensitive and cruel. On one of her visits, when Dana finds out that Rufus has sold many of the slaves without regard for family ties, Carrie, the cook, tells her, "He's no good. He's all grown up now and part of the system. He could feel for us a little when his father was running things—when he wasn't entirely free himself. But now he's in charge. And I guess he had to do something right away to prove it."[8]

As Dana spends more time on the plantation, experiencing firsthand the degradation and brutality of slavery, she is shocked to find out how easily she sometimes forgets what it is like to be free and how easily and quickly she forgives Rufus for his senseless, cruel treatment of herself and others. Like the other slaves, she sometimes finds she even likes Rufus. At the slaves' cornhusking party, Rufus provides a little whiskey to help the party along:

> Rufus came out to play hero for providing such a good meal, and the people gave him the praise he wanted. Then they made gross jokes about him behind his back. Strangely they seemed to like him, hold him in contempt and fear him all at the same time. This confused me because I felt just about the same mixture of emotions myself. I had thought my feelings were complicated because he and I had such a strange relationship. But then slavery of any kind fostered strange relationships.[9]

In the end, Dana has to kill Rufus to be free of slavery. But it is hard, surprisingly hard:

> He lay with his head on my shoulder, his left arm around me, his right hand still holding my hand, and slowly, I realized how easy it would be for me to continue to be still and forgive him even this. So easy, in spite of all my talk. But it would be so hard to raise the knife, drive it into the flesh I had saved so many times. So hard to kill. . . .

He was not hurting me, would not hurt me if I remained as I was. He was not his father, old and ugly, brutal and disgusting. He smelled of soap, as though he had bathed recently—for me? The red hair was neatly combed and a little damp. I would never be to him what Tess had been to his father—a thing passed around like the whisky jug at a husking. He wouldn't do that to me or sell me or . . .

No.

I could feel the knife in my hand, still slippery with perspiration. A slave was a slave. Anything could be done to her. And Rufus was Rufus—erratic, alternately generous and vicious. I could accept him as my ancestor, my younger brother, my friend, but not as my master, and not as my lover. He had understood that once.

I twisted sharply, broke away from him. He caught me, trying not to hurt me. I was aware of him trying not to hurt me even as I raised the knife, even as I sank it into his side.[10]

Dana is able to kill Rufus because she knows "a slave is a slave. Anything can be done to her." But how is she able to interpret this information in such a way as to take it to provide reason for killing him? Suppose she did not have access to her twentieth-century perspective, one in which the wrongness of slavery is taken for granted and African Americans, at least in theory, can have the same aspirations as white Americans. She might nevertheless have seen the real injustice of her situation. She might nevertheless, as did Sethe, have chosen to act on her claim to humanity, to resist weighing her options on the standards available to her under slavery, even though doing so might mean death. But she would not have been able to do this without a rather powerful imagination and an enormous amount of personal courage.

In Butler's science fiction novel, an alternative evolving story is available to Dana. Dana has access, through time travel, to her twentieth-century California way of being, a way of being involving its own form and continuity. As a plantation slave, however, without such a context, Dana would have had to invent something like it if she were to deliberate as she does and at great cost. Even with her knowledge of what it is like to be free, Dana has to *struggle* to *remember* what it feels like to be in control of her life. On the plantation, Dana does not accept slavery. She defies the authorities to the extent that she can—for example, by teaching people to read. And by doing so, Dana does choose and act in a way that responds to an alternative evolving story—the evolving story of African-American struggle for emancipation. But even so, Dana sometimes subordinates herself, loses her sense of self, and almost forgets what it is like to be free. Responsiveness to the evolving story—even the evolving moral story of resistance to racist oppression—does not, for Dana at that time in those relationships, include the possibility of possessing real self-respect or human dignity. It cannot, for these are not imaginable in such terms. Only as she lays claim to an alternative way of being, an existence she has, in fact, experienced, is she able to kill to escape from—indeed, even to fully identify—the inhumanity of slavery.

Without the science fiction context, Dana's killing Rufus might appear, from her community's or even her own perspective, to have had no point. She would not have been likely to have achieved freedom in this way. She would have been severely punished, not only losing the privileges she possessed as Rufus's mistress but suffering extreme physical and emotional brutality as well. She could even have lost her life as a result. On one, not too implausible interpretation of her choice, such an action would not advance Dana's interests—her interests in security, physical well-being, and so on. Her choice would have been like Sethe's choice to kill her children or the mother's choice in *Jazz* to steal the ring: We could identify the rationality of her choice by appealing to moral imagination and to facts about the nature of her situation under a systemically racist social arrangement. We can interpret the choice in light of the thoroughgoing wrongness of the system as a whole and in light of the chooser's objective interest in the bringing about of a more humane society. But in terms of the existing system and the limits such a system places on the imaginability of the chooser's real interests in human flourishing, it would be hard to see how such an act can be considered one that best advances the chooser's aims and desires. For it would be easy to say of the mother in *Jazz* or, say, of Dick Gregory that what they do only confirms racist stereotypes and can only worsen their own situation in a racist society. Certainly, we want to attribute rationality to such choices, for such choices *are* rational as acts of resistance to inhumane social structures and behaviors. But for the individual who makes the choice, to whom the conceptual resources required for attribution of rationality may not be immediately available, there is the real risk, at best, of being considered crazy—even by herself—and, at worst, of losing everything that remains to her.

Sethe, for instance, has to struggle to claim the significance of her choice. Paul D. says of Sethe's choice that "more important than what Sethe had done was what she claimed."[11] In Paul D.'s view, Sethe's love is "too thick" for a "used-to-be slave." He points out that her thick love "didn't work": Her boys are gone, one girl is dead and "the other won't leave the yard."[12] But in Sethe's view, her action did work. It worked because her children were not enslaved. Sethe claims the reasonableness of her resistance, of her choice, by claiming the meaningfulness of certain values—such as "thick love"—and the significance of certain ends—such as avoiding slavery. In doing so, she claims an alternative set of values and meanings than that to which Paul D. appeals. But as she says to Paul D., the cost is great: "I took one journey and I paid for the ticket, but let me tell you something Paul D. Garner: It cost too much. Do you hear me? It cost too much."[13]

Identifying the right sort of moral component in questions of individual rational deliberation, at least sometimes, requires distance provided in important part by moral and political theory about the kind of society that exists and about what *ought* to exist instead—indeed, by social and moral vision. Such distance is also provided in another part by powerful moral imagination of, or actual claim to, alternative ways of being of a certain sort, of a genuinely more humane sort. Nussbaum is right to suggest that morality is better thought of as concern for the contingencies of an evolving story—at least better thought of this way than as an "ideal perspective," defined independently of consideration of contingent relations. This seems right as a recognition of the radical contingency of rational standards on particular circumstances and relations. But Aristotle's claim that it is the human good we are seeking and not the good of some other being only provides reason for dispatching the Archangel if we take for granted the notion of "human good"—that is, if we assume that our best theories about the human good are largely adequate. To the extent that the human good, as defined by prominent evolving stories, may *already* be that of "some other being," at least for some people, the Archangel's distance is desirable: If the general notion "human," for instance, does not include certain kinds of people, the rationality of these people's actions *will* require identifying the good of some other being, for they themselves—given existing general conceptions of humans and their goods—*are,* it turns out, other beings. For some people, the rationality of some sorts of choices presupposes the possibility of *discovering* how what is defined as the human good by an evolving story is not, in fact, humanly good.

In developing the metaphor of improvisation, Nussbaum claims that "the jazz player, actively forging continuity, must choose in full awareness of and responsibility to the historical traditions of the form, and actively honor at every moment, her commitments to her fellow musicians, *whom she had better know as well as possible as unique individuals*" (p. 94, emphasis added). But in Dana's case, she is only able to deliberate properly about her situation because she can know Rufus as *other than* a unique individual. If she had only been able to know him as a unique individual, she might not have been able to kill him. She is able to kill him because she knows him as a *type.* True, he is different from his father in certain respects. He is not "old and ugly, brutal and disgusting." But because Dana is able to know Rufus also as a type, as a slave master, she is able to disregard these differences or at least to see that as regards her real interests, they are irrelevant.

Nussbaum thinks "each friend is to be cherished for his or her own sake, not simply as the instantiation of the universal value, friendship" (p. 82). But it is not always clear what it means to cherish someone for his or her own sake. In important cases, it seems, cherishing someone for his or her own sake may require seeing that person as an instantiation of a kind, as a kind of subordinated or arbitrarily privileged person. For as I pointed out in Chapter 5, a person's social role can make salient to a person's identity individual features that are largely irrelevant to that person's individuality. Appreciating an individual's individuality in such cases at least requires an acknowledgment of the general social norms and values that explain such salience. Cherishing someone for her own sake may require understanding the individual's situation in more general terms, terms involving appeal to or identification of certain universal values. If Dana had not been able to appeal to the right sort of universal values to see exactly what Rufus really was an instantiation of, she would not have been able to claim her freedom or perhaps even to remember her self-worth.

Dana's perspective in the story is, in some respects, more like that of the Archangel than the Prole, scanning the situation from the "distance" of who she is in twentieth-century California. Her "distance" constitutes grounds for interpreting particular attachments differently from what would likely have been possible for someone not possessing such a perspective. Because of her occasional access to another life, she is able to detach herself from some of her partialities, responsibilities, and intuitions as these develop in her life as a slave; at least, she is able to identify them *as* partialities defined by slave life and hence to more appropriately understand their significance. Dana has to be able to scan things from a distance if she is to be able to properly classify her particular experiences and relations, to give them the right sort of interpretation. Nussbaum accounts for nonarbitrariness by suggesting that "in ethical terms . . . the perceiver brings to the new situation a history of general conceptions and commitments, and a host of past obligations and affiliations (some general, some particular), all of which contribute to and help to constitute her evolving conception of good living" (p. 94). In cases, though, in which there is a question about how the history upon which those general conceptions and commitments depend is defined, about the appropriateness of the story on the basis of which some conceptions and commitments become salient and others do not, the evolving story metaphor by itself seems limited. Something needs to be said about the nature of the conceptual and practical tradition that is presupposed by and ultimately justifies such an evolving story.

Perhaps particularly in the case of literature, *moral* as distinct from aesthetic evaluation sometimes requires the capacity to look at an evolving story from something similar to an archangelic, otherworldly perspective. Consider Toni Morrison's enlightening discussion of American literature in *Playing in the Dark: Whiteness and the Literary Imagination*.[14] National literatures, she reminds us, "seem to end up describing and inscribing what is really on the national mind."[15] They help to construct, as Anthony Appiah puts it, the unifying story in terms of which people acquire cultural identities and on the basis of which they interpret the world.[16] Now, one might think blacks just don't appear in American literature, that American literature is not about them, that they "signified little or nothing in the imagination of white American writers."[17] But Morrison says that when she approached American literature from her position and inclinations as a writer, fully self-conscious of her own struggles with and reactions to racial ideology, she saw things differently:

> It is as if I had been looking at a fishbowl—the glide and flick of the golden scales, the green tip, the bolt of white careening back from the gills; the castles at the bottom, surrounded by pebbles and tiny, intricate fronds of green; the barely disturbed water, the flecks of waste and food, the tranquil bubbles travelling to the surface—and suddenly I saw the bowl, the structure that transparently (and invisibly) permits the ordered life it contains to exist in the larger world. In other words, I began to rely on my knowledge of how books get written, how language arrives; my sense of how and why writers abandon or take on certain aspects of their project. I began to rely on my understanding of what the linguistic struggle requires of writers and what they make of the surprise that is the inevitable concomitant of the act of creation. What became transparent were the self-evident ways that Americans choose to talk about themselves through and within a sometimes allegorical, sometimes metaphorical, but always choked representation of an Africanist presence.[18]

In American literature, according to Morrison, powerful images of impenetrable whiteness "appear almost always in conjunction with representations of black or Africanist people who are dead, impotent or under complete control . . . a dark, abiding presence that moves the hearts and texts of American literature with fear and longing . . . from which our early literature seemed unable to extricate itself."[19]

For example, what was the sense of freedom and individuality that was so central to, as Morrison puts it, "that well-fondled phrase 'the American Dream'"? In a long passage from an investigation of European settlers in the process of becoming Americans, William Dunbar—a well-educated, upper-class Scotsman—described his experience of "a sense of authority and autonomy that he had not known before, a force that flowed from his absolute control over the lives of others."[20] Dunbar's plantation, we are told, was mild by the standards of the times: "But 4,000 miles from the sources of culture, alone on the far periphery of British civilization where physical survival was a daily struggle, where ruthless exploitation was a way of life, and where disorder, violence, and human degradation were commonplace, he had triumphed by *successful adaptation*."[21] The authority and autonomy Dunbar had not known before, that central theme and presumption of American literature, is defined in terms of boundedness, the subordination, the denial of African Americans: "It was this Africanism, deployed as rawness and savagery, that provided the staging ground and arena for the quintessential American identity."[22]

Morrison describes how writers like Poe, Hemingway, and Twain were responsive to and constrained by the "evolving story" of the "American Dream." In *Huckleberry Finn,* the slave Jim is humiliated and tormented by the two children, Huck and Tom. Moreover, Huck and Tom humiliate Jim *after* we, the readers, have come to know Jim as a moral agent, as a caring father and a sensitive man:

> If Jim had been a white ex-convict befriended by Huck, the ending could not have been imagined or written: because it would not have been possible for two children to play so painfully with the life of a white man (regardless of his class, education or fugitiveness) once he had been revealed to us as a moral adult. Jim's slave status makes play and deferment possible—but it also dramatizes, in style and mode of narration, the connection between slavery and the achievement (in actual and imaginary terms) of freedom. Jim seems unassertive, loving, irrational, passionate, dependent, inarticulate. . . . It is not what Jim seems that warrants inquiry, but what Mark Twain, Huck and Tom need from him that should solicit our attention.[23]

What Mark Twain, Huck, and Tom need from Jim is his unfreedom. What is overlooked in discussions of this novel, Morrison argues, is that "there is no way, given the confines of the novel, for Huck to mature into a moral human being *in America* without Jim."[24] It would have been impossible in imaginative terms for Jim to go free because *Huck's* freedom and authority presume the subordination of this black man.

The point is not that Poe, Hemingway, or Twain were racist, even if they were. The point is also not, of course, that this is bad literature. If this were so, the issue at hand would be much less interesting. It would be easier and less troublesome if we could treat the complicity of American literature in the fabrication of racism as the result of bad writers or of writers of a particularly deficient moral character. But this is not the case. Indeed, Morrison suggests that it would have been harder for these works to have constituted "good" literature if they had *not* been complicit in the fabrication of racism: When Willa Cather attempted in *Sapphira and the Slave Girl* to directly address, at least to some extent, the dependency of white identity on the enslavement of African Americans, the novel "fails."[25] It fails, if it does, Morrison says, because there is no available language, no resources within the evolving story of the American Dream, to clarify or even name the problems with which the author deals.[26] *Sapphira and the Slave Girl* is treated by critics as flawed in execution and vision. But in Morrison's view, it was precisely Cather's attempt to address the power and license a white mistress has over her female slaves that explains, at least in part, the novel's "failure."

It seems unlikely that we can dismiss Poe, Hemingway, and Twain *as* writers, whatever we now think of their values and commitments and of the implications of their storytelling for the development and preservation of the white American Dream. Morrison speaks of American literature as literature that she both revered and loathed. Indeed, it would appear that one can sometimes acknowledge and reject the directions of thought and imagination that constrain an act of storytelling while nonetheless, perhaps at another level, admiring and even being thrilled by the marvel of the storytelling itself. If one admires Faulkner, say, in one's youth and then later comes to identify the misogyny involved in Faulkner's novels, it is not always the case that one thereby changes one's views about the merits of the storytelling or even ceases to continue to enjoy such stories.

Perhaps one might say that the occasional discrepancy between aesthetic and moral judgment is explained in terms of the complexity of artistic achievement. Perhaps although one might acknowledge the misogyny, say, of Faulkner's writing, one might nonetheless appreciate its other moral achievements. Perhaps the occasional promotions of misogyny are outweighed by moral and artistic achievements involving other values.

Morrison's point, though, is that understanding of morality itself is at stake in the white American Dream. Her point is not that occasional examples of racist thinking coexist with the development, through literature, of such values as autonomy, freedom, and respect for individuality. Rather, her point is that the major themes and presumptions of American literature are "made possible by, shaped by, activated by a complex awareness and employment of a constituted Africanism."[27] The making of a new American man in American literature, she argues, is the making of a new white American man, and that very identity, that cultural identity which is presupposed in moral thinking, presumes and depends on the subordination and dehumanization of African Americans. Again, it would be much easier to say that these great writers just made some mistakes, that in some particular aspects of their artistic practice they appealed to the *wrong* moral vision. But in fact, as Nussbaum suggests, artistic achievement consists in part in the fact that the images involved *move* us, that they are beautiful. And Morrison's point about literary imagination is that it is precisely because stories *need* to be able to move, to appeal to the literary imagination, that artists *had* to appeal to a certain developing moral vision—one that, as it turns out, there are good reasons to think morally questionable.

Rationality and Moral Imagination

What does this mean for the nature of rational deliberation? It looks as though in some cases, the capacity to act on one's *real* interests—interests, for instance, in genuine autonomy and self-respect—requires not *responsiveness* to an evolving story but rather precisely the opposite—namely, the capacity, position, or imagination to *not* respond to the "evolving story . . . [with] its own form and continuity," at least to not respond in a particular way (p. 94). Moreover, it looks as though the capacity to resist being defined, and hence importantly motivated, by an evolving story requires struggle to develop and to *claim* the possibility of an alternative evolving story, often, in effect, of an impossible dream.

Dana's decision to kill Rufus and escape from slavery strikes readers, I would think, as a rational choice, as an example of rational deliberation. For by doing so she is able to reclaim her freedom. But suppose, as would be the case in less extraordinary circumstances, Dana's choice had not resulted in immediate freedom. Indeed, suppose her choice had not resulted in freedom for her at all but instead on further loss of her freedom. Would we then have thought her choice rational?

Individual choices that lead in the direction of real emancipation are often of precisely this sort. Revolutionaries who make choices on the basis of commitments to liberation, for instance, do not always or even often live to see the realization of their goals. As individuals, they may not only realize few of their personal desires and interests; they are also likely to suffer enormously. One might think, of course, that these kinds of choices are *morally* justified, that if we do not dismiss them as crazy it is because they are justified in terms of abstract moral ideals, such as freedom, justice, and so on. But it just does not seem to be true that individuals who make such choices are motivated entirely by moral considerations. They are also, and perhaps more strongly and importantly, *personally* motivated—that is, motivated by idiosyncratic commitments and interests people possess regardless of whether such commitments and interests are morally justifiable.

Even without the science fiction context, Dana might be understood to have deliberated rationally in her individual interests. Without access to a twentieth-century California way of being, Dana would have been in something like the position of Sethe. She would have been in a position in which although such a choice might not have had immediate positive, tangible results for her, it could have made it possible for her to *dream* of such results. And in a situation in which certain options are impossible even to dream, the bringing about of the imaginability of such possibilities can be personally empowering, even if such conceivability, as is often the case, itself entails suffering. For if it were to become possible for her just to *dream* that which in other terms *is*, in fact, impossible, she might have been able to deliberate about herself and eventually to act in ways, and to influence others to act in ways, that *expressed* the possibility of such a dream.

Morrison writes that it was only as she herself became a writer that she was able to begin to identify the ways in which American literature has been complicit in the promotion of racism: "Both [writing and reading] require being alert and ready for unaccountable beauty, for the intricateness or simple elegance of the writer's imagination . . . of the writer's notions of risk and safety, the serene achievement of, or sweaty fight for, meaning and response-ability."[28] Understanding Dana's choice is made easy by the science fiction context—the existence of an already developed alternative system of meanings and values. If Dana had not been able to appeal to her twentieth-century self, she would not only have had to appeal to then unacceptable beliefs about the rightness for her of the pursuit of dignity and self-respect; she would also have had, as Sethe did, to struggle for the meanings and values that would allow her to *care enough* about such beliefs to act on them once she possessed them—the "sweaty fight for meaning and response-ability." It is true, as Nussbaum suggests, that rationality is not just a propositional grasp of facts. But it is also not primarily a question of the relationship between grasp of facts and capacity for perception or of the significance of the one over the other; rather, it is at least sometimes a question of struggle for the meanings and values that allow certain facts to *be* facts in the first place.

We might understand Dana's appeal to an alternative "evolving story," a perspective that looks more Archangelic than Prolean, as indicating the significance of moral theory, the appeal to general moral ideals and concepts in the attribution of importance to some particular relations and perceptions and not others. But whereas Dana does appeal to an alternative perspective, the kind of appeal she is able to make, or the kinds of theoretical ideals and concepts she is able to employ, is made possible in this case by her personal involvement in the evolving story of slavery, by her personal relations and commitments to that story. In other words, it looks as though Dana's explanations of events, explanations upon which the rationality of her choice depends, become possible in part precisely because of her individual struggle to resist the consequences of slavery. It is Dana's personal situation within the plantation story—her relationship to Rufus and the other slaves, the emotions and feelings she experiences as a result of such relationships—that explains how she is able to give to her twentieth-century self the significance she does, namely, the motivation to kill in order to be free.

Indeed, Dana is able to appropriately understand and interpret the theory available to her only because she *has* been moved by the very evolving story she is now in a position to resist. It is because Dana *has* responded to such an evolving story that she is now *able* to resist in the way she does, that she is able to *identify* the real danger of her situation. Even as she raises her knife, even as she sinks it into his side, Dana is aware "of him trying not to hurt me."[29] The understanding that allows Dana to kill Rufus is understanding not just of slavery as a moral wrong, the abstract understanding many who have no experience of slavery possess; rather, it is understanding of the ways in which slavery, and, of course, any racist social system, *makes* meaningful and acceptable the practices and attitudes that sustain it. Dana understands that it is precisely what *seems* right to her under such conditions that must be resisted and precisely because humiliating practices *can* be made to seem right to her that she must resist in the way she does.

Grasp of facts is not enough for rational deliberation. But neither is the primacy of perception, even together with appreciation of relevant facts. In some cases, rational deliberation requires struggle to bring about the meanings and values that make the discovery of a certain kind of perception possible. And part of that process of bringing about meanings and values consists in individual struggle to claim human worth to the extent that it can be claimed in a particular situation. In the science fiction example, Dana only has to recognize the significance of who she is in the twentieth century for how she interprets Rufus's "kindness." For anyone else—for Toni Morrison, for Sethe—it has to be possible to imagine *being* some other way and then, on top of that, to claim, and to continue to claim, the significance of being in such a way for how one understands the myriad personal relations and impressions that define who one is within the evolving story one depends on in day-to-day practice.

Nussbaum argues that the moral achievement of literature, of appeal to experience, often consists in the capacity of certain configurations of events to *move*. She acknowledges, of course, that it is not just a question of capacity to move: "Adam's image of the sea creature, too, satisfies, is right, in part because it fulfills his sense of what a father owes an adult daughter" (p. 155). Rightness is not constituted solely by beauty but also by the "standing terms" of the evolving story—general moral principles. Thus, moral achievement is not just "an artwork embroidered for its own intrinsic aesthetic character, without regard to principle and commitment" (p. 155). It must be beauty that responds to "external" moral constraints.

The point here is that in some cases it is the capacity to be moved in a particular way, as well as the valuing of that capacity, that itself provides grounds for the discovery of the "standing terms" that make such beauty more than just an "artwork embroidered for its own intrinsic aesthetic character." That is, it is certain kinds of valuing and committing of oneself, ones that do indeed constitute claims to human worth and dignity, that explain a person's *discovering* certain moral possibilities. The fact that Dana's choice to do as she did could have been individually rational even if, as in Sethe's case, she were not to acquire her actual freedom suggests that individual rationality is defined not just by relations of an evolving story but also by facts about what it means to be claiming real human worth, as opposed to what appears to be human worth, in a particular situation. Nussbaum points out that on Aristotle's conception, what is good for someone as an individual is what is good for her as a human being (p. 95). But to the extent that certain evolving stories make the real humanity of some individuals *unimaginable,* something needs to be said about what is involved in discovering the *right* understanding of human flourishing. What Nussbaum's account of the moral component of individual rationality seems to overlook is that in some societies people have to have the courage to make certain moral claims and to believe them strongly enough to act on them before they can discover the general moral conceptions that could justify such claims.

The fact that people do, in fact, stake everything on such claims, as Sethe did, and that their doing so often explains the acquiring of social and moral understanding suggests that we sometimes do *discover* what human flourishing really means as we engage effectively with moral argument and conflict. It would appear that in metaethics and epistemology, as in natural science, we acquire understanding through abductive inference—that is, by looking for the best explanations of what we do in practice and of our considered, intuitively plausible understanding of what we do in practice. And as I suggested in discussing Hacking, individuals sometimes make claims to value, to the moral significance of certain personal experiences and perceptions, as a result of which it becomes possible more generally to understand important social phenomena more appropriately. These sorts of examples suggest that some widely accepted moral and metaphysical notions do *not* provide the best explanations. I would suggest, for instance, that general assumptions that moral facts are *not* discoverable can be shown to lack explanatory power as regards examples of social change and plausible intuitions about what transpires in such change.

Consider, for instance, the social understanding that has been developing in recent years, in some parts of North America at least, about sexual harassment and date rape. Individuals, such as Anita Hill, who attempted to make charges of sexual harassment, to carry out the naming of such behavior, did so by claiming a certain significance for their own personal perceptions and experiences. Now, there are some, of course, who think the introduction of concepts such as "sexual harassment" and "date rape" can be explained entirely by political interest. But such views obscure the fact that it is possible to argue—and people do, in fact, argue—on the basis of reason and empirical evidence that what is sometimes thought to be sexual harassment is not really sexual harassment. As I tried to point out in relation to essentialism-constructivism debates in Chapter 6, the interest relativity of social kinds does not by itself preclude the objectivity of such kinds, unless one assumes an indefensible, foundationalist conception of what objectivity means. As Boyd argues, it is true about social kinds, as it is about natural kinds, that it is facts about the structure of society and about the human beings who make it up that explain the success of inductive generalizations and explanations involving social kinds, when they are successful; such success is not explained by the fact that any or all members of a society accept certain definitions of such kinds.[30] The fact that certain understandings of "sexual harassment" and "date rape" allow us to make more effective generalizations and to offer more adequate explanations of certain social phenomena is not best explained by the hypothesis that feminists invented such terms entirely as a result of their political interests; such success would appear to be better explained by the hypothesis that facts about human beings and their well-being—such as that the behaviors described by "sexual harassment" and "date rape" do indeed undermine possibilities for human flourishing for some people—have been discovered.

In the example I mentioned briefly in the introductory chapter, LeRoi Jones was *moved* by the celebrating crowd—"that wild, mad crowd," like a circus. He was moved by the "unbelievable joy and excitement," by the sight of "people made beautiful because of [an idea]." Yet when Jones first arrived in Cuba, like many before and after him, he was "extremely paranoid," intending to avoid the official itinerary and to see for himself: "I was determined not to be 'taken.' . . . I felt immediately sure that the make was on."[31] The explanation for his transformation seems to lie not so much in the information he acquired while in Cuba nor even in his personal perceptions. Rather, when Jones finds himself moved by the fact that "people still *can* move," he places value that, in his case, can only be explained by moral imagination, by the recognition of alternative conceptions of what is and what might be—depending upon the development of such alternatives—morally reasonable. It is value that is difficult, perhaps even impossible, to make sense of in terms of the beliefs that ground his initial concern "not to be 'taken.'" When Jones returns to the United States understanding his own entire belief system to involve lies and the influence of propaganda, it is not because his personal experience with the crowds was beautiful, was moving, for he could have had such an experience and then, upon later reflection, dismissed it as crazy; rather, it was because having experienced such beauty, Jones took it to be significant. Jones claimed the significance, the value; he then had to *discover* the "standing terms" that could explain such significance.

Rational deliberation often requires a claim to specific sorts of valuing *first*—in particular, valuing of more adequate ways of being *human*—even if they are currently understood as crazy. To the extent that what is valued actually *is* a more adequate way of being, such valuing can *explain* the development of rational standards and more appropriate concepts. In Chapter 2, I argued that it is difficult to give an account of the individual rationality of pursuing human flourishing for some cases without considering the role of nonpropositional understanding in defining rational choice. In particular, I suggested that on an adequate idealization, objective ends or real interests should be defined in terms of what an individual would choose for herself if she were able to consider her available options in light of understanding she would acquire if she were personally transformed or if her society were socially transformed—in other words, if she had access to relevant nonpropositional, as well as propositional, information. I also suggested at that point that such an idealization would begin to fail to make sense, which is why, in part, the question of rationality has to be considered a question also about integrity. For it is often the acquisition of a more adequate sense of self itself that constitutes the bringing about of more appropriate epistemic conditions. The significance people sometimes claim for personal experiences and perceptions, in the kinds of cases discussed here, would appear to be explained by nonpropositional understanding. Indeed, as I suggested in Chapter 2, it would be hard to explain the fact that we know much at all about deep-rooted systemic oppression without appealing to nonpropositional understanding. For it is part of the success of ideological oppression, as I have tried to indicate throughout this book, that systemic discrimination is the behavioral norm, part of the social definition, and hence difficult to talk about, often even to oneself.

Standards of rationality are often *discovered* when people have the courage to make certain moral claims and to believe them strongly enough to act on them without available moral justification. And this does not mean just any kind of moral claim can generate standards of rationality as long as we work hard enough at telling the right sorts of stories about such claims to value. For whereas it might seem that we could generate stories ad infinitum, it is not true that just any kind of story we might tell about the moral significance of particular perceptions and experiences does, in fact, explain the pursuit of human flourishing for the people involved. For, as already argued, there are facts about the matter of what does and what does not promote the well-being of specific people in specific societies at a certain time, facts that can, through appeal to theory and empirical investigation, be discovered. Thus, ultimately, the explanation for why some evolving stories are better than others has to do with facts about what is required to bring about the understandability and possibility of the pursuit of real human flourishing within a particular situation, where the objective content of "human flourishing" is taken to depend on the relationship between its use in a process of ongoing investigation and facts about the actual structures of the social and physical world, just as is, arguably, the case for any other general concept.

The Return of the Archangel?

Nussbaum may be right in response to Hare that moral philosophy is not best expressed by the image of a being with "superhuman powers of thought, superhuman knowledge and no human weaknesses" (p. 44). But the contrary is no better if human power, human knowledge, and human weaknesses rest on a conception of human that only applies to some social members. The opposition between these metaphors, however, may be misleading. Whereas rational deliberation does require attention to details, it is often necessary to take, or at least to move toward, a "distanced" theoretical perspective to be able to see which particular details are relevant and for what purpose.

I have suggested that the moral component of individual rationality is ultimately explained in terms of facts about human flourishing, many of which still need to be discovered. For in some important cases, individual choice is rational in terms of possibilities for freedom that are yet to be brought about, of which courage is required even to dream. How, then, do we understand the Archangel if what is significant about the Archangel for rational deliberation is the capacity to see things from a distance, to identify particular relations and commitments for their real significance as regards the pursuit of human flourishing?

Toni Morrison says that in reading Marie Cardinal's "autobiographical novel," *The Words to Say It,* she insisted on pursuing one question: "What was the narrative moment, the specular even spectacular scene that convinced [Cardinal] that she was in danger of collapse?"[32] The answer, it turns out, is Cardinal's attendance at a Louis Armstrong concert, her experience of "one precise, *unique* note, tracing a sound whose path was almost *painful,* so absolutely necessary had its *equilibrium* and *duration* become; it *tore at the nerves* of those . . . who followed it."[33] The "unbearable equilibrium," Morrison suggests, causes Cardinal to run into the street. Perhaps the question that needs to be raised about improvisation as a metaphor explaining the significance of personal relations for rational deliberation is the question Morrison raises about Cardinal's experience: When do equilibrium and duration, balance and permanence become "wonderful tropes for the illness" that can break up the life of someone like Cardinal, a sensitive young girl?[34] It is true, as Nussbaum's discussion of the sea creature suggests, that in some cases equilibrium and balance ignite moments of moral discovery. In other cases, however—perhaps in the case of Morrison herself—it is precisely *because* a certain equilibrium and balance ignite directions of thought and imagination, because they *can* move people not just to act and think in certain ways but also to find such ways meaningful, that they become tropes for illness.

In Cardinal's case, we find out, the problem is not one of responsiveness or nonresponsiveness to a particular evolving story; rather, it is one about the kind of story it is and how she gets defined within it. Cardinal, we find out, is in turmoil because of her identification, on the one hand, with Algerian people with whom she grew up and her association, on the other, with the white French powers intending to destroy Algeria. Her "problem," it turns out, has its roots in the fact that she "was a colonialist, a white child, loving and loved by Arabs, but warned against them in relationships other than distant and controlled ones."[35]

In some cases, as in Cardinal's, equilibrium and balance become tropes for illness. For the equilibrium and balance are defined by a unifying story of a particular sort, the relevant moral assumptions of which are not likely to be made explicit. And in cases in which one comes to recognize that such a story constitutes, as Fanon says, a "restructuring of the self," the only adequate response is complete resistance to such a system—moreover, forceful and persistent resistance. If such resistance is not possible or at least not perceived to be possible, perhaps the only other available response is death—of one sort or another. The choices available to Sethe, for instance, amounted to various sorts of death.

The Archangel, with its distanced perspective, might be understood as the defining or redefining of equilibrium and balance. Contrary to Nussbaum, what does seem to have primacy in some cases of rational deliberation is the capacity to be able to scan a situation from a distance, as the Archangel is supposed to do, to appeal to general moral theories and concepts to identify the situation for what it is. Rational deliberation requires the capacity to *name* the sort of unity that exists. In Chapter 6, I argued that it does not make sense to talk about the appreciation of difference without acknowledging the dependence of judgments about relevant sorts of difference upon assumptions about the nature of social unity in general. Although I acknowledged and have tried to explicate the important philosophical insights involved in discussions of "difference," I suggested that unless commitments to particular unifying pictures are acknowledged and defended, emphases on "difference" risk reinforcing arbitrary and oppressive systems of domination in just the way liberal appeals to social unity (on the basis of a priori assumptions about how a society is defined) are accused of doing.[36] What seems to be important about Hare's appeal to the Archangel is that defining rational standards—moral or nonmoral—depends on an assumption about the nature of the whole. It requires an appeal to some general picture of how the world is unified, to a notion of the sort of picture it is that defines similarities and differences and of what sort of picture it ought to be. What is left out of Hare's treatment of the Archangel, though, is any acknowledgment of the ways in which the discovery of the right sorts of unifying pictures depends on the moral and epistemic significance of personal relations and commitments and on individuals' courage in claiming such significance.

Aristotle suggested that Archangels are not useful for understanding morality because it is the human good we are looking for, not the good of some other being. The problem, though, is that to the extent that in an oppressive social system the human good *is* already that of some other being, the Archangel is indeed useful. In cases in which individuals come to identify entire practical and conceptual systems of meanings as being of a particular moral sort, to identify, that is, the existence of a particular evolving unifying story, their doing so would appear to have to do with insistence on the significance of some particular aspect of an individual's motivational system—her interests, desires, and commitments. In Marie Cardinal's case, it was her feeling for Algeria. Because of her feeling for Algeria, her emotional commitments put her in *dis*equilibrium, in unbalance. And that recognition of unbalance *constitutes* a kind of discovery, at least the possibility of naming the social unity that makes some things significant and others not. In cases in which an entire unifying system is identified *as unhealthy*—as in the case of Sethe, Toni Morrison, Frantz Fanon, and LeRoi Jones—the disequilibrium is explained by a claim to *human* value, to *self-worth*. Thus, the Archangel, or the possibility of the Archangel, is not necessarily an intellectual position, at least not in the first instance; indeed, often it *cannot* be an intellectual position. Rather, it is a way of being—a claim to humanness—that is not accommodated by an existing evolving story and that requires the search for alternative meanings and values—alternative stories—to be expressed and acted upon.

Rationality Once Again

The more serious mistake in the picture of rationality assumed by the idealizations discussed in the initial chapters of this book is that the picture gets wrong the metaphysics of individual development. It gets wrong both the nature of individual development and the nature of self-knowledge. I tried to point out in earlier chapters that in defining rational choice in terms of what an individual does with information, the standard picture assumes that in some sense it is unproblematic who the individual is.

The Aristotelian view of rationality defended by Nussbaum also takes for granted questions about who the person is, in particular the adequacy of the sense of integrity individuals acquire as the result of a society being one way rather than another. For Nussbaum, the particular is prior to the general in that the improvising actor "persistently permits discovery and surprise, even a surprise that might cause serious reversal in her entire ethical conception" (p. 91). According to Nussbaum, storytelling is significant for rational deliberation because it not only accommodates aspects of practical reasoning better than does an abstract treatise but it also *elicits* a response: "By identifying with them and allowing ourselves to be surprised (an attitude of mind that story-telling fosters and develops), we become more responsive to our own life's adventure, more willing to see and be touched by life" (p. 162). But again, Toni Morrison points out that the moral significance of the surprise that is elicited by good storytelling depends not on the constraints of the evolving story but rather on identifying the evolving story for what it is in general and, importantly, on identifying the *kind* of person whose response such surprise is. When Morrison identifies "the bowl, the structure that transparently (and invisibly) permits the ordered life it contains to exist in the larger world," she says she "began to rely on my understanding of what the linguistic struggle requires of writers and what they make of the surprise that is the inevitable concomitant of the act of creation."[37] What she discovers about this "bowl," the literary imagination expressed by such surprise, is the "sometimes allegorical, sometimes metaphorical, but always choked representation of an Africanist presence."[38]

Aristotle and Nussbaum do not appear to recognize that at least in unjust societies and perhaps in general, real (as opposed to what we might think constitutes) moral insight depends on certain kinds of perceptions, often on certain *kinds* of people with specific sorts of commitments. In cases in which a society has developed traditions of injustice against particular social groups, in which some groups of people systematically and historically dominate others, the identification of possibilities for moral progress will require forceful and persistent resistance to practical and conceptual traditions that rationalize, on a daily basis and in individual lives, the continuation and promotion of such injustice. However, to the extent that such systems of meanings are presupposed in most people's deliberations, both moral and nonmoral, indeed, are presupposed in most people's assumptions about who they are, motivation for such resistance is often explained by certain *individuals'* quite specific perceptions—of instances of freedom, love, control, beauty—and their willingness and capacity to claim meaningfulness for such perceptions.

In conclusion, the question of why some particular perceptions matter and others do not depends on an often apparently impossible dream—the possibility of more humane, more just, more equitable social relations and of specific individuals' situatedness within them. In other words, it is ultimately relative to a broader moral vision, perhaps one that cannot even be completely articulated in recognizable terms, that some particular perceptions, commitments, and relations acquire epistemic and moral significance. Moreover, it is sometimes *only* in relation to such a vision that *some* relations and commitments can acquire significance. The problem with the "distancing" view is not that it involves distancing but rather that it involves distancing *as opposed to* involvement. For in many cases, rational standards *do* require a distanced perspective; they require, as the Archangel is taken to express, scanning a situation from a distance and being able to see the larger picture for what it is morally. The possibility of such scanning, however, often requires the development of alternative norms and values; moreover, it often requires personal and social transformation. The fact that we acquire rational standards through involvement in practice does not suggest that there is something wrong with the image of the "distanced" Archangel, even of its primacy; rather, it suggests that there is something wrong with a theoretical model that takes the definition of standards to be the central issue rather than, as often seems to be the case, the ongoing pursuit of the more adequate ways of being that can make the right sorts of standards imaginable.

Epilogue

At the Feminist Ethics and Social Policy conference in Pittsburgh in November 1993, a number of prominent North American feminists criticized the work of three Cuban feminists for apparently overlooking differences among women. In their paper "Women and Participation in Cuba," Amelia Suárez, Inés Rodriguez, and Sonia Enjamio described their work with women in three municipalities in Havana, in particular their conclusions about what sorts of changes need to be brought about in order that women's equality in Cuba be more than merely formal.[1] But their language was universalistic. They spoke about the condition of women generally in Cuba and about the human condition.

Universalistic discourse is worrying to some feminist theorists because such discourse indicates tendencies to define general concepts like "women" a priori—that is, in advance of empirical political investigation and struggle. Sojourner Truth's question, "Ain't I a woman?" was intended to point out that in 1851 the general concept "women" referred only to white women. Spelman argues, correctly, that the tendency to define terms a priori—to look for fixed essences—undermines the capacity of political theory to represent the interests of the less dominant. But many have taken such arguments to mean that universalistic concepts and theories should be mistrusted in general rather than, as *is* implied, that certain kinds of universalization—those involving dependence upon false beliefs—should be mistrusted.

The case against the Cubans could be made even stronger. The worry of the critics was that in making universalistic statements, the Cuban scholars were running the *risk* of imposing unity on experience and precluding the appreciation of difference. Worse than this, one might think, is that some Cuban intellectuals *argue* that specific sorts of unity *should* be imposed on groups of people *in order to* make some possibilities meaningless and difficult to understand.

In "Cuba Nexos y Rupturas: Tres Décadas de Cultura en la Revolución," a paper I mentioned briefly in Chapter 6, art historian Raquel Mendieta Costa argues that after the revolution in 1959, social values had to be *brought about* by Cuban artists and historians.[2] The enormous social changes introduced by the revolution were not just changes but what she calls an encounter with history. According to Mendieta, "Reality was transformed into a picture, a landscape of successive and dizzying images, as if the imagination of Marxist theory, incarnated in history, produced a transfiguration of what such images could make known ... in order to transform reality itself, where for the first time the great American utopia was realized in acts and concrete undertakings."[3] Mendieta points out that in 1960s there was an incredible flourishing of the arts, including, as in cinema, the development of arts that had no precedent in Cuba. Yet, she says, it couldn't have been otherwise: Profound economic, social, and political changes radically altered the face of the Cuban situation, and artistic and literary culture could do no less than demonstrate this transformative process. Artists and writers sought, through genres and languages previously little explored, to translate the complex events that were occurring day by day.[4]

The activities of artists of the 1960s, Mendieta argues, constituted an essential gesture of opposition to the values that characterized the republican state: New social values such as anti-imperialism, Latin Americanism, third worldism, antiracism, struggle for the revindication of the popular masses—for instance, full employment, low rent, free health care and education, redistribution of land to the peasants—constituted real and daily values that began to create a new tradition, a new social psychology.[5] These artists, to the extent that they were able to bring these values to life, to make them understandable and applicable, were transforming the conceptual resources of a people—in fact, were creating a new sense of what that society was about, a new sense of national identity. As Mendieta says, artistic and literary activity after the revolution was not just transformative; it constituted the creating of a picture, a landscape of images that produced a transfiguration of what could be known and what *could be done*.

In liberal democratic traditions, many are uneasy about the idea of imposing a sense of national identity on a people. But it was not only true that the government encouraged artists and writers to promote certain values, to retell the history of Cuba. It has been an important part of Cuban education for the past thirty-five years to teach young people values, to instruct students in what sort of persons they should be, not just morally but also personally and politically.[6] It is openly urged that all curricula should follow an ideology, that ideology should be present in all programs.[7] From a liberal democratic perspective, this immediately looks like a denial of individuality and autonomy, the essence of the denial of individual liberty that, critics charge, characterizes communism.

In discussing familiar conceptions of individual interests, I have tried to explain the philosophical roots of the assumption that *imposing* on people a sense of who they are, or imposing on people in almost any way at all, constitutes a denial of autonomy: Liberals assume, following Mill, that it is better for people to act on their own values, whatever they are, as long as their actions are carefully thought out and sufficiently well informed. According to liberal democratic traditions, it will not do to intervene in people's affairs on grounds that the people involved would, in fact, accept the choices in question if only they were somehow converted to aims and values other than their original ones. For if we accept this, the arguments go, it will become justifiable to indoctrinate people in any way at all as long as it can be shown that after processes of psychological pressure and intimidation, the people involved would themselves accept the values imposed.

The assumption is that respecting people's autonomy involves respecting people's freedom to act on their settled values and aims without interference other than the providing of appropriate resources. But in discussing Toni Morrison's *Playing in the Dark,*[8] I have tried to suggest that the idea of unfettered individualism just *is* the justification for the denial of individual autonomy, at least if we live, as there seems reason to think we do, in an unjust society. National literatures, Morrison reminds us, "seem to end up describing and inscribing what is really on the national mind" (p. 14). Her point is that the unifying story constructed by American literature presupposes the boundedness, subordination, and denial of African Americans: "It was this Africanism, deployed as rawness and savagery, that provided the staging ground and arena for the quintessential American identity" (p. 44).

If this is so, the difference between concern for individuals in the North American and the Cuban systems is that in the Cuban context the social imposition of value and meanings and the effects of such imposition on what people can understand and do are recognized and addressed both politically and morally, whereas in liberal democratic traditions, because such imposition is not acknowledged, they are not. Whether such issues are addressed appropriately in the Cuban situation is another question, one I will not try to answer. The point I have been trying to make in this book is that it is a mistake to think that such issues about values and vision cannot be addressed appropriately or at least that there are not good reasons for thinking that some ways of addressing such issues are better than others. I have tried to suggest that intuitions about reasonableness in both individual and social deliberation *presuppose* judgments that some conceptions of human well-being, of human flourishing, are better than others, even though such assumptions are often not explicitly acknowledged or defended. I have also suggested that if moral truths about what constitutes human dignity and respect cannot be and are not discovered and developed through argument and appeal to evidence, important judgments about reasonableness—both individual and social—are unfounded.

Personal stories based on individual difference have been significant in North American feminist politics because personal storytelling often constitutes the introduction into theory of practical possibilities that, according to a dominant social narrative, cannot even be imagined. I have suggested that such emphasis on personal storytelling in North American feminism is both morally and epistemologically significant. But it need not be the *individual* herself who begins to perceive things differently and then decides to act in ways that make the telling of a more adequate alternative story possible. Sometimes political change happens *first*. At a meeting of the *Casa de las Mujeres* in municipality Cerro, Havana, sixty-four-year-old Teresa told us that at the time of the Cuban revolution she was a thirty-year-old illiterate domestic worker with two small children.[9] As she recounts her story, it was not any epiphanous personal insight that began the transformative path as a result of which she became the leader of her union, achieved advanced qualification in her technical field, and eventually represented Cuba abroad at international conferences; rather, it was the series of social changes that presented her with educational possibilities, as well as intense social and political indoctrination aimed at convincing the public in general that women, including black women like herself, can and should be educated. Cuba's recognized success in such areas as antiracism, education, and health reform is at least partly a result of an ongoing effort throughout the past thirty-five years to *impose* certain values on society, to *bring about* a specific sense of national identity.

In both the North American and the Cuban contexts, a national-social identity is imposed on people so that some possibilities are conceivable and doable and others are not. And in both cases, a *moral* vision is imposed according to which some directions of thought and action become meaningless, even unimaginable. The difference is that in the Cuban context, the imposition of moral vision is acknowledged and discussed. In liberal democratic traditions, it is not acknowledged, or at least it is not acknowledged as individually and politically important. Worse than this, though, there is a risk that in liberal democratic traditions, the arbitrary imposition of a particular moral vision *cannot* be effectively addressed: To the extent that individuality is assumed to consist in living one's life "from the inside" with true beliefs, any attempt to bring about the changes to norms and values required for the pursuit of real autonomy by most social members is *already* regarded as a threat to autonomy. The practical danger of the kind of view of individual rationality and interests I have been discussing and criticizing is that the right sorts of questions regarding autonomy—questions about moral vision, its discovery and development—cannot even be raised.

The fact that some feminists at the Pittsburgh conference would want to see in the universalistic theorizing of Cuban women an ignorance of differences among women is a misconstrual of the entire issue of "difference" in feminist theory and its relation to radical social change. Moreover, given the rejection in some North American feminist theory of standard liberal conceptions of autonomy, the embracing by the Cuban women of the general social and moral issues that determine possibilities for individuality should be appealing. It is true, for instance, that Morrison's "difference" from the racist white American Dream constitutes a basis for telling alternative stories. But Morrison's awareness of her difference is not, in fact, an awareness of individuality, at least not in the first instance. Rather, it is an awareness of the nature of the larger picture that makes it unimaginable for people like her to be individuals at all. Before she became a writer, before she became "mindful of those places where imagination sabotages itself, locks its own gates, pollutes its own vision" (p. xi), she thought the black people just weren't there in the picture. But then she became aware of "the bowl, the structure that transparently (and invisibly) permits the ordered life it contains to exist in the larger world." She became aware of the larger picture, the whole, and at that point she saw what was more important—"the self-evident ways that Americans choose to talk about themselves through and within a sometimes allegorical, sometimes metaphorical, but always choked representation of an Africanist presence" (p. 17).

To the extent that they become interesting and useful, issues of difference are about differences from those dominant social norms and values that constitute an oppressive social system, norms and values that need to be discovered. According to the terms provided by the American Dream, Toni Morrison is different in terms of her nonexistence: She is just not there in the picture. But in terms of her moral judgment that the American Dream is *wrong,* she is different in terms of the unfair representation she receives in this picture and its consequences for her human possibilities. And it is this difference that is important. The real differences are not those differences that are defined as differences by the American Dream or whatever the unifying picture may happen to be but rather those that are defined in terms of a moral judgment about that unifying picture—namely, that it is *wrong,* if it is, and how. Thus, the concern about "difference," at least in its political usefulness, is a concern about general social and moral vision—what it is and what it ought to be.

If the Cuban women are disregarding difference in the sense that differences have become interesting in North American feminism, the fact that they use universalistic language provides no evidence of this. For their project is one of building a more just society in general, the whole in terms of which relevant sorts of differences become identifiable, a project that itself requires emphasizing differences. If we were to make a judgment about their disregard of relevant sorts of differences, we would need to know something about the kind of general moral picture they are directed by, information that was not provided in the paper but that could, of course, be acquired through empirical investigation into the history, social structures, global situation, values, and so on, of the Cuban situation. The worry about universalistic discourse is that it risks taking for granted the dubious moral commitments of certain traditions. But to the extent that differences relevant to criticizing such traditions depend on moral judgments *about* that tradition, universalistic statements—statements depending on assumptions about universal human goods—are also involved in emancipatory struggle against such traditions.

The women who wrote the paper presented at the Feminist Ethics conference in Pittsburgh were fourteen and fifteen years old at the time of the Cuban revolution. Each of them has participated all her life in organizations such as the Cuban Federation of Women, organizations aimed at channeling the political participation of the masses.[10] They have lived and worked with the idea that democracy requires that adequate material conditions be brought about before people can even identify, let alone express, their interests. The work they are currently doing in the Havana municipalities is work aimed at demonstrating that although Cuba has made enormous gains in women's equality, there remain informal problems of equality—more subtle sorts of problems having to do with identity, with how women see themselves, and with how they are treated according to existing social norms.[11] It is work aimed at deepening understanding of equality by examining ever more complex aspects of social relations in a struggle for socialist values—social relations that are often rather different from those of "liberal democratic" societies. The fact that their work is aimed at identifying means of improving general conditions in times of economic crisis is no indication of failure to recognize the importance of difference in struggles for equality. Rather, it is an acknowledgment of the fact that, as Mendieta takes to be uncontroversial, value and norms often need to be *brought about* before people can begin to identify the right sorts of similarities and differences.

Notes

Introduction

1. LeRoi Jones, "Cuba Libre," reprinted in Jones, *Home: Social Essays* (New York: William Morrow, 1966), p. 16, cited in Van Gosse, *Where the Boys Are: Cuba, Cold War America and the Making of a New Left* (New York: Verso Press, 1993), p. 185.

2. Jones, "Cuba Libre," p. 61.

3. Ibid., p. 62.

4. See, e.g., P. Kitcher, "The Naturalists Return," *Philosophical Review* 101, no. 1 (January 1992), esp. pp. 110–114.

5. Thomas Kuhn, *The Structure of Scientific Revolutions* (Chicago: University of Chicago Press, 1962), p. 66.

6. Quoted in Michard-Marchal, *Sexisme et sciences humaines: pratique linguistic du rapport de sexage* (Lille: Presses universitaires de Lille, 1982), p. 7, cited in Lise Noël, *Intolerance: The Parameters of Oppression* (Montreal and Kingston: McGill–Queen's University Press, 1994), p. 27; emphasis added.

7. Claudia Card, "Introduction," in Card, ed., *Feminist Ethics* (Lawrence: University Press of Kansas, 1991), p. 25.

8. Frantz Fanon, "The Fact of Blackness," in *Black Skin, White Masks* (New York: Grove Press, 1967), pp. 109–140, reprinted in D. T. Goldberg, ed., *The Anatomy of Racism* (Minneapolis: University of Minnesota Press, 1990), p. 108.

9. Ibid., p. 109.

10. Toni Morrison, *Beloved* (New York: Penguin Books, 1988).

11. Toni Morrison, *Playing in the Dark: Whiteness and the Literary Imagination* (New York: Vintage Books, 1992), p. 44.

12. Fanon, "The Fact of Blackness," p. 109; emphasis added.

13. Ibid.

14. Jones, "Cuba Libre," p. 61.

Chapter 1

1. Marilyn Frye, *Willful Virgin* (Freedom, Calif.: Crossing Press, 1992), p. 7.

2. Drucilla Cornell, *Beyond Accommodation: Ethical Feminism, Deconstruction and the Law* (New York: Routledge, 1991); "What Takes Place in the Dark," *Differences: A Journal of Feminist Cultural Studies* 42 (Summer 1992): 45–71.

3. Toni Morrison, *Beloved* (New York: Penguin Books, 1988).

4. Elizabeth V. Spelman, *Inessential Woman: Problems of Exclusion in Feminist Thought* (Boston: Beacon Press, 1988), pp. 1–3.

5. Ibid., p. 1.

6. David Hume, *Enquiries Concerning Human Understanding and Concerning the Principles of Morals,* 2d ed. (Oxford: Oxford University Press, 1902), sections 5, 7.

7. Cornell, *Beyond,* p. 3.

8. Cornell, "What Takes Place in the Dark."

9. Ibid., pp. 62–64.

10. Ibid., p. 62.

11. Philip Kitcher, *Abusing Science: The Case Against Creationism* (Cambridge: MIT Press, 1984), esp. pp. 50–54.

12. Ibid., p. 50.

13. E.g., ibid., pp. 45–54.

14. Cornell, *Beyond,* pp. 186–188, 194–195.

15. Ibid., p. 194.

16. Ibid., p. 195.

17. Ibid.

18. Ibid.

19. Morrison, *Beloved,* p. 164.

20. Barbara Herman, "Agency, Attachment and Difference," in John Deigh, ed., *Ethics and Personality* (Chicago: University of Chicago Press, 1992), pp. 61–63.

21. Morrison, *Beloved,* p. 162.

22. Ibid.

23. For an important argument against the use of the concept of tragedy to describe slavery, see Elizabeth V. Spelman, "Slavery and Tragedy," in Roger S. Gottlieb, ed., *Radical Philosophy: Tradition, Counter-Tradition, Politics* (Philadelphia: Temple University Press, 1993), pp. 221–244.

24. See, e.g., Richard Boyd, "Scientific Realism and Naturalistic Epistemology," *PSA 1980* 2 (1980): 613–662.

25. Morrison, *Beloved,* p. 162.

26. Ibid., p. 45.

27. H. Putnam, "The Analytic and the Synthetic," in Putnam, *Mind, Language and Reality: Philosophical Papers, Volume 2* (New York: Cambridge University Press, 1975), pp. 33–69.

28. Cornell, *Beyond,* p. 196.

29. Morrison, *Beloved,* p. 165.

30. Ibid., p. 162.

31. Ibid., p. 163.

32. Ibid., p. 45.

33. Ibid., p. 164.

34. E.g., Angela Gilliam, "Women's Equality and National Liberation," in Chandra Mohanty, Ann Russo, and Lourdes Torres, eds., *Third World Women and the Politics of Feminism* (Bloomington: Indiana University Press, 1991), pp. 215–236.

35. Donna Haraway, "Reading Buchi Emecheta," in Haraway, *Simians, Cyborgs and Women* (New York: Routledge, 1991), p. 113.

36. For an overview of developments in naturalistic epistemology, see Philip Kitcher, "The Naturalists Return," *Philosophical Review* 101 (January 1992): 53–114.

37. Morrison, *Beloved*, p. 273.

38. See R. Boyd, "How to Be a Moral Realist," in G. Sayre-McCord, ed., *Essays on Moral Realism* (Ithaca, N.Y.: Cornell University Press, 1988), pp. 181–228, for discussion of the implications for moral objectivity of rejecting foundationalist epistemology.

39. See, e.g., Kitcher, "The Naturalists Return," esp. pp. 110–114.

Chapter 2

1. Gramsci makes this point in his discussion of intellectuals. "Organic intellectuals," those whose ideas closely reflect the actual situation, need to be able to formulate their ideas in terms of the perceptions of the "traditional" intellectuals, those, such as church leaders, professors, and so on, who are recognized by society as intellectuals. See "The Intellectuals," in Q. Hoare and G. Nowell Smith, eds., *Selections from the Prison Notebooks of Antonio Gramsci* (New York: International Publishers, 1983 [1971]), pp. 3–14.

2. There are other pictures of individual rationality available. See Peter Railton, "Moral Realism," *Philosophical Review* 95, no. 2 (April 1986), esp. pp. 166–171, for reasons for thinking this instrumental conception is the most plausible, despite its problems.

3. See, e.g., Rolf Sartorius, ed., *Paternalism* (Minneapolis: University of Minnesota Press, 1983); John Rawls, *A Theory of Justice* (Cambridge: Harvard University Press, 1971), pp. 248ff.

4. Rawls, *A Theory*, pp. 416f. Similar views have been advanced by Henry Sidgwick, *The Methods of Ethics* (London: Macmillan & Co., 1907); Richard Brandt, *A Theory of the Right and the Good* (Oxford: Clarendon Press, 1979); and R. M. Hare, *Moral Thinking* (Oxford: Clarendon Press, 1981).

5. Rawls, *A Theory*, pp. 248–250.

6. Joel Feinberg, "Legal Paternalism," *Canadian Journal of Philosophy* 1, no. 1 (1971): 106–124, reprinted in Sartorius, *Paternalism*, pp. 3–18.

7. Ibid., pp. 9–11.

8. Thomas Hill Jr., "Servility and Self-Respect," *The Monist* 57 (1973): 87.

9. Rawls, *A Theory*, p. 417; John Rawls, "Kantian Constructivism in Moral Theory," *Journal of Philosophy* 77, no. 9 (1980): 517–572.

10. See, e.g, Barbara Herman, "Agency, Attachment and Difference," in John Deigh, ed., *Ethics and Personality* (Chicago: University of Chicago Press, 1992), esp. pp. 60–63.

11. See especially Rawls, *A Theory*, pp. 248–250. In fact, liberal accounts allow significant criticism of a person's particular desires—even strongly held ones—but they stop at criticism of the standards and perspective according to which the current person assesses her desires and options. This is the case with Brandt's version, discussed later.

12. Dorothy Allison, *Skin: Talking About Sex, Class and Literature* (Ithaca, N.Y.: Firebrand Books, 1994), p. 206.

13. Rawls, *A Theory,* pp. 416–418.

14. Ibid., p. 420.

15. Richard Brandt, *A Theory of the Right and the Good* (Oxford: Clarendon Press, 1979).

16. Ibid., esp. pp. 88f.

17. Ibid., p. 111.

18. Ibid., p. 113.

19. Ibid.

20. Ibid., p. 117.

21. Ibid., p. 112.

22. Barbara Christian, "What Celie Knows That You Should Know," in David T. Goldberg, ed., *The Anatomy of Racism* (Minneapolis: University of Minnesota Press, 1990), p. 135.

23. Ibid.

24. Ibid., pp. 141–142.

25. Gilbert Ryle, *The Concept of Mind* (London: Penguin Books, 1949).

26. Milton Fisk, "Can the Cuban Revolution Survive Without Democracy?" paper presented at the fifth annual Society for Cuban and North American Philosophers, University of Havana, June 1993.

27. For instance, Cuban feminist Maritza Sosa argues that a prominent U.S. feminist's claim that there is no sexual democracy in Cuba fails to consider the relevant differences between Cuban society, history, traditions, values, and so on, and those of the capitalist United States. Maritza Sosa, "¿Democracia sin Mujeres? Reflexiones Sobre la Relación Género-Poder en Cuba," paper presented at the Sixth Conference of Cuban and North American Philosophers and Social Scientists, Havana, Cuba, June 15, 1994.

28. María Lugones, "Playfulness, 'World'-Travelling, and Loving Perception," *Hypatia* 2, no. 2 (Summer 1987): 3–19.

29. Ibid., p. 17.

30. Nkiru Nzegwu, "Gender Equality in a Dual-Sex System: The Case of Onitsha," *Canadian Journal of Law and Jurisprudence* 7, no. 1 (January 1994): 73–96; "O Africa: Gender Imperialism in Academia," in Obioma Nnameka and Oyeronke Oyewumi, eds., *African Women and Imperialism* (London: Routledge, forthcoming); "Sweeping Out Africa with Mother Europe's Broom: A Post-Colonial Sacrifice for Appiah," paper presented at the American Philosophical Association, Boston, Massachusetts, December 28, 1994, and at the Fernand Braudel Centre and the Institute of Global Studies, Binghamton, New York, February 2, 1995.

31. Alice Walker, *Meridian* (New York: Pocket Books, 1976), pp. 199–200.

32. Ibid.

33. See Thomas Kuhn, *The Structure of Scientific Revolutions* (Chicago: University of Chicago Press, 1962).

34. For discussion of scientific intuitions and their explanation, see Richard Boyd, "Scientific Realism and Naturalistic Epistemology," *PSA 1980* (1980): 613–662; and "How to Be a Moral Realist," in G. Sayre-McCord, ed., *Essays on Moral Realism* (Ithaca, N.Y.: Cornell University Press, 1988), pp. 181–228.

35. In particular, Boyd, "Scientific Realism and Naturalistic Epistemology"; "How to Be a Moral Realist"; "On the Current Status of Scientific Realism," *Erkenntnis* 19, nos. 1, 2, and 3 (1983): 45–90.

36. Virginia Woolf, *Three Guineas* (New York: Harcourt, Brace, Jovanovich, 1966), p. 62.

37. See, e.g., Peter Railton, "Marx and the Objectivity of Science," *PSA 1984* (1984): 813–825, reprinted in R. Boyd, P. Gaspar, and J. D. Trout, eds., *The Philosophy of Science* (Cambridge: MIT Press, 1991), pp. 763–773.

38. Anthony Appiah, "The Invention of Africa," in Appiah, *In My Father's House* (New York: Oxford University Press, 1992), p. 15.

Chapter 3

1. Peter Railton, "Moral Realism," *Philosophical Review* 95, no. 2 (April 1986): 163–207; "Facts and Values," *Philosophical Topics* 14, no. 2 (October 1986): 5–31. Whereas Railton's account is primarily of an individual's good, the definition of an objective end for a person provides the criteria for defining rational choice. See in particular, "Moral," pp. 186–189, 190–191.

2. John Rawls, *A Theory of Justice* (Cambridge: Harvard University Press, 1971), pp. 417f.; Henry Sidgwick, *The Methods of Ethics* (London: Macmillan & Co., 1907); Richard Brandt, *A Theory of the Right and the Good* (Oxford: Clarendon Press, 1979); R. M. Hare, *Moral Thinking* (Oxford: Clarendon Press, 1981).

3. Railton, "Facts," p. 11.

4. Ibid.

5. Railton, "Moral," p. 174.

6. Ibid.

7. Railton, "Facts," p. 16.

8. See, e.g., Railton, "Moral," p. 182, and "Facts," pp. 13–15.

9. Railton, "Facts," pp. 15–16.

10. Railton, "Moral," pp. 173f.

11. Ibid., pp. 173–174.

12. Railton, "Facts," pp. 16f.

13. Railton, "Moral," p. 180.

14. Ibid., p. 193.

15. Ibid., pp. 174–175.

16. Ibid., p. 188.

17. Rawls, *A Theory,* pp. 248f.

18. Railton, "Facts," p. 15.

19. Ibid.

20. Ibid., pp. 19–20.

21. Ibid., p. 20.

22. Ibid., p. 23.

23. Ibid., p. 20.

24. Toni Morrison, *Beloved* (New York: Penguin Books, 1988), p. 164.

25. Ibid.

26. Toni Morrison, *Playing in the Dark: Whiteness and the Literary Imagination* (New York: Vintage Books, 1992).

27. Ibid., p. 72.

28. See Railton, "Facts," p. 30, n. 12. See also J. David Velleman, "Brandt's Theory of 'Good,'" *Philosophical Review* 97, no. 3 (July 1988): 353–371, the published version of the paper Railton refers to (see Velleman, p. 353, n. 1).

29. See Railton's characterization of the issue in terms of moral rightness for a society that parallels his account of individual rationality. Criteria for assessing the relative merits of particular choices are generated by the theoretical specification of a social point of view. Railton, "Moral," p. 191.

30. Rawls, *A Theory,* pp. 552–554.

31. Dorothy Allison, *Skin: Talking About Sex, Class and Literature* (Ithaca, N.Y.: Firebrand Books, 1994), p. 111.

32. Arlene Stairs, "The Cultural Negotiation of Indigenous Education: Between Microethnography and Model-Building," *Peabody Journal of Education* 69, no. 2 (Winter 1994): 154–171. Also, "Human Development as Cultural Negotiation: Indigenous Lessons on Becoming a Teacher," paper presented at the annual meeting of the American Educational Research Association, New Orleans, April 1994.

33. Allison, *Skin,* p. 94.

34. Peter Railton, "Alienation, Consequentialism, and the Demands of Morality," *Philosophy and Public Affairs* 13, no. 2 (1984): 166–169.

35. Stephen Darwall, Allan Gibbard, and Peter Railton, "Toward *Fin de Siècle* Ethics: Some Trends," *Philosophical Review* 101, no. 1 (January 1992): 182.

Chapter 4

1. Toni Morrison, "Introduction," in Morrison, ed., *Race-ing, Justice, En-gendering Power* (New York: Pantheon Books, 1992), p. xi.

2. Will Kymlicka, *Liberalism, Community and Culture* (Oxford: Clarendon Press, 1991). Page references within the text are to this work.

3. John Danley, "Liberalism, Aboriginal Rights, and Cultural Minorities," *Philosophy and Public Affairs* 20, no. 2 (1991): 168–185.

4. Marilyn Frye distinguishes between oppression and suffering. See, e.g., "Oppression," in Frye, *Politics of Reality* (Trumansberg, N.Y.: Crossing Press, 1983), pp. 1–16. Groups are oppressed when they are systematically denied access to opportunities and goods. German Canadians may be a minority in Canada and they may suffer as a result of differences in culture, but they are not an oppressed minority. Native people and African Canadians are, however, oppressed groups.

5. Will Kymlicka, "Liberal Individualism and Liberal Neutrality," *Ethics* 99, no. 4 (July 1989): 890.

6. John Rawls, *A Theory of Justice* (Cambridge: Harvard University Press, 1971), p. 329, cited in ibid., p. 886.

7. Adina Schwartz, "Moral Neutrality and Primary Goods," *Ethics* 83 (1973): 302; and Thomas Nagel, "Rawls on Justice," *Philosophical Review* 82 (1973): 228–229, cited in Kymlicka, "Liberal Individualism," p. 891 (the source of this quote).

8. Kymlicka, "Liberal Individualism," pp. 895–896, n. 29.

9. Claudia Card, "Gender and Moral Luck," in Owen Flanagan and Amelie Rorty, eds., *Identity, Character and Morality* (Cambridge: MIT Press, 1990), pp. 199–218.

10. Nancy Sherman, "The Place of Emotions in Kantian Morality," in Flanagan and Rorty, eds., *Identity, Character and Morality*, pp. 166–168.

11. Luce Irigaray, "The Power of Discourse and the Subordination of the Feminine," in Margaret Whitford, ed., *The Irigaray Reader* (Cambridge: Basil Blackwell, 1991), p. 128.

12. Morrison, "Introduction," p. xi.

13. Patricia J. Williams, *The Alchemy of Race and Rights: Diary of a Law Professor* (Cambridge: Harvard University Press, 1991), p. 222.

14. See, e.g., Will Kymlicka, "Two Theories of Justice," *Inquiry* 33 (1990): 112.

15. Ibid., p. 115.

16. Ian Hacking, "Making Up People," in Edward Stein, ed., *Forms of Desire: Sexual Orientation and the Social Constructionist Controversy* (New York: Routledge, 1990), p. 80.

17. Frantz Fanon, "The Fact of Blackness," in David Goldberg, ed., *The Anatomy of Racism* (Minneapolis: University of Minnesota Press, 1990), p. 109.

18. C. Michard-Marchal, *Sexisme et sciences humaines: pratique linguistic du rapport de sexage* (Lille: Presses Universitaires de Lille, 1982), p. 7, cited in Lise Noël, *Intolerance: The Parameters of Oppression* (Montreal and Kingston: McGill–Queen's University Press, 1994), p. 27; emphasis added. Noël's book contains a wealth of examples of such invisibility.

19. Interview following presentation of film on PBS.

20. Toni Morrison, *Playing in the Dark: Whiteness and the Literary Imagination* (New York: Vintage Books, 1992).

21. Barbara Smith, "Queer Politics: Where's the Revolution?" *The Nation,* July 5, 1993, p. 13.

22. Anthony Appiah, "The Myth of an African World," in Appiah, *In My Father's House* (New York: Oxford University Press, 1992), pp. 73–84. For important criticism of Appiah's views on identity, relations to Africa, and cross-cultural understanding, see Nkiru Nzegwu, "Sweeping Out Africa with Mother Europe's Broom: A Post-Colonial Sacrifice for Appiah," paper presented at the American Philosophical Association, Boston, Massachusetts, December 28, 1994.

23. See, e.g., Diana Fuss, *Essentially Speaking: Feminism, Nature and Difference* (New York: Routledge, 1989); Joan Scott and Judith Butler, eds., *Feminists Theorize the Political* (New York: Routledge, 1992); Diana Fuss, ed., *Inside/Out: Lesbian Theories, Gay Theories* (New York: Routledge, 1991); Appiah, *In My Father's House;* Judith Butler, *Gender Trouble* (New York: Routledge, 1990).

24. Kymlicka sets out two conditions that, as he himself acknowledges, are not very helpful: Membership in a cultural community is defined by (1) an objective component dealing with such things as a common language and heritage, and (2) a subjective component dealing with self-identification with the group (p. 179, no. 2).

25. Rosemary Brown, *Being Brown: A Very Public Life* (Toronto: Random House of Canada, 1989).

26. See, e.g., R. N. Boyd, "Metaphor and Theory Change," in A. Ortony, ed., *Metaphor and Thought* (New York: Cambridge University Press, 1979), pp.

348–408; "Scientific Realism and Naturalistic Epistemology," *PSA 80* 2 (1980): 613–662; "On the Current Status of Scientific Realism," *Erkenntnis* 19, nos. 1, 2, and 3 (1983): 45–90; and Philip Kitcher, *The Advancement of Science* (New York: Oxford University Press, 1993).

Chapter 5

1. See, e.g., David Gauthier, "The Liberal Individual," in Shlomo Avineri and Avner de-Shalit, eds., *Communitarianism and Individualism* (New York: Oxford University Press, 1992), pp. 151–164.

2. Thomas Hill Jr., "Servility and Self-Respect," *The Monist* 57, no. 1 (1973): 87–104, reprinted in Thomas Hill Jr., *Autonomy and Self-Respect* (New York: Cambridge University Press, 1991), pp. 4–18.

3. Toni Morrison, "Introduction," in Morrison, ed., *Race-ing, Justice, En-gendering Power* (New York: Pantheon Books, 1992), pp. xiv–xv.

4. Lynne McFall, "Integrity," *Ethics* 98, no. 7 (October 1987): 5–20, reprinted in John Deigh, ed., *Ethics and Personality* (Chicago: University of Chicago Press, 1992), p. 79.

5. Amelie O. Rorty and David Wong, "Aspects of Identity and Agency," in Owen Flanagan and Amelie O. Rorty, eds., *Identity, Character and Morality* (Cambridge: MIT Press, 1990), pp. 19–36.

6. Sydney Shoemaker, *Self-Knowledge and Self-Identity* (Ithaca, N.Y.: Cornell University Press, 1963); D. Parfit, *Reasons and Persons* (Oxford: Oxford University Press, 1984); M. Sandel, *Liberalism and the Limits of Justice* (New York: Cambridge University Press, 1982); A. MacIntyre, *After Virtue* (Notre Dame: University of Notre Dame Press, 1984), and *Whose Justice? Which Rationality?* (Notre Dame: University of Notre Dame Press, 1988); H. Frankfurt, "The Freedom of the Will and the Concept of the Person," *Journal of Philosophy* 68, no. 1 (1971): 5–20; C. Taylor, "Responsibility for Self," in A. O. Rorty, ed., *The Identities of Persons* (Los Angeles: University of California Press, 1976), pp. 22–50.

7. Flanagan and Rorty, "Introduction," in *Identity, Character*, p. 3.

8. John Rawls, "Justice as Fairness: Political Not Metaphysical," *Philosophy and Public Affairs* 14, no. 3 (Summer 1985): 232–233.

9. Rorty and Wong, "Aspects," p. 23.

10. I am indebted to Patricia J. Williams, *The Alchemy of Race and Rights: Diary of a Law Professor* (Cambridge: Harvard University Press, 1991), pp. 136f., for this example.

11. Ibid., pp. 137–138.

12. Ibid., p. 144.

13. Morrison, "Introduction," p. xv.

14. Ibid., p. xiii.

15. Ibid., pp. xv–xvi.

16. Ibid., p. xvi.

17. Ibid.

18. See Wanda Coleman, "Remembering Latasha: Blacks, Immigrants and America," *The Nation*, February 15, 1993, p. 187.

19. Victoria Davion, "Integrity and Radical Change," in Claudia Card, ed., *Feminist Ethics* (Lawrence: University Press of Kansas, 1991), pp. 180–194.

20. McFall, "Integrity," in Deigh, ed., *Ethics and Personality*, pp. 88, 90.

21. Davion, "Integrity," p. 181.

22. Ibid., p. 182.

23. Ibid., p. 183.

24. Sarah Lucia Hoagland, *Lesbian Ethics* (Palo Alto: Institute of Lesbian Studies, 1988), esp. ch. 2.

25. Mab Sebrest, *My Mama's Dead Squirrel: Lesbian Essays on Southern Culture* (Ithaca, N.Y.: Firebrand Books, 1985), p. 20.

26. As in J. L. Mackie, "The Subjectivity of Values," in Mackie, *Ethics: Inventing Right and Wrong* (London: Penguin Books, 1977), pp. 15–49.

27. See, e.g., Nicholas Sturgeon, "Moral Explanations," in David Copp and David Zimmerman, eds., *Morality, Reason, and Truth* (Totowa, N.J.: Rowman and Allenheld, 1985), pp. 49–78, reprinted in Geoffrey Sayre-McCord, ed., *Essays on Moral Realism* (Ithaca, N.Y.: Cornell University Press, 1988), p. 242.

28. For an important example, see Haideh Moghissi, "Racism and Sexism in Academic Practice: A Case Study," in H. Afshar and M. Mynard, eds., *Dynamics of Gender and Race: Some Feminist Intervention* (London: Taylor and Francis, 1994), pp. 222–234.

29. Lynne McFall, "What's Wrong with Bitterness?" in Card, ed., *Feminist Ethics*, pp. 146–154, quote on p. 154.

30. Ibid., p. 146.

31. Ibid., p. 148.

32. Ibid.

33. Ibid., p. 153.

34. Ibid., p. 148.

35. Ronald de Sousa, *The Rationality of Emotions* (Cambridge: MIT Press, 1987), p. 259, cited in ibid., p. 154.

36. Sue Campbell, "Being Dismissed: The Politics of Emotional Expression," *Hypatia* 9, no. 3 (Summer 1994): 54.

37. Ibid., p. 53.

38. Ibid., p. 52.

39. Dorothy Allison, *Bastard Out of Carolina* (New York: Penguin Books, 1992). I am grateful to Elizabeth Hanson for this example.

40. Ibid., pp. 97–98.

41. Jon Elster, "Norms of Revenge," *Ethics* 100, no. 4 (July 1990): 862–885, reprinted in Deigh, ed., *Ethics and Personality*, pp. 155–178.

42. Ibid., p. 155.

43. Ibid., p. 159.

44. Ibid., p. 165.

45. Ibid., p. 176.

46. Ibid., p. 165.

47. Ibid., pp. 158–159.

48. Ibid., p. 176.

49. Ibid., p. 161.

50. Ibid., p. 178.

Chapter 6

1. See, e.g., Iris Young, *Justice and the Politics of Difference* (Princeton: Princeton University Press, 1988).

2. Elizabeth V. Spelman, *Inessential Woman: Problems of Exclusion in Feminist Thought* (Boston: Beacon Press, 1988).

3. Donna Haraway, "Ecce Homo, Ain't (Arn't) I a Woman, and Inappropriate/d Others: The Human in a Post-Humanist Landscape," in Judith Butler and Joan Scott, eds., *Feminists Theorize the Political* (New York: Routledge, 1992), pp. 86–100.

4. Ibid., p. 88.

5. See Ernst Mayr, *Populations, Species, and Evolution* (Cambridge: Harvard University Press, 1970), p. 4, and *The Growth of Biological Thought* (Cambridge: Harvard University Press, 1982), p. 256.

6. Ian Hacking argues that the tradition of natural kinds should be traced not to Locke but to Mill (Ian Hacking, "A Tradition of Natural Kinds," *Philosophical Studies* 61, nos. 1, 2, and 3 [1991]: 109–126, and "On Boyd," *Philosophical Studies* 61, nos. 1, 2, and 3 [1991]: 149–154). For reasons that cannot be fully spelled out here, I find the connection some feminists make to Locke (see, e.g., Diana Fuss, *Essentially Speaking: Feminism, Nature and Difference* [New York: Routledge, 1989], pp. 4–5) defensible and useful. For one thing, the tension in Locke between an epistemologically motivated inclination toward nominalism and the need to account for classification practices is paralleled, arguably, by an ongoing tension within feminist theory between a resistance to "metaphysics" and the need for an account of "real" gender categories. See, e.g., D. Cornell, *Beyond Accommodation: Ethical Feminism, Deconstruction and the Law* (New York: Routledge, 1991), pp. 3, 166.

7. John Locke, *An Essay Concerning Human Understanding* (Oxford: Oxford University Press, 1975 [1689]), esp. IV, iii, p. 25.

8. Elizabeth Grosz, "Conclusion: A Note on Essentialism and Difference," in Sneja Gunew, ed., *Feminist Knowledge: Critique and Construct* (New York: Routledge, 1990), p. 334.

9. Spelman, *Inessential Woman*, p. x.

10. Fuss, *Essentially Speaking*, pp. 2–3.

11. Donna Haraway, "Situated Knowledges," in Haraway, *Simians, Cyborgs and Women: The Reinvention of Nature* (New York: Routledge, 1991), p. 187.

12. Ibid., p. 191.

13. Ibid.

14. Ibid.

15. Claudia Card, "Introduction," in Card, ed., *Feminist Ethics* (Lawrence: University Press of Kansas, 1991), p. 25.

16. Haraway, "Ecce," p. 86.

17. Ibid., p. 92.

18. Ibid.

19. Ibid.

20. Ibid., p. 93.

21. Christina Sommers, commentary on Marilyn Friedman's "They Lived Happily Ever After: Sommers on Women and Marriage," presented at American

Philosophical Association, Eastern Division, Boston, Massachusetts, December 28, 1990.

22. In reference to debate about equity hiring policies at the general meeting of the Canadian Philosophical Association Convention in Charlottetown, Prince Edward Island, May 1992.

23. Haraway, "Ecce," p. 93.

24. Ibid., p. 91.

25. Ibid., p. 98.

26. Fuss, *Essentially,* pp. 2–3.

27. Haraway, "Ecce," p. 88.

28. Raquel Mendieta Costa, "Cuba Nexos y Rupturas: Tres Décadas de Cultura en La Revolución," paper presented at the Fifth Meeting of Cuban and North American Philosophers, Havana, Cuba, June 21, 1993; "De la Isla a la Nación," *Revista Proposiciones,* Año, Edición no. 1 (1994): 16–29.

29. Haideh Moghissi, *Populism and Feminism in Iran: Women's Struggle in a Male-Defined Revolutionary Movement* (New York: St. Martin's Press, 1994). See also "Women, Modernization and Revolution in Iran," *Review of Radical Political Economics* 23, nos. 3 and 4 (1991): 205–223.

30. Moghissi, *Populism,* p. 2.

31. Fuss, *Essentially,* p. 5.

32. See, e.g., Linda Alcoff and Elizabeth Potter, "Introduction," in Alcoff and Potter, eds., *Feminist Epistemologies* (New York: Routledge, 1993), pp. 1–14.

33. Although radical constructivism, as Haraway argues, has been dominant in feminist—particularly postmodernist—theory, there are some notable exceptions. See, for instance, Lorraine Code, *What Can She Know? Feminist Theory and the Construction of Knowledge* (Ithaca, N.Y.: Cornell University Press, 1991); and Lynne Hankinson Nelson, *Who Knows? From Quine to a Feminist Empiricism* (Philadelphia: Temple University Press, 1991).

34. Kuhn's neo-Kantian constructivism is more complex and sophisticated than some kinds of feminist constructivisms. Haraway sometimes seems to be referring to constructivism as the view that knowledge claims are nothing but a working out of power relationships.

35. Thomas Kuhn, *The Structure of Scientific Revolutions* (Chicago: University of Chicago Press, 1962).

36. See, e.g., R. Boyd, "Scientific Realism and Naturalistic Epistemology," *PSA 80* 2 (1980): 613–662; "On the Current Status of Scientific Realism," *Erkenntnis* 19, nos. 1, 2, and 3 (1983): 45–90.

37. Philip Kitcher, "Social Knowledge," paper presented at the American Philosophical Association meeting, New York, December 30, 1992.

38. E.g., Alvin Goldman, "A Causal Theory of Knowing," *Journal of Philosophy* 64 (1967): 357–372; W.V.O. Quine, "Natural Kinds," in Quine, *Ontological Relativity and Other Essays* (New York: Columbia University Press, 1969), pp. 114–138. Louise Antony has recently pointed this out.

39. E.g., R. Boyd, "Metaphor and Theory Change," in A. Ortony, ed., *Metaphor and Thought* (New York: Cambridge University Press, 1979), pp. 348–408; "Scientific Realism and Naturalistic Epistemology"; "On the Current Status of the Issue of Scientific Realism."

40. Stephen Jay Gould, *Wonderful Life: The Burgess Shale and the Nature of History* (New York: W. W. Norton, 1989).

41. Ibid., pp. 48–51.

42. Ibid., p. 51.

43. Will Kymlicka, *Liberalism, Community and Culture* (Oxford: Clarendon Press, 1991).

44. Toni Morrison, ed., *Race-ing, Justice, En-gendering Power* (New York: Pantheon Books, 1992), p. xii.

45. Mayr, *Populations, Species, and Evolution; The Growth of Biological Thought.*

46. Mayr, *The Growth of Biological Thought,* pp. 147–209.

47. Sydney Shoemaker, "Causality and Properties," in P. van Inwagen, ed., *Essays in Honor of Richard Taylor* (Dordrecht, Holland: D. Reidel Press, 1980), pp. 206–233.

48. R. Boyd, "Realism, Conventionality and 'Realism About,'" in G. Boolos, ed., *Meaning and Method: Essays in Honor of H. Putnam* (Cambridge: Cambridge University Press, 1990), p. 176.

49. Edward Stein, ed., *Forms of Desire: Sexual Orientation and the Social Constructionist Controversy* (New York: Routledge, 1990), pp. 325–355.

50. Ibid., pp. 350–353.

51. Boyd, "Realism, Conventionality and 'Realism About.'"

52. Fuss, *Essentially,* p. 2.

53. "Quebec Town Finds Ways to Oppose Racist Rally," *Globe and Mail,* August 1, 1992, p. A5.

54. I am grateful to Jennifer Parks for this example (Jennifer Parks, "Respect for Life, Respect for Women, and the Treatment of Spare Human Embryos," M.A. Thesis, Queen's University, 1992).

Chapter 7

1. Audre Lorde, *Sister Outsider: Essays and Speeches by Audre Lorde* (Trumansberg, N.Y.: Crossing Press, 1984), p. 57.

2. Ibid., p. 56.

3. Ibid., p. 55.

4. Ibid.

5. Dorothy Allison, *Skin: Talking About Sex, Class and Literature* (Ithaca, N.Y.: Firebrand Books, 1994), p. 94.

6. Ibid., p. 112.

7. Ibid., p. 100.

8. Stephen Darwall, Allan Gibbard, and Peter Railton, "Toward *Fin de Siècle* Ethics," *Philosophical Review* 101, no. 1 (January 1992): 181–182.

9. Angela Gilliam, "Women's Equality and National Liberation," in Chandra Mohanty, Ann Russo, and Lourdes Torres, eds., *Third World Women and the Politics of Feminism* (Bloomington: Indiana University Press, 1991), p. 218.

10. Ibid.

11. Peter Railton discusses these sorts of examples in "Alienation, Consequentialism and the Demands of Morality," *Philosophy and Public Affairs* 13, no. 2 (1984): 134–171.

12. Richard Miller, *Moral Differences: Truth, Justice and Conscience in a World of Conflict* (Princeton: Princeton University Press, 1992), chs. 9–11. Page references in the text are to this edition.

13. Toni Morrison, *Jazz* (New York: Alfred A. Knopf, 1992), pp. 202–203.

14. Dick Gregory with Robert Lipsyte, *Nigger* (New York: E. P. Dutton, 1964), p. 49. I am grateful to Susan Franzosa for this example.

15. Patricia J. Williams, *The Alchemy of Race and Rights: Diary of a Law Professor* (Cambridge: Harvard University Press, 1991), p. 222.

16. Mab Segrest, *My Mama's Dead Squirrel: Lesbian Essays on Southern Culture* (Ithaca, N.Y.: Firebrand Books, 1985), p. 153.

17. Ibid., p. 20.

18. Darwall, Gibbard, and Railton, "Toward *Fin de Siècle* Ethics," p. 182.

19. Charles Mills, "Old Worlds, New Worlds," paper presented at Guelph University, Guelph, Ontario, May 5, 1993. See also Mills, *The Racial Contract,* forthcoming.

20. Sarah Hoagland, *Lesbian Ethics* (Palo Alto: Institute of Lesbian Studies, 1988), esp. ch. 2.

21. Ifi Amadiume, *Male Daughters, Female Husbands: Gender and Sex in an African Society* (London: Zed Press, 1987), p. 7.

22. Nkiru Nzegwu, "Gender Equality in a Dual-Sex System: The Case of Onitsha," *Canadian Journal of Law and Jurisprudence* 7, no. 1 (January 1994): 73–96.

23. Judith Van Allen, "'Sitting on a Man': Colonialism and the Lost Political Institutions of Igbo Women," *Canadian Journal of African Studies* 6, no. 2 (1972): 165–181.

24. Ian Hacking, "Making Up People," in Edward Stein, ed., *Forms of Desire: Sexual Orientation and the Social Constructionist Controversy* (New York: Routledge, 1990), pp. 69–88.

25. Susan Franzosa, "Authoring the Educated Self: Educational Autobiography and Resistance," *Educational Theory* 42, no. 4 (1992): 404.

26. Hacking, "Making Up People," p. 80.

27. Ibid., p. 79.

28. Arnold Davidson, "Sex and the Emergence of Sexuality," in Stein, ed., *Forms,* esp. pp. 96–98.

29. Ibid., p. 97.

30. John Boswell, "Categories, Experience and Sexuality," in Stein, ed., *Forms,* pp. 133–174.

31. Hacking, "Making Up People," pp. 78–79.

32. Boswell, "Categories," pp. 145–146.

33. Lorde, *Sister,* p. 55.

34. Ibid.

35. Virginia Woolf, *Moments of Being,* ed. Jeanne Schulkind (Sussex: University Press, 1976). I am grateful to Susan Franzosa for referring me to this text.

36. Jeanne Schulkind, "Introduction," in ibid., p. 19.

37. Ibid.

38. I have benefited from discussions with Jane Isaacs-Doyle for the ideas in this section.

Chapter 8

1. M. C. Nussbaum, *Love's Knowledge: Essays on Philosophy and Literature* (New York: Oxford University Press, 1990), p. 74. References within the text are to this edition.

2. Henry James, *The Golden Bowl* (New York: Scribner's, 1909).

3. R. M. Hare, *Moral Thinking: Its Levels, Methods and Point* (Oxford: Clarendon Press, 1981), pp. 44–64.

4. Ibid., p. 44.

5. Ibid.

6. Ibid., p. 45.

7. Octavia E. Butler, *Kindred* (Boston: Beacon Press, 1979).

8. Ibid., p. 223.

9. Ibid., pp. 229–230.

10. Ibid., p. 260.

11. Toni Morrison, *Beloved* (New York: Penguin Books, 1988), p. 202.

12. Ibid.

13. Ibid., p. 18.

14. Toni Morrison, *Playing in the Dark: Whiteness and the Literary Imagination* (New York: Vintage Books, 1992).

15. Ibid., p. 14.

16. Anthony Appiah, *In My Father's House: Africa in the Philosophy of Culture* (New York: Oxford University Press, 1992).

17. Morrison, *Playing*, p. 15.

18. Ibid., p. 17.

19. Ibid., p. 33.

20. Ibid., p. 42.

21. Ibid. (emphasis added).

22. Ibid., p. 44.

23. Ibid., p. 57.

24. Ibid., p. 56.

25. Willa Cather, *Sapphira and the Slave Girl* (Toronto: Random, 1975).

26. Ibid., p. 23.

27. Ibid., p. 44.

28. Ibid., p. xi.

29. Butler, *Kindred*, p. 260.

30. R. Boyd, "What is Realism 'Realism About?'" in G. Boolos, ed., *Meaning and Method: Essays in Honor of H. Putnam* (Cambridge: Cambridge University Press, 1990), pp. 171–195.

31. Van Gosse, *Where the Boys Are: Cuba, Cold War America and the Making of a New Left* (New York: Verso Press, 1993), p. 185.

32. Morrison, *Playing,* p. vi.

33. Ibid., pp. vii–viii (emphasis added by Morrison). Original source is Marie Cardinal, *The Words To Say It* (Cambridge, Mass.: Van Vactor and Goodheart, 1984).

34. Ibid., p. viii.

35. Ibid., p. ix.

36. E.g., Iris Marion Young, *Justice and the Politics of Difference* (Princeton, N.J.: Princeton University Press, 1988).

37. Morrison, *Playing,* p. 17.

38. Ibid.

Epilogue

1. Paper presented at Feminist Ethics and Social Policy conference in Pittsburgh, November 5, 1993, read by Rita Manning (my translation).

2. Raquel Mendieta Costa, "Cuba Nexos y Rupturas: Tres Décadas de Cultura en la Revolución," paper presented at the Fifth Meeting of Cuban and North American Philosophers, Havana, Cuba, June 21, 1993 (my translation).

3. Ibid., p. 3.

4. Ibid., pp. 3–4.

5. Ibid., p. 2.

6. Nancy Arteaga Chacón, "Los Valores Morales, lugar y papel en la sociedad socialista cubana," paper presented at the sixth annual Society of Cuba and North American Philosophers and Social Scientists, University of Havana, Cuba, June 15, 1994.

7. Lissette Mendora, "La Formación de Valores," paper presented at the Fac. Ciencias Sociales, Instituto Superior Politécnico José A. Echeverría, Havana, Cuba, June 22, 1994.

8. Toni Morrison, *Playing in the Dark: Whiteness and the Literary Imagination* (New York: Vintage Books, 1992). Page references within the text are to this work.

9. See Vicki Skeels and Susan Babbitt, eds., *"The Revolution Gave Me Humanity": Cuban Women and Social Justice* (forthcoming).

10. See, for instance, Olga Fernandez Riós, "Cuba: Reevaluación de la Democracia desde una perspectiva tercermundista," *Ko Eyu Latinoamericano: Revista de Análisis Político-Cultural,* Ene-Mar 94, no. 67 (1994): 45–52.

11. Amelia Suárez and Lourdes Perez, "La Mujer en la Municipalidad," paper presented at the sixth annual Society of Cuba and North American Philosophers and Social Scientists, University of Havana, Cuba, June 16, 1994.

Bibliography

Alcoff, Linda, and Elizabeth Potter, eds. 1993. *Feminist Epistemologies* (New York: Routledge).

Allen, Judith Van. 1972. "'Sitting on a Man': Colonialism and the Lost Political Institutions of Igbo Women," *Canadian Journal of African Studies* 6, no. 2: 165–181.

Allison, Dorothy. 1992. *Bastard Out of Carolina* (New York: Penguin Books).

———. 1994. *Skin: Talking About Sex, Class and Literature* (Ithaca, N.Y.: Firebrand Books).

Amadiume, Ifi. 1987. *Male Daughters, Female Husbands: Gender and Sex in an African Society* (London: Zed Press).

Antony, Louise, and Charlotte Witt, eds. 1993. *A Mind of One's Own: Feminist Essays on Reason and Objectivity* (Boulder: Westview Press).

Appiah, Anthony. 1992. *In My Father's House: Africa in the Philosophy of Culture* (New York: Oxford University Press).

Arteaga Chacón, Nancy. 1994. "Los Valores Morales, lugar y papel en la sociedad socialista cubana." Paper presented at the sixth annual Society of Cuba and North American Philosophers and Social Scientists, University of Havana, Cuba, June 15.

Boswell, John. 1992. "Categories, Experience, and Sexuality." In Edward Stein, ed., *Forms of Desire* (New York: Routledge), pp. 133–174.

Boyd, Richard. 1979. "Metaphor and Theory Change." In A. Ortony, ed., *Metaphor and Thought* (New York: Cambridge University Press), pp. 348–408.

———. 1980. "Scientific Realism and Naturalistic Epistemology." *PSA 1980* 2: 613–662.

———. 1983. "On the Current Status of Scientific Realism." *Erkenntnis* 19, nos. 1, 2, and 3: 45–90.

———. 1988. "How to Be a Moral Realist." In G. Sayre-McCord, ed., *Essays on Moral Realism* (Ithaca, N.Y.: Cornell University Press), pp. 181–228.

———. 1990. "Realism, Conventionality and 'Realism About.'" In G. Boolos, ed., *Meaning and Method: Essays in Honor of H. Putnam* (Cambridge: Cambridge University Press), pp. 171–195.

Brandt, Richard. 1979. *A Theory of the Right and the Good* (Oxford: Clarendon Press).

Brown, Rosemary. 1989. *Being Brown: A Very Public Life* (Toronto: Random House of Canada).

Butler, Octavia E. 1979. *Kindred* (Boston: Beacon Press).

Campbell, Sue. 1994. "Being Dismissed: The Politics of Emotional Expression." *Hypatia* 9, no. 3 (Summer): 46–65.

Card, Claudia. 1990. "Gender and Moral Luck." In Owen Flanagan and Amelie Rorty, eds., *Identity, Character and Morality* (Cambridge: MIT Press), pp. 199–218.

——, ed. 1991. *Feminist Ethics* (Lawrence: University Press of Kansas).

Christian, Barbara. 1990. "What Celie Knows That You Should Know." In David T. Goldberg, ed., *The Anatomy of Racism* (Minneapolis: University of Minnesota Press), pp. 135–145.

Code, Lorraine. 1991. *What Can She Know? Feminist Theory and the Construction of Knowledge* (Ithaca, N.Y.: Cornell University Press).

Cornell, Drucilla. 1991. *Beyond Accommodation: Ethical Feminism, Deconstruction and the Law* (New York: Routledge).

——. 1992. "What Takes Place in the Dark." *Differences: A Journal of Feminist Cultural Studies* 42 (Summer): 45–71.

Danley, John. 1991. "Liberalism, Aboriginal Rights, and Cultural Minorities." *Philosophy and Public Affairs* 20, no. 2: 168–185.

Darwall, Stephen, Allan Gibbard, and Peter Railton. 1992. "Toward *Fin de Siècle* Ethics." *Philosophical Review* 101, no. 1 (January): 115–189.

Davion, Victoria. 1991. "Integrity and Radical Change." In Claudia Card, ed., *Feminist Ethics* (Lawrence: University Press of Kansas), pp. 180–194.

de Sousa, Ronald. 1987. *The Rationality of Emotions* (Cambridge: MIT Press).

Elster, Jon. 1990. "Norms of Revenge." *Ethics* 100, no. 4 (July): 862–885, reprinted in John Deigh, ed., *Ethics and Personality* (Chicago: University of Chicago Press, 1992), pp. 155–178.

Fanon, Frantz. 1990. "The Fact of Blackness." In Fanon, *Black Skins, White Masks* (New York: Grove Press, 1967), pp. 109–140, reprinted in D. T. Goldberg, ed., *The Anatomy of Racism* (Minneapolis: University of Minnesota Press), pp. 108–126.

Feinberg, Joel. 1971. "Legal Paternalism." *Canadian Journal of Philosophy* 1, no. 1: 106–124.

Fernandez Riós, Olga. 1994. "Cuba: Reevaluación de la Democracia desde una perspectiva tercermundista." *Ko Eyu Latinoamericano: Revista de Análisis Político-Cultural,* Ene-Mar 67: 45–52.

Frankfurt, H. 1971. "The Freedom of the Will and the Concept of the Person." *Journal of Philosophy* 68, no. 1: 5–20

Franzosa, Susan. 1992. "Authoring the Educated Self: Educational Autobiography and Resistance." *Educational Theory* 42, no. 4: 395–412.

Frye, Marilyn. 1983. *Politics of Reality* (Trumansberg, N.Y.: Crossing Press).

——. 1992. *Willful Virgin* (Freedom, Calif.: Crossing Press).

Fuss, Diana. 1989. *Essentially Speaking: Feminism, Nature and Difference* (New York: Routledge).

——, ed. 1991. *Inside/Out: Lesbian Theories, Gay Theories* (New York: Routledge).

Gauthier, David. 1992. "The Liberal Individual." In Shlomo Avineri and Avner de-Shalit, eds., *Communitarianism and Individualism* (New York: Oxford University Press), pp. 151–164.

Gilliam, Angela. 1991. "Women's Equality and National Liberation." In Chandra Mohanty, Ann Russo, and Lourdes Torres, eds., *Third World Women and the*

Politics of Feminism (Bloomington: Indiana University Press), pp. 215–236.

Goldman, Alvin. 1967. "A Causal Theory of Knowledge." *Journal of Philosophy* 64: 357–372.

Gosse, Van. 1993. *Where the Boys Are: Cuba, Cold War America and the Making of a New Left* (New York: Verso Press).

Gould, Stephen Jay. 1989. *Wonderful Life: The Burgess Shale and the Nature of History* (New York: W. W. Norton).

Gramsci, Antonio. 1983 [1971]. "The Intellectuals." In Q. Hoare and G. Nowell Smith, eds., *Selections from the Prison Notebooks of Antonio Gramsci* (New York: International Publishers), pp. 3–14.

Gregory, Dick, with Robert Lipsyte. 1964. *Nigger* (New York: E. P. Dutton).

Gunew, Sneja, ed. 1990. *Feminist Knowledge: Critique and Construct* (New York: Routledge).

Hacking, Ian. 1990. "Making Up People." In Edward Stein, ed., *Forms of Desire: Sexual Orientation and the Social Constructionist Controversy* (New York: Routledge), pp. 69–88.

———. 1991. "A Tradition of Natural Kinds." *Philosophical Studies* 61, nos. 1, 2, and 3: 109–126.

———. 1991. "On Boyd." *Philosophical Studies* 61, nos. 1, 2, and 3: 149–154.

Haraway, Donna. 1991. "Reading Buchi Emecheta." In Haraway, *Simians, Cyborgs and Women: The Reinvention of Nature* (New York: Routledge), pp. 109–126.

———. 1991. "Situated Knowledges." In Haraway, *Simians, Cyborgs and Women: The Reinvention of Nature* (New York: Routledge), pp. 183–202.

———. 1992. "Ecce Homo, Ain't (Arn't) I a Woman, and Inappropriate/d Others: The Human in a Post-Humanist Landscape." In Judith Butler and Joan Scott, eds., *Feminists Theorize the Political* (New York: Routledge), pp. 86–100.

Hare, R. M. 1981. *Moral Thinking: Its Level, Methods and Point* (Oxford: Clarendon Press).

Herman, Barbara. 1992. "Agency, Attachment and Difference." In John Deigh, ed., *Ethics and Personality* (Chicago: University of Chicago Press), pp. 41–64.

Hill, Thomas Jr. 1973. "Servility and Self-Respect," *The Monist* 57, no. 1: 87–104.

———. 1991. *Autonomy and Self-Respect* (New York: Cambridge University Press).

Hoagland, Sarah. 1988. *Lesbian Ethics* (Palo Alto: Institute of Lesbian Studies).

Irigaray, Luce. 1991. "The Power of Discourse and the Subordination of the Feminine." In Margaret Whitford, ed., *The Irigaray Reader* (Cambridge: Basil Blackwell), pp. 118–133.

Jones, Leroi. 1966. "Cuba Libre," reprinted in Jones, *Home: Social Essays* (New York: William Morrow), pp. 11–62.

Kitcher, Philip. 1984. *Abusing Science: The Case Against Creationism* (Cambridge: MIT Press).

———. 1992. "The Naturalists Return." *Philosophical Review* 101, no. 1 (January): 53–114.

———. 1993. *The Advancement of Science* (New York: Oxford University Press).

Kuhn, Thomas. 1962. *The Structure of Scientific Revolutions* (Chicago: University of Chicago Press).

Kymlicka, Will. 1989. "Liberal Individualism and Liberal Neutrality." *Ethics* 99, no. 4 (July): 883–905.

———. 1991. *Liberalism, Community and Culture* (Oxford: Clarendon Press).

Lorde, Audre. 1984. *Sister Outsider: Essays and Speeches by Audre Lorde* (Trumansberg, N.Y.: Crossing Press).

Lugones, María. 1987. "Playfulness, 'World'-Travelling, and Loving Perception." *Hypatia* 2, no. 2 (Summer): 3–19.

MacIntyre, A. 1984. *After Virtue* (Notre Dame: University of Notre Dame Press).

———. 1988. *Whose Justice Which Rationality?* (Notre Dame: University of Notre Dame Press).

Mackie, J. L. 1977. "The Subjectivity of Values." In *Ethics: Inventing Right and Wrong* (London: Penguin Books), pp. 15–49.

Mayr, Ernst. 1970. *Populations, Species, and Evolution* (Cambridge: Harvard University Press).

———. 1982. *The Growth of Biological Thought* (Cambridge: Harvard University Press).

McFall, Lynne. 1987. "Integrity." *Ethics* 98, no. 1 (October): 5–20, reprinted in John Deigh, ed., *Ethics and Personality* (Chicago: University of Chicago Press, 1992), pp. 79–94.

———. 1991. "What's Wrong with Bitterness?" In Claudia Card, ed., *Feminist Ethics* (Lawrence: University Press of Kansas), pp. 146–160.

Mendieta Costa, Raquel. 1993. "Cuba, Nexos y Rupturas: Tres Décadas de Cultura en La Revolución." Paper presented at the Fifth Meeting of Cuban and North American Philosophers, Havana, Cuba, June 21.

———. 1994. "De la Isla a la Nación." *Revista Proposiciones* Año 1, Edición no. 1: 16 29.

Mendora, Lissette. 1994. "La Formación de Valores." Paper presented at the Fac. Ciencias Sociales, Instituto Superior Politécnico José A. Echeverría, Havana, Cuba, June 22.

Miller, Richard. 1992. *Moral Differences: Truth, Justice and Conscience in a World of Conflict* (Princeton: Princeton University Press).

Mills, Charles. 1993. "Old Worlds, New Worlds." Paper presented at Guelph University, Guelph, Ontario, May 5.

Moghissi, Haideh. 1991. "Women, Modernization and Revolution in Iran." *Review of Radical Political Economics* 23, nos. 3 and 4: 205–223.

———. 1994. *Populism and Feminism in Iran: Women's Struggle in a Male-Defined Revolutionary Movement* (New York: St. Martin's Press).

———. 1994. "Racism and Sexism in Academic Practice: A Case Study." In H. Afshar and M. Mynard, eds., *Dynamics of Gender and Race: Some Feminist Intervention* (London: Taylor and Francis), pp. 222–234.

Morrison, Toni. 1988. *Beloved* (New York: Penguin Books).

———. 1992. *Jazz* (New York: Alfred A. Knopf).

———. 1992. *Playing in the Dark: Whiteness and the Literary Imagination* (New York: Vintage Books).

———, ed. 1992. *Race-ing, Justice, En-gendering Power: Essays on Anita Hill, Clarence Thomas, and the Construction of Social Reality* (New York: Pantheon Books).

Nelson, Lynne Hankinson. 1991. *Who Knows? From Quine to a Feminist Empiricism* (Philadelphia: Temple University Press).

Noël, Lise. 1994. *Intolerance: The Parameters of Oppression* (Montreal and Kingston: McGill–Queen's University Press).

Nussbaum, M. C. 1990. *Love's Knowledge: Essays on Philosophy and Literature* (New York: Oxford University Press).

Nzegwu, Nkiru. 1994. "Gender Equality in a Dual-Sex System: The Case of Onitsha." *Canadian Journal of Law and Jurisprudence* 7, no. 1 (January): 73–96.

———. 1994. "Sweeping Out Africa with Mother Europe's Broom: A Post-Colonial Sacrifice for Appiah." Paper presented at the American Philosophical Association, Boston, Massachusetts, December 28.

———. 1995. "O Africa: Gender Imperialism in Academia." In Obioma Nnameka and Oyeronke Oyewumi, eds., *African Women and Imperialism* (Trenton, N.J.: Africa World Press).

Parfit, D. 1984. *Reasons and Persons* (Oxford: Oxford University Press).

Quine, W. V. 1969. "Natural Kinds." In Quine, *Ontological Relativity and Other Essays* (New York: Columbia University Press), pp. 114–138.

Railton, Peter. 1984. "Alienation, Consequentialism, and the Demands of Morality." *Philosophy and Public Affairs* 13, no. 2: 134–171.

———. 1984. "Marx and the Objectivity of Science." *PSA 1984* 2: 813–825, reprinted in R. Boyd, P. Gaspar, and J. D. Trout, eds., *The Philosophy of Science* (Cambridge: MIT Press, 1991), pp. 763–773.

———. 1986. "Facts and Values." *Philosophical Topics* 14, no. 2 (October): 5–31.

———. 1986. "Moral Realism." *Philosophical Review* 95, no. 2 (April): 163–207.

Rawls, John. 1971. *A Theory of Justice* (Cambridge: Harvard University Press).

———. 1980. "Kantian Constructivism in Moral Theory." *Journal of Philosophy* 77, no. 9: 517–572.

———. 1985. "Justice as Fairness: Political Not Metaphysical." *Philosophy and Public Affairs* 14, no. 3 (Summer): 223–251.

Rich, Adrienne. 1979. *On Lies, Secrets, and Silence: Selected Prose 1966–1978* (New York: W. W. Norton).

Rorty, Amelie O., and David Wong. 1990. "Aspects of Identity and Agency." In Owen Flanagan and Amelie O. Rorty, eds., *Identity, Character and Morality* (Cambridge: MIT Press), pp. 19–36.

Ryle, Gilbert. 1949. *The Concept of Mind* (London: Penguin Books).

Sandel, M. 1982. *Liberalism and the Limits of Justice* (New York: Cambridge University Press).

Sartorius, Rolf, ed. 1983. *Paternalism* (Minneapolis: University of Minnesota Press).

Scott, Joan, and Judith Butler, eds. 1992. *Feminists Theorize the Political* (New York: Routledge).

Segrest, Mab. 1985. *My Mama's Dead Squirrel: Lesbian Essays on Southern Culture* (Ithaca, N.Y.: Firebrand Books).

Sherman, Nancy. 1990. "The Place of Emotions in Kantian Morality." In Owen Flanagan and Amelie Rorty, eds., *Identity, Character and Morality* (Cambridge: MIT Press), pp. 149–172.

Shoemaker, Sydney. 1963. *Self-Knowledge and Self-Identity* (Ithaca, N.Y.: Cornell University Press).

―――. 1980. "Causality and Properties." In P. van Inwagen, ed., *Essays in Honor of Richard Taylor* (Dordrecht, Holland: D. Reidel Press), pp. 206–233.

Sidgwick, Henry. 1907. *The Methods of Ethics* (London: Macmillan & Co.).

Sosa, Maritza. 1994. "¿Democracia sin Mujeres? Reflexiones Sobre la Relación Género-Poder en Cuba." Paper presented at the Sixth Conference of Cuban and North American Philosophers and Social Scientists, Havana, Cuba, June 15.

Spelman, Elizabeth V. 1988. *Inessential Woman: Problems of Exclusion in Feminist Thought* (Boston: Beacon Press).

―――. 1993. "Slavery and Tragedy." In Roger S. Gottlieb, ed., *Radical Philosophy: Tradition, Counter-Tradition, Politics* (Philadelphia: Temple University Press), pp. 221–244.

Stairs, Arlene. 1994. "The Cultural Negotiation of Indigenous Education: Between Microethnography and Model-Building." *Peabody Journal of Education* 69, no. 2 (Winter): 154–171.

―――. 1994. "Human Development as Cultural Negotiation: Indigenous Lessons on Becoming a Teacher." Paper presented at the annual meeting of the American Educational Research Association, New Orleans, April.

Stein, Edward, ed. 1990. *Forms of Desire: Sexual Orientation and the Social Constructionist Controversy* (New York: Routledge).

Sturgeon, Nicholas. 1988. "Moral Explanations." In David Copp and David Zimmerman, eds., *Morality, Reason, and Truth* (Totowa, N.J.: Rowman and Allenheld, 1985), pp. 49–78, reprinted in Geoffrey Sayre-McCord, ed., *Essays on Moral Realism* (Ithaca, N.Y.: Cornell University Press), pp. 229–255.

Suárez, Amelia, Sonia Enjamio, and Inés Rodríguez. 1993. "La Mujer en la Municipalidad." Paper presented at Feminist Ethics and Social Policy conference, University of Pittsburgh, November 7.

Velleman, J. David. 1988. "Brandt's Theory of 'Good.'" *Philosophical Review* 97, no. 3 (July): 353–371.

Walker, Alice. 1976. *Meridian* (New York: Pocket Books).

Whitford, Margaret, ed. 1991. *The Irigaray Reader* (Cambridge: Basil Blackwell).

Williams, Patricia J. 1991. *The Alchemy of Race and Rights: Diary of a Law Professor* (Cambridge: Harvard University Press).

Woolf, Virginia. 1966. *Three Guineas* (New York: Harcourt, Brace, Jovanovich).

―――. 1976. *Moments of Being*, ed. Jeanne Schulkind (Sussex: University Press).

Young, Iris. 1988. *Justice and the Politics of Difference* (Princeton, N.J.: Princeton University Press).

About the Book and Author

CONVENTIONAL WISDOM AND COMMONSENSE morality tend to take the integrity of persons for granted. But for people in systematically unjust societies, self-respect and human dignity may prove to be impossible dreams.

Susan Babbitt explores the implications of this insight, arguing that in the face of systemic injustice, individual and social rationality may require the transformation rather than the realization of deep-seated aims, interests, and values. In particular, under such conditions, she argues, the cultivation and ongoing exercise of moral imagination is necessary to discover and defend a more humane social vision.

Impossible Dreams is one of those rare books that fruitfully combines discourses that were previously largely separate: feminist and antiracist political theory, analytic ethics and philosophy of mind, and a wide range of non-philosophical literature on the lives of oppressed peoples around the world. It is both the object lesson in reaching across academic barriers and a demonstration of how the best of feminist philosophy can be in conversation with the best of "mainstream" philosophy—as well as affect the lives of real people.

Susan E. Babbitt is assistant professor of philosophy at Queen's University in Kingston, Ontario.

Index